Prestige in Academic Life

The achievement of academic excellence is inherently competitive. Deliberate government policies, globalisation and changes in communication technologies mean that competitiveness in the academic world is sharper than ever before. At the centre of this is the seeking of prestige, at all levels from the national system to the individual. *Prestige in Academic Life* aims to increase understanding of motivation in universities by exploring the part that prestige plays, for good and ill. The book's focus on motivation and prestige helps to answer fundamental questions that run through much discussion on universities, such as why some problems are never solved; why change can be so difficult to achieve; and how individuals and groups can enable it to happen.

Issues explored include:

- What role does prestige play in academic life?
- How does prestige play out in the working lives of academics, students, administrators and institutional leaders?
- How can the positive aspects of prestige be encouraged and the negative ones diminished?

University leaders and managers, academics, administrators and students, indeed all who are interested in universities, will find this valuable reading. It will help those in leadership positions to enhance the efficiency, effectiveness and wellbeing of their institutions, and will support academic staff in negotiating their career path.

Paul Blackmore is Professor of Higher Education in the International Centre for University Policy Research, Policy Institute at King's, at King's College London.

Prestige in Academic Life

Excellence and exclusion

Paul Blackmore

LONDON AND NEW YORK

First published 2016
by Routledge
2 Park Square, Milton Park, Abingdon, Oxon OX14 4RN

and by Routledge
711 Third Avenue, New York, NY 10017

Routledge is an imprint of the Taylor & Francis Group, an informa business

© 2016 Paul Blackmore

The right of Paul Blackmore to be identified as author of this work has been asserted by him in accordance with sections 77 and 78 of the Copyright, Designs and Patents Act 1988.

All rights reserved. No part of this book may be reprinted or reproduced or utilised in any form or by any electronic, mechanical, or other means, now known or hereafter invented, including photocopying and recording, or in any information storage or retrieval system, without permission in writing from the publishers.

Trademark notice: Product or corporate names may be trademarks or registered trademarks, and are used only for identification and explanation without intent to infringe.

British Library Cataloguing in Publication Data
A catalogue record for this book is available from the British Library

Library of Congress Cataloging in Publication Data
Names: Blackmore, Paul, 1954-Title: Prestige in academic life : excellence and exclusion / Paul Blackmore.Description: New York : Routledge, 2016. | Includes bibliographical references and index.Identifiers: LCCN 2015029500| ISBN 9781138884939 (hardback) | ISBN 9781315715780 (ebook) | ISBN 9781138884946 (pbk.)Subjects: LCSH: College teachers--Professional relationships. | Scholars--Professional relationships. | Academic achievement--Social aspects. | Occupational prestige. Classification: LCC LB1778 .B48 2016 | DDC 378.1/2--dc23LC record available at http://lccn.loc.gov/2015029500

ISBN: 978-1-138-88493-9 (hbk)
ISBN: 978-1-138-88494-6 (pbk)
ISBN: 978-1-315-71578-0 (ebk)

Typeset in Galliard
by Saxon Graphics Ltd, Derby

Contents

1 Why talk about prestige? 1

2 Prestige and the organisation 17

3 Psychology of prestige 39

4 Globalisation and national systems 54

5 National prestige: global hubs 72

6 League tables and international clubs 84

7 Necessary myths: universities and knowledge 102

8 Necessary myths: the university as economic powerhouse 118

9 Heads of institutions and prestige 139

10 Students and prestige 155

11 Prestige in academic life: excellence and exclusion 171

Index 186

Chapter 1

Why talk about prestige?

The presence of prestige

University leaders scan league tables anxiously, wanting to know that their institution has the highest possible standing. Some aspire to be world class; others seek a more modest niche. Entire research teams are enticed from one institution to another, with promises of additional rewards and better facilities. Researchers bid feverishly and against the odds for the next crumb of funding, preferring a few thousand pounds from a highly respected source to ten times the amount from one that is less highly ranked. Teachers are encouraged to apply for prizes for excellence in teaching by showing that they are better than the colleagues with whom they often share their work. Some prefer not to single themselves out in this way. Parents and students seek out the best university that they can afford. In all directions the academy is increasingly competitive, and a more traditional rhetoric of collegiality seems threadbare. Academic life itself, it could be argued, was always a competition: nobody wants to produce second-rate research, to have a commonplace idea. For students too there are, in the short term, only so many places available in the institutions that hold the highest prestige. Academic excellence is therefore inherently competitive. However, that competitiveness is more obvious than ever before, encouraged by deliberate government policy in many countries and also by changes in communication technologies and the globalisation of higher education. At the centre of all of this is prestige, at all levels from the national system to the individual.

A historical perspective

Prestige has featured in human life for some considerable time. The pyramids of Egypt and Mexico, the Parthenon of Athens, the Colosseum in Rome and Beijing's Forbidden City all had a prestige function. The distribution of power and wealth and ability, and the social positioning related to it, are universal aspects of an organised society. There may be some value in taking a historical perspective, in that differing social and cultural conditions may influence what is held to be prestigious. There are particular sources of change too: technological change provides additional ways in which prestige can be generated and expressed.

Universities have existed in societies from feudal times, through agricultural and industrial revolutions, periods of political and social unrest, world war and globalisation. They have reflected and at times contributed to those changes. Universities have helped to bring new forms of knowledge into being and have had to accommodate them. We can see differing conceptions of the purposes and forms of universities through succeeding waves of their establishment. In Britain, the oldest universities were joined by redbricks and civics in the nineteenth century, plateglass institutions in the 1960s and former polytechnics in the 1990s. Australia has its sandstones, gumtrees and moderns, Scotland its ancients, old and new, the US its doctorate-granting universities, its master's and baccalaureate colleges. Each new wave has entailed a difficult and for some an imperfectly achieved ascent into respectability, to find a contested place in the academic sun. Disciplines too have differing histories of engagement in universities. Where universities once existed principally to study divinity and law, there has been vast growth over a long period in the pure and applied sciences and in the humanities and social sciences. Professions have also found their way into the university, in a process that has both conferred an academic status on the profession and also, it could be argued, increased the influence of the academy.

With this expansion of disciplines, professions and functions have come many more staff of more varied kinds. The role of the academic has grown and changed in focus. In many places the academic role has split apart although in others it was never united. Prestige is at stake here too. The basis of an academic role's claim to professionalism – even whether it has or should have one – has long been a matter of debate and more recently the object of policy in many countries. A professional administration now manages many aspects of universities, drawing in staff with a vast range of skills that are required in any large modern organisation. In any university, professional and administrative staff now outnumber academic staff and the line between is increasingly blurred. The decline of donnish dominion was signalled many years ago, but whilst academic authority overall may have been eroded, universities continue to present a complex picture of power and prestige among their tribes and territories. The role of the student has also changed through time and currently is gaining in prominence.

The value of prestige as an aid to analysis is that it offers insight into the working of organisations, groups and individuals, through an examination of that which has the highest acclaim and how it has been developed and sustained. Many of the prestige concerns that can be identified today have existed for a very long time. The past may often seem a more stable place, with clearer, more widely shared and less contested views of what was prestigious than in what is experienced as the teeming present. An account of prestige becomes more difficult. Prestige exists most comfortably at times of stability rather than change. It could be argued that the conception of prestige includes the idea of stability, so that part of the art of developing prestige today is in projecting a sense of stability whilst remaining contemporary in a time of change. At the same time as serenity is projected, prestige is often won and maintained through fierce struggle, and can be lost as well as gained.

Defining prestige

Prestige is a term in wide and common use, but is not easy to define or to locate. James English, exploring contemporary growth in literary prizes, asks some key questions: 'Where does prestige reside? In things? In people? In relationships between things and people?' (2005, 3). Prestige does not reside in a person, although a role or function that a person has or performs may be prestigious. Thus there is prestige inherent in a kingship or a presidency that is separable from the holder of the role. A person may have attributes or possessions or achievements that lend prestige. Similarly, nothing of itself can be prestigious. Prestige is a social phenomenon, conferred by those who hold something in esteem. Prestige requires more than one person to value something. A group of people must agree if it is to acquire that status. That group does not have to be large, and prestigiousness does not require the agreement of everyone in a community. It needs only enough people to form a body who share particular valuations. Indeed, as will be suggested later, one way of estimating the boundaries of a community is by noting where a shared agreement of what is deemed prestigious breaks down. Thus prestige occurs where something is valued highly by a group of people, and association with that thing confers raised status on an individual or group. So an account of prestige deals with: what is prestigious; who is associated with it; who values it; and the various relationships, processes and states of being that are related to it. Prestige is thus both a psychological and a sociological issue. It has to do with how and what people think, as well as what they do and how they relate to others.

A number of other, at least as well-established terms appear to be available. Fame, reputation, status, standing, approbation and credibility have related meanings. Each term draws attention to particular aspects of excellence and social position whilst downplaying others. Listing them points up the difficulty of working with words that are in daily use, each of them carrying a cluster of meanings and implications, and each of them shifting subtly in meaning from one context to another. Some of these apparent synonyms listed above are not suitable. Status and standing emphasise the possessor of prestige, approbation the awarding of approval. Fame is too general: most prestige has a more specific field of application.

Reputation is a possible competitor. The *Oxford English Dictionary* says that reputation is 'the beliefs or opinions that are generally held about someone or something'. Thus reputation may be good or bad, or simply neutral. The definition contains the idea that reputation exists in beliefs and opinions: it is people who confer reputation. The same source says that prestige refers to 'widespread respect and admiration felt for someone or something on the basis of a perception of their achievements or quality', suggesting a difference between reputation and prestige. A feeling of respect or admiration can only be positive. Unlike reputation, there is no such thing as bad prestige. Negative prestige would be expressed in different terms: notoriety or even infamy. This raises questions about how many people have to hold something prestigious, and whether some communities might see something as prestigious whilst others would not. A second difference is that prestige stands somewhere beyond reputation. Something of the highest reputation might achieve a level of regard where it would be termed prestigious, and that high regard would probably be held by many. A third difference is not reflected in the definitions, but can be found in its derivation. A good reputation has an air of solidity and worth. A person who did something, or did not do something, in order to protect or advance their reputation would feel comfortable to do that and to know that others knew what they had done and why. Prestige is a difficult term, with a range of meanings in use. Its origin in the Latin word 'praestigium', meaning 'trick' or 'stratagem', suggests one difficulty with it: we do not always like to admit that we do anything in order to gain or retain prestige. The word carries connotations of caring more for appearance than for substance, of over-valuing the opinions of others. Thus it can be a pejorative term. A person who actively seeks prestige may be thought to be selfish, to be reaching out for things that are better offered than grasped at. Despite that, many uses of the term are not adversely critical – to speak of a prestigious prize is not to demean it, but simply to say that many desire it and hold it in esteem. Even those who deride prestige-seeking tend to be critical not of the thing but of those who regard it as prestigious. In researching prestige, the equivocal nature of people's relationship with the idea of prestige is challenging. Interviewees may be reluctant to describe anything that they do as 'prestige-seeking'. The connotations of the term threaten to get in the way of an investigation.

So the term prestige expresses the further reaches of reputation, and carries with it the twin notions of competitiveness and equivocality. In summary, then, something has prestige if enough people who are sufficiently connected to know one another's views can all agree that it is prestigious. For that to happen, the thing must be relatively scarce. Something possessed by all cannot be prestigious, unless the possession takes place in a relatively closed community, in which case the absence of that thing beyond the community provides the sense of scarcity. Thus, for example, a group of professors may all have high and equivalent status within that group, because every one of that group has something that others outside the group may not have.

In Pursuit of Prestige (Brewer et al., 2002) is probably the most extensive and coherent attempt to operationalise the idea of prestige in the field of strategy in US higher education, exploring the apparent paradox that US higher education is widely admired around the world and yet is seen within the country as being wasteful and inefficient. The writers do so by claiming that there are key differences in institutions' strategic intentions and by making a distinction between prestige and reputation. Prestige is said to be: measured in relationship to others; much more influenced by faculty and others inside the institution; slow to depreciate; a 'rival good', in that the attainment of it necessarily means that someone else suffers a loss of it; and entailing a search for something that is limited in supply. In comparison, reputation is: an absolute term; much more influenced by what customers want; can be increased quickly but also decreases quickly unless maintained; a 'non-rival' good; and can increase in supply at a system level. Therefore, reputation can be gained that is not at the expense of a competitor. The writers go on to propose that institutions are either prestigious, prestige-seeking or concerned with reputation. It is also noted that there are hybrid institutions, in which some parts might aim at prestige and others at reputation.

The writers make a number of valuable points about prestige within an organisation. Firstly, they comment that prestige is very costly and has to be built up over a long period of time, often at the expense of spending that might lead to reputational gain. For example, one might decide to divert resources from student provision and into research. Secondly they suggest that prestige institutions are focused more closely on their own internal values rather than on meeting external standards and needs. Reputation-seeking institutions, on the other hand, will be more concerned to satisfy customers and are likely to be quicker to adapt to customers' needs. They are also not as engaged with league table rankings and other signs of prestige. The writers note that private institutions are far less likely to engage in prestige-generating activities than public ones. They suggest that this can be explained by the nature of governance arrangements. Since prestige is costly to achieve and entails risk, institutions that are governed by members of faculty are likely to favour spending on prestige items, because those taking the decisions receive the benefits but do not directly bear the costs or the risks.

Reputation held at an individual level contains some assumption or implication about personal qualities that are known because they inform observed behaviour, including attitudes. Indeed reputation may be based entirely on others' perceptions of an individual's personal qualities. Thus, Othello laments the loss of his reputation, by which he means the way others have seen him behave as a gentleman and an army officer. Prestige is silent on personal qualities. A prestigious person is not necessarily virtuous, punctual or reliable, for example. The components of prestige are external to the individual and consist of association with various forms of capital. This perhaps explains why prestige seems an unattractive concept with which individuals are sometimes reluctant to be associated.

Possible paradigms

Although universities have always been places of contestation, for the institution, for its constituent academic entities and for those who work and study in them, there may be some value in sketching two higher education paradigms, reflecting some of the major changes that have taken place in recent years and that continue today. Broadly, higher education in many countries has moved from a relatively elite and implicitly understood and agreed conception of its nature and purpose to a much more complex and contested one. In a more competitive climate, prestige has become an even more important means of achieving position and distinctiveness (see Table 1.1).

Ron Barnett has suggested that the kinds of knowledge that are valued in a university have shifted. At the centre is a change to a more instrumental view of a university's purpose, from 'knowing that' to 'knowing how', from pure to applied, from problem-making to problem-solving, from knowledge as process to knowledge as product, and from a disinterested to a pragmatic stance (1994, 49). It can be argued that the status of the most prestigious forms of knowledge, in university terms, is under threat. Peter Scott named another related and socially complex change when he commented that the British higher education system had undergone 'massification' but its instincts were still elite and small-scale (1995). From educating only a fraction of a population, most national education systems have expanded substantially over the last thirty years, admitting a larger and more varied range of students. Elitism still exists, strongly in tension with a trend towards inclusivity. With this expansion of universities' purposes have come a larger number of stakeholders, each of whose wishes has, at some level, to be satisfied. A university has a wider range of possible ways of being: to be research intensive or teaching intensive, academically or professionally orientated, local or national or international, or may attempt to be some or all of these. Thus the development and projection of prestige is an increasingly complex business. A related trend is towards explicitness, in a number of fields. Institutions are expected to have mission statements to express what have in the past been unspoken understandings; curricula are increasingly defined in terms of pre-specified learning outcomes; research has to show that it has achieved impact. Far less is implicit, and this affects the ways in which prestige is communicated and understood, because much that is prestigious is implicit, both in the nature of its supposed excellence, and in the ways that people know it. Greater government interest in the outcomes and outputs of universities, expressed through changes in funding and governance, have led to a trend in some nation states that one writer has described as a move from collegial to managerial (Bergquist, 1992) and

Table 1.1 Prestige paradigms

Former	Future
Knowing that	Knowing how
Elite education	Mass education
Few stakeholders	Many stakeholders
Implicit	Explicit
Collegium	Enterprise
National	International
Hierarchy	Network

another from collegium to enterprise (McNay, 1995). These express related tendencies: away from members of faculty being autonomous individuals and towards being directly managed employees; and of the university having a closer relationship with business and commerce and a stronger concern for wealth creation. A further prestige dimension, already mentioned, is between the national and the international. Here we can see a shift for some, but not all, institutions. Only in the last twenty years has higher education emerged as being strongly international, with the ambitions of some nation states to develop themselves as 'global hubs' and the popularisation of the idea of the 'world-class university' reflected in international league tables. The greatest contemporary challenge in conceptualising prestige comes from the ways in which communication and learning technologies are transforming the speed of communication, the generation and flow of knowledge, and the formation of communities and interest groups that transcend organisational structures and national boundaries. Hierarchy, a comfortable way of framing prestige, does not disappear, but the metaphor of the network is now at least as powerful a way of understanding human interaction, and the working of prestige can often better be understood by that means.

Any general statement about something as complex as a university, that can be viewed from so many perspectives, can only be illuminative rather than definitive, is likely to be at best only partially true and may be mythical, although myth can of course be very powerful. These are not either/or states, and any shift is a change in emphasis. What can be seen is a university as a site of tension, with arguments and counter-arguments run and re-run, as existing, often implicit, notions of prestige act as brakes on change.

Current concerns

The shifts identified above play out in a number of ways that can in part be understood through their prestige aspects, in different locations and at different system levels. The pursuit, deployment and recognition of prestige is often an important factor, sometimes occurring as a deliberate means of gaining advantage, sometimes a set of implicit beliefs and values that may impede planned change. Firstly, at a global level, the demand for higher education is increasing rapidly. Many countries are developing or reforming their higher education systems. The introduction and growth in influence of international university league tables offers evidence that higher education has, for many universities, become a global issue, with increasing flows of both faculty and students across national boundaries. This provides another arena in which universities can seek prestige. There may be beneficial effects, providing the stimulus of competition and reducing complacency among those institutions that sit at the top of their national league tables. These changes bring with them the possibility of malign effects, too, in that making comparisons among universities that work in very different national, social and political settings is extremely difficult and value-laden, and is likely to favour particular kinds of institution. Many universities have, and are likely to continue to have, a local mission, and will not do well in global tables, but may be judged by them. Thus league tables generate crude signals of prestige that may be interpreted in ways that may not have been intended by their compilers. Higher education systems and individual institutions are likely to be developed with reference to existing systems and institutions elsewhere, particularly those that are believed to be prestigious. The international dimension of prestige carries with it a probability that aspects of policy and practice may be transferred from one system to another, whether or not they are appropriate. An obvious example might be the temptation for a university in a developing – or indeed a developed – country with pressing local needs to focus instead on forms of research with no local benefit.

There is a worldwide trend within nation states to see universities as contributors to economic growth, and so many institutions are now increasingly attuned to the money economy. This produces the contested space of academic capitalism, where some traditional academic values are challenged, for example in the valuations of basic and applied research. To what degree does money drive what is valued in universities and thus behaviour within them? Many universities depend heavily on their national government for funding, and all of them, ultimately, for permission to continue as recognised educational institutions. Universities cannot afford to pursue an independent mission if they have continually to apply to government for funding. However, government policy requirements are often likely to be shorter term in aspiration than are the traditions of an institution or the preferences of those who work in them. Government may direct attention to ends that generate reputation rather than prestige. This leads to interesting questions about the extent to which economic concerns, fuelled often by globalisation, together with the increasingly interventionist habits of government, change the nature of prestige patterns in universities, and indeed whether prestige patterns can be or are led by economic relations. Here it is suggested that the relationship is a complex one, as enterprising members of faculty accommodate their own aims within a changing policy and funding context, often through creative leadership and management.

When governments invest in higher education in the belief that it will stimulate growth, through the production of a highly educated workforce and application of the outcomes of excellent research, there is a clear tension between the pursuit of knowledge for its own sake and for an economic purpose. Many universities now seek to describe the distinctive nature of their curricula, often in ways that relate the curriculum to employment. Again, prestige has a part to play. It is now commonplace for universities to declare a belief in providing an interdisciplinary experience for their undergraduates, on the grounds that problems in the world require a number of disciplines to be brought to bear, if they are to be understood and solved. For this to happen, faculty must themselves be open to interdisciplinary approaches. However, as is discussed later, in many areas there can be risk to an academic career if it crosses disciplinary boundaries. How can we encourage students to be interdisciplinary if faculty are not? When faculty value basic research over applied, or prefer to teach mono-disciplinary programmes or to teach without any direct concern for students' workplace expertise, issues of prestige may be in play.

Students, too, in an increasingly marketised higher education system, have choices to make about what and where to study. For some, international choices are more available than ever before. Students have an increasing amount of comparative data available to them, often in the form of rankings that tell them where the greatest prestige is to be gained. Universities work hard to present themselves in the best possible light, selecting carefully from league table positions and other badges of quality. A student's decision on where to apply to study may be a reputation- or a prestige-based one.

Communicating prestige

Staff, students and institutions all face the effects of instant worldwide communication, which bring not only more data that can be used comparatively, but also and partly as a result, a trend towards greater explicitness that then provides an incentive for marketing and branding. Governments recognise that communication can mean being economical with the truth, can mean spin and, at worst, misinformation. So, and especially in the UK, government seeks to make universities more transparent to those who have an interest in them. Data must be published widely so that prospective parents, students, research funders and commercial customers know exactly what they are buying. Journalists, too, know that competitions make good copy, because there are always winners and losers. The more competitions there are, the more news can be generated. League tables exist for just about everything, attempting to measure all aspects of academic life – the amount spent on libraries, research funding earned, Nobel prizes, highest classification degrees, class sizes, faculty with doctorates, faculty with teaching qualifications. If it can be measured, and even if it cannot be measured, everything finds its way into vast exercises that seek to show that one university is better than another, that one department in Ruritanian studies outshines all others, that one group of students is more employable than another. Vast amounts of data are gathered, managed, manipulated, presented, interpreted, believed, disbelieved and acted upon. When governments encourage and require the publication of comparative data, they are intervening to manage perceptions of quality, usually, at least within its own borders, seeking to ensure that prestige is genuinely merited and poor performance is clearly identified. The response at institutional level may be a striving for excellence. However, it may be one of performativity, so that the institution concentrates on improving only that which is being directly measured. It may also be one of accommodation, with a token compliance that enables more enduring beliefs, values and behaviours to be maintained.

So, national systems, institutions, departments, research teams and individual faculty, professional staff and students are concerned about their standing in the eyes of others. Governments want more from universities. Universities take marketing far more seriously. Faculty present their accomplishments in increasingly professional forms to promotions committees. Students learn how to present themselves to other universities and to employers. It is not good enough to do something well. It has to be known that one has done it well and indeed better than anyone else. With so much at stake, and so many competing interests at play, a policy when implemented will not necessarily achieve its intentions. At all levels, educational communities are complex social entities, not command economies. Thinking about prestige offers a way of understanding what happens and what does not happen, and can offer a guide for action.

Prestige economies

How does one make sense of what is happening as universities and all those connected with them become increasingly and overtly competitive? One way is to take the metaphor of the market and to try to explore and explain what happens in universities in market terms. Nations compete in an international market to be seen as the safest and most cost-effective provider of higher education. Universities compete in teaching, research and consultancy markets to show that they are the best at whatever they are trying to do. Faculty compete for the best research funding and the most able students. Students seek the best degree they can obtain from the highest-rated university to which they can gain admission. However, these are not, directly, money markets, but ones in which prestige is at stake.

The idea of a prestige economy has existed for at least sixty years as a means of describing the ways in which things that a group of people hold to be valuable are developed, possessed, exchanged and depleted, although interest in prestige as a social phenomenon is much older. The notion of a prestige economy was originally developed by anthropologists to describe the ways in which tribes engaged in activities that appeared to carry prestige, although money was not involved (Bascom,1948; Herskovits, 1948). In recent years the concept has been applied to literary prizes (English, 2005) and to various aspects of academic life (Blackmore and Kandiko, 2012). The 'economy' aspect suggests a market of a kind. However, 'prestige' indicates a particular kind of market, one in which what is recognised and traded does not necessarily have a direct financial value. It may consist of whatever is valued. Markets have products, which may be relatively concrete, in the form of books and articles, keynote addresses, Nobel prizes and degree awards. Each of these products has features that characterise it, that may give it a competitive edge, marking it out from other products. Markets also involve relationships, and social connections can themselves be prestigious.

The market is a beguiling but dangerous metaphor. Aspects of academic life may not be describable entirely in terms of products or markets. Some of the work that universities do cannot, in the end, be fully proceduralised. We cannot all agree on the purpose of a university. Indeed, if we could, one could argue that the institution would no longer be a university, since one function of it may be to question the status quo, including the university's own purpose. The 'products' of universities are not always easy to predict, either in quantity or quality. We do not know how to guarantee good research outcomes. We cannot guarantee academic brilliance, although we can probably describe broad competence. We do not know what is the best way to teach anything, for a number of reasons, including the immense variability in the needs and learning styles of those who learn, but also because what is to be learnt may not be entirely describable and may not be possible fully to assess. Amid this uncertainty, a market metaphor can still be applied. However, since the products in the marketplace cannot fully be described, and may derive some of their attractiveness from being ineffable, the market may be a very subtle and nuanced one.

More fundamentally, one has to consider whether some aspects of human motivation do not fit into a conventional market metaphor at all. The member of faculty who continues to give priority to teaching even when it is obvious that promotion goes to those who spend their time on research does not fit. The faculty member who prefers to work in a field that has no prospect of attracting significant research funding but instead to follow his or her intellectual passion does not fit either. Here, and elsewhere, there is clearly a disjuncture between the idea of the market and the motivating power of money, which is the usual currency of markets. Money is not the sole motivator and the nature of the return on investment is not always clear. If these are markets, they are of a particular kind. Individual and collective enthusiasm and altruism play a role too.

The idea of an economy points to the social aspects of prestige, but the working of a prestige economy cannot be explained in purely sociological terms. The psychology of prestige is equally important, helping to explain why prestige is such a fundamental part of human life. Firstly, an agreement about what is prestigious saves the burden and effort of making choices. If what is excellent has already been defined, this can be taken as a given, and also removes the possibility of making mistaken choices. Secondly, the adoption of an agreed standard by a community has the function of reducing possible conflicts. When a prestige object, defined as any entity which is held to have high status, has been identified, it becomes possible to adapt beliefs and behaviours in order to associate with that which has a high value. By aligning with others who accord prestige in similar ways, the individual can join a community of the like-minded, and benefit from this further form of association. Bourdieu (1984) has proposed that judgements of aesthetic taste offer ways in which a person can gain social standing. The existence of prestige objects also offers the opportunity for acquisitiveness and competition, since it provides a currency for trading and for displaying higher social positioning. For all of these reasons and more, prestige is a deeply rooted and enduring feature of human social existence that it is therefore worth exploring.

Why write about prestige

Why explore prestige in academic life? An obvious reason is simply that it is interesting. There may be an audience for another book that explores the strangenesses of academic life, and that has the purpose only of describing it. However, there is risk in this apparently innocent pursuit. Prestige may have good or bad effects. Universities may, partly for prestige reasons, seek to produce the best possible research and the most highly educated undergraduates. Prestige may accompany, may even drive, a desire for quality, and this may be broadly beneficial. However, for prestige reasons universities may also perhaps be tempted to neglect some of the less fashionable or glamorous aspects of their mission, such as their responsibilities to local communities, when international league tables beckon. Individuals may seek to gain an unmerited prestige advantage over colleagues, perhaps by underhand means. Thus there is a danger in appearing to celebrate every quirky social practice. Some prestige-driven behaviour is bad behaviour, at both institutional and individual levels, for example if it protects vested interest or excludes people of ability, and it deserves to be named as such. Therefore, this book is not intended to be a celebration of the oddities of academic life.

An instrumental answer is that life is more complex in universities than ever before. The notion of prestige becomes more significant in relation to the degree of economic pressure exerted on a socio-cultural system. In universities, not only are academic staff required to be more productive overall, but the nature of what is produced is more heavily influenced externally, for example by recent concerns in the UK for research to have 'impact', an aim that favours some kinds of research over others. When resources become relatively more scarce and pressures to produce particular outputs intensify, this is likely not only to increase existing tensions in what is valued (for example between research and teaching, or between pure and applied research) but also to stimulate more intense rivalry in that competition for resources and recognition. Struggles for prestige will intensify. It also becomes more relevant because those who seek to increase the efficiency and effectiveness of an institution need to find ways in which this can be achieved. Policymakers, leaders and managers who seek to influence universities and faculty can only do so if they know what they are dealing with. One of the most important aspects is the motivation of people, individually and in groups. Otherwise those with change intentions are working in the dark, not knowing how particular actions are likely to be interpreted, or what responses there may be to a given stimulus. An understanding of what is prestigious offers a means of doing this. Then the aims of change initiatives are more likely to be achieved.

Alternatively, one might move beyond this ethically neutral position. If it is believed that universities should be places that contribute positively to the world, supporting a number of liberal values, then universities must themselves uphold those values. It is easy to sound pious, but examples can make the point: there would probably be broad agreement within universities that an institution's local community outreach initiative is worthwhile even though it makes no contribution to the institution's global league table position, or that team effort should be encouraged as well as individual achievement, or that faculty should see an enthusiasm for teaching as a potential career advantage, not an impediment. However, prevailing prestige patterns may inhibit the achievement of these desirable intentions. So, once again at the risk of piety, the book does have a moral purpose, in that certain liberal values are held to be important, both for a society and for a university within it. The values are not new and not particularly controversial, for they are part of the history and the rhetoric of higher education. They include a commitment to free speech under the law, open enquiry, rational debate, tolerance of others and of their views, equality of opportunity, and inclusion of all those who can benefit from higher education, insofar as is possible.

This book seeks therefore to be more than *descriptive*, in that it suggests what might be done to ensure either that an individual entity prospers or that the group or collection of groups taken together can manage or perhaps reduce the malign effects of prestige. Here it is claimed that although there might be broad agreement about the desirability of enacting these values in university life, in practice behaviours may not always support them and indeed may work actively against them. The bad effects of a concern for prestige cannot be done away with entirely through adjustments to governance and procedures. These latter can set the stage and direct some of the actions, but actors may continue to work in ways that gain individual and group advantage. Prestige is a social phenomenon, in which much is implicit, and it works in ways that may be quite unconscious for individuals. Thus those widely supported ideals of universities can be developed and safeguarded only if the issues that are explored here are acknowledged and dealt with, so that aspects of prestige involving motivation and affiliation and identity are understood and are worked with to a beneficial end.

Prestige exists in a relational way, whereas reputation can be quality based. Thus, as Brewer *et al.* (2002) have pointed out, for some people to have prestige means that others do not have it, whilst all can have a good reputation provided they meet a standard. This exposes to charges of elitism those who attempt to show others how to gain prestige when, from one political perspective, one might argue that it is more desirable to level everyone up rather than to help a few to get ahead of the others. A counter-argument might be that prestige exists in any case. Some people have it on an undeserved basis, through the inheritance of great wealth, for example, or otherwise find themselves in a position where it is relatively easy to accrue prestige. Popularising the idea of prestige as something distinct from reputation and that can be generated in different ways gives everyone the opportunity to gain prestige if they wish it, by being aware of how it differs from reputation and by knowing how to set about generating it. The naming and describing of prestige also makes it easier to safeguard against the potentially negative impact of prestige. If a decision is made for prestige rather than reputational reasons, that is then known, and one can decide whether that is the kind of decision one wishes to see made. For example, those awarding research grants may be concerned that the best ideas are rewarded rather than the best-known researchers. A blind reviewing process is usually adopted to ensure a level playing field for all applicants. There may be other reasons for making an award to an applicant with prestige, for example by generating positive publicity because a major 'name' is thus associated with the sponsoring organisation. However, at least this then becomes an open decision that can be debated.

About the book

The book travels over familiar territory, but in an unfamiliar way. The reason for examining academic prestige, apart from its intrinsic interest, is to find ways of increasing the efficiency, effectiveness and wellbeing of institutions and of those who work in them. A huge range of literature both theoretical and applied already does this job and is drawn on here. A policy literature sets the political and financial context of universities. A philosophical one considers their possible purposes, often taking an historical perspective. A strongly dystopian strand of commentary laments the actual or imminent death of the university and argues for a return to previous values. Work exists on disciplines, interdisciplinarity, academic cultures and academic careers. The quest for respectability that characterises the interaction between universities and actual and would-be professions has been extensively discussed. A leadership literature considers strategic matters, particularly the management of change, often in collegial settings where formal line management is weak. Of course there is also a major body of literature on generic leadership and management, dealing with the nature and forms of organisation, the theory and practice of leadership, and roles, functions and motivation in the workplace.

The assumption here is that an understanding of what motivates people *in academic life*, and the thoughtful management of the working environment in the light of that understanding, is likely to be beneficial. In doing so this book works slightly against the contemporary grain by considering universities to be particular places. This is not to argue that universities are unique, but that a number of issues come together with considerable force in a university and therefore merit special attention. The book's focus on prestige helps to expose some of the hidden aspects of motivation, when things are done for reasons that the doers may not like to admit even to themselves. Finally, by including all levels of prestige, from the international through to the individual academic, the book tries to show how pervasive prestige is, and how all levels are interconnected. An overarching set of terms or a framework may assist understanding. There is, however, a danger of fixing too much upon a single framework, so that a framework may then drive perceptions rather than the reverse. This book is quite eclectic in its sources and in the understandings it seeks to achieve.

The particular focus is on prestige itself. In wanting to understand how and why individuals act, I am principally interested in the prestige that an individual or larger entity accrues, probably over a long time, as a result of association with various items that are prestigious or that enable the generation of prestige. So I am focusing on prestige as a resource that is an index of standing in a field and that facilitates the gaining of various permissions. The term 'prestige economy' extends that personal status-gaining by describing the system within which that gaining has to take place. As such it is particularly useful in examining why individuals do what they do in an organisational setting, where prestige operates at other levels, at those of the team, department and organisation.

The book aims to be distinctive in a number of ways. It has a focus on the idea of prestige, rather than reputation or status, and emphasises the implicit and covert as well as the explicit aspects of gaining an advanced position in a domain. It acknowledges that prestige is an issue that draws from both sociology and psychology, since it deals with how and what people think, as well as what they do and how they relate to others. It deals with prestige in an holistic way, examining system, institutional, departmental and individual aspects, and exploring the beliefs, values and behaviours of academic leaders, members of faculty, university administrators and students, working from a single conceptual base.

Prestige pervades much of individual and organisational life. Its scale and complexity mean that its study requires focus. Something may present itself as a problem at an individual or group or organisational or system level when the situation we desire does not exist, or a change process we have set going does not do what we wanted. Not all of these are the concern of this book. It becomes a prestige issue if an intention is frustrated by other values and behaviours that are rated more highly than those that are being promoted. It is not a prestige issue if there are just not enough resources to do a job, unless of course the lack of resources can be explained in terms of prestige. Having placed limits on the scope of the book, one has to widen the remit again by noting that many prestige-related motivations may not be consciously realised or, if they are, may not be admitted.

So the aim of this book is to understand higher education better, by applying the idea of prestige to it. A by-product is that ideas about prestige may then be applicable in other settings. The purpose of doing so is to contribute to ways in which systems, institutions and individuals can work in ways that are morally and ethically congruent with some of the widely espoused values of universities. Stages include some conceptual clarification of what is, or might be, meant by prestige, followed by consideration of how it exists and what its effects are within higher education. Both of the above are achieved through literature review and through interviews with highly experienced leaders of and commentators on higher education internationally. The process has been iterative – the many discussions that have led to this book have involved the testing of definitions and the exploration of contexts, so both have been open to change, and continue to be so.

A conceptual base is offered in two chapters. 'Prestige and the organisation' takes a broadly sociological perspective, drawing extensively on Bourdieu as probably the most useful source of terms that help to frame discussion. The following chapter, 'Psychology of prestige', takes a psychological perspective, exploring some of the reasons that humans are inevitably evaluative in their relationships with the world. Chapter 4 establishes the processes of globalisation as the broad context for prestige concerns. This theme is further explored in Chapter 5, which examines activity in a number of nations states to establish themselves as 'global hubs' for higher education, and in Chapter 6, dealing with the growth and consequences of ranking and league tables, particularly those that are international in scope. The institutional level is introduced by Chapter 7, on the views of vice-chancellors, informed by a study of the experiences and views of twenty heads of higher education institutions in the UK. Two further chapters consider a number of beliefs and values that tend to be held in universities and that are associated with the prestige of universities as a whole and of activities and interest groups within them. These have to do with the kinds of knowledge with which the institution deals and the economic contribution that universities may make. Chapter 10 explores the ways in which students make their choices of institutions to which to apply. A concluding chapter draws the discussion together, summarising some key concerns and suggesting further areas of interest.

References

Barnett, R. (1994) *The limits of competence*. Buckingham: Society for Research into Higher Education/Open University Press.

Bascom, W. (1948) Ponapean prestige economy, in *Southwestern Journal of Anthropology* 4, 2, Summer: 211–21.

Bergquist, W. (1992) *The four cultures of the academy*. San Francisco: Jossey Bass.

Blackmore, P. and Kandiko, C.B. (2012) Motivation in academic life: A prestige economy, in *Research in Post-Compulsory Education* 16, 4: 399–411.

Bourdieu, P. (1984) *Distinction: A social critique of the judgment of taste*, trans. Richard Nice. Cambridge, MA: Harvard University Press.

Brewer, D., Gates, S. and Goldman, C. (2002) *In pursuit of prestige: Strategy and competition in US higher education*. London: Transaction Publishers.

English, J.F. (2005) *The economy of prestige*. Cambridge, MA: Harvard University Press.

Herskovits, M.J. (1948) *Man and his works: The science of cultural anthropology*. New York: A.A. Knopf.

McNay, I. (1995) From the collegial academy to corporate enterprise: The changing cultures of universities, in T. Schuller (ed.), *The Changing University?*: 105–15. Buckingham: Society for Research into Higher Education/Open University Press.

Scott, P. (1995) *The meanings of mass higher education*. Buckingham: Society for Research into Higher Education/Open University Press.

Chapter 2

Prestige and the organisation

Towards a framework for prestige

A university climbs three places in the Shanghai Jiao Tung world rankings; another is declared the most successful of those founded in the last fifty years. Bands of universities bask in the glow of being Ivy League, Russell Group or Sandstone. Others find peers with whom they can claim to be the most innovative, entrepreneurial or inclusive. A new vice-chancellor is appointed, reaching the top of the slippery pole of university leadership. Another moves to head a national body and opinions are divided as to whether this is promotion, escape or retirement. A physics department is judged the best in the UK. Entire research teams are poached by universities desperate to buy a lead over their competitors. An academic gains a three-year research award guaranteeing peace to research and freedom from other activities; another gains a national teaching award. A prospective student pores over university websites, torn because the course she really wants to take is at a lowly rated institution. In all of these cases, somebody gains something that is scarce, and others acknowledge it has value, forming the core triumvirate of prestige. Each of them raises questions about the nature of prestige and about how these components are related. The book looks more broadly, too, at the social settings within which this takes place, and uses the idea of a prestige economy as a location for prestige. This prompts further questions about the nature of a prestige economy, including its boundaries and connections, how it comes into being and how it works, and also about the extent to which it is a useful concept. Definition can remove some ambiguities but the terms remain contestable and problematic, since prestige is a social construct, as is the idea of a prestige economy. Both are valuable terms but ideologically loaded ones, partly because they carry with them the implication of competition and the metaphor of a market. They may help to illuminate some aspects of organisational life but they will throw others into shadow. So the metaphor of a prestige economy is being used for its explanatory value but with an awareness that it brings difficulties with it, which are explored later.

This chapter considers these issues, guided by what has been written about prestige and about related issues such as motivation, and also by some outcomes of empirical work. First of all there is the 'where' of prestige, bridging the individual and the social, exploring the nature of the places where prestige-valuing happens, both at a system level and locally, where individuals and groups interact constantly. Then there is the 'who' question, including not only those who have prestige or recognise it, but those who deal in it and those who do not have it. The 'what' of prestige includes the possessions, artefacts, connections and capabilities that provide prestige in an academic environment. This connects with the 'how' of prestige, the processes that make prestige something dynamic, not static, something that involves many people in activity. Much of the work that has a bearing on prestige is rooted either in sociology or in psychology. An exploration of organisations and the people in them requires the insights of both. This chapter takes a largely sociological approach, but the two cannot fully be separated.

Views of organisation

Discussion of organisations may tend to foreground the more mechanistic aspects – formal positions, rules and procedures. It may be helpful to think of organisations through a range of metaphors, and by so doing indicate possible perspectives and ways in which prestige may be understood. Table 2.1 suggests four possible metaphors, the aspects of organisation that are thus highlighted and some of the items that may be signals of prestige.

A formal, mechanistic view can be seen in the descriptions that institutions publish of their purposes. Institutional standing is signalled by mechanistic means, by titles and salaries for individuals and by space, budget size and reporting lines for an organisational unit. It is probably the most obvious place to look for outward signs of prestige, but not the only one. Prestige may also be signalled

Table 2.1 Views of an organisation and related prestige

	Assumes/foregrounds	Prestige items
Mechanism	Formal structures; buildings; formal positions; internal organisation; rules and procedures	Mission statement; physical spaces; job titles; location in organisation; department size; budget
Culture	Social aspects; interaction; form and style of communication; individual ways of being	Ceremonial symbols and activities; set-piece events
Network	Dispersed groupings; connections; communication methods	Social capital; reputation; approbation of shared interest group; influence
Political system	Self-interest; negotiation; decision-making; backstage activity	Span of authority; budget size; relationship to formal leadership; power; allies; ability to persuade and coerce

and negotiated through social means. The extent to which deference to an individual is to be expected, or criticism may be voiced, is in part a prestige issue. Prestige is signalled socially, from the pomp of set-piece events through to the choreography of conversation. A network view challenges conventional organisational structures, and can express better the fluidity of relationships in a complex world with rapid and ubiquitous means of communication. Prestige may arise much more from the approbation of those who are networked together, rather than from positioning in a formal system or structure. Finally, prestige is a scarce commodity, a manifestation of power, its possession bringing permissions and advantage. It is likely to be actively sought, leading to negotiation, bargaining and alliance. Thus prestige may be highly visible, or implicit in conversational rules. It may follow organisational boundaries or transcend them. Each of these metaphors can contribute to an holistic view of prestige in an organisation.

National systems, institutions, disciplines, professions, departments and individual lives provide a structural context for academic work and prestige, suggesting organisational levels at which any of the metaphors may be useful. An entire national system may compete internationally – the recent development of 'global hubs' is explored later. An institution is in a national prestige economy, represented through league tables that purport to bring objectivity to judgements about overall institutional quality. Within the institution, faculties and schools may compete with one another for resources and influence, and may, because of perceptions of relative status, be more or less willing to work together. Individual members of faculty seek to develop their own careers in a culture that often praises collegiality but rewards individual achievement.

However, the various levels of prestige do not always work as discrete systems. Tensions may be generated between levels, with a prestige economy at one level influencing another, sometimes quite dramatically. For example, the emergence of the 'world-class' university has led many institutions to aspire to be highly placed in international league tables, with consequences for what is valued and resourced within an institution. A change in the rules of what counts as research – such as the UK government's current concern for research that has demonstrable impact – changes the rules of the research game and may also over time change what is held to be prestigious. The availability of funding for particular kinds of teaching – for example undergraduate as opposed to postgraduate teaching – may influence perceptions of the relative attractiveness of developing provision at one level rather than another and with it the incentive for individual staff to be involved. So prestige economies can be viewed in terms of interconnected layers. An individual may be affected by prestige issues being played out at a number of levels. However, these are not always smooth processes of influence. Prestige patterns at one level may be quite resistant to change that is driven by different values at another level. Thus a government that emphasises student employability may not find all university staff to be quick to see it as their priority. An individual's or a group's sense of identity may be influential.

Identity

Contemporary sociological interpretations tend to stress the fluidity of identity, whilst acknowledging the importance of a real or apparent continuity that comes about through an individual maintaining a coherent thread of a story about themselves. A sense of continuous identity provides security for an individual and guards against anxiety. That sense of identity makes it easier to know what to think and what to do when there is no time or motivation to decide. Thus Giddens has referred to self-identity as: 'the sustaining of coherent, yet continuously revised, biographical narratives' (1991, 5), pointing to the need for individuals to make personal sense of themselves and their lives and noting the dynamic nature of that sense of self, which has to adjust in order to accommodate changes of many kinds.

However, self-identity is not generated solely by an individual acting in isolation. Importantly for social conceptions, such as prestige, it occurs partly through an interaction with others. Bruner, for example, comments that it is 'affected not only by your own interpretations of yourself but by the interpretation others offer of your version' (1991, 34). To some extent, then, our sense of who we are is influenced by what we think others think of us, and some part of it may be negotiated moment by moment. Thus self-identity is closely connected with the social and cultural environment. Bourdieu bridged the individual and the social with the influential term 'habitus' describing 'a system of shared social dispositions and cognitive structures which generates perceptions, appreciations and actions' (1984, 279).

These are broad points about identity that can relate to any exploration of people in organisations. In discussion of academic life, a related claim has been made about the influence of the academic discipline on the individual. Mary Henkel comments that from the academic community comes not only a place to be known and valued but the voice through which it can be done, for a discipline 'provides the language in which individuals understand themselves and interpret their world' (2000, 15), a point returned to later in considering issues in interdisciplinarity. This sense of identity can powerfully influence what people believe should be the shape of their working life and, specifically, what they think they should be doing with their time. This may differ from one discipline to another, as Henkel noted when surveying academics' sense of their own identity: 'Academics in English and History departments were the most likely to see their role in terms of integration of research, teaching and, in some cases, administration as well ... The ideal science career was to continue in research throughout' (Henkel, 2000, 182–3).

Thus faculty who are nominally employed for the same purposes, and who may have the same formal contract of employment, may have very different senses of what they value, and what the role entails, with a consequence for what they are likely to be inclined to spend time on. Some sense of the expectation that an individual might have about his or her career can be seen in the following description of an ideal career, taken from a recent investigation into prestige in universities:

> when you're associate professor or senior you can take a risk because you have tenure and you can go off in all sorts of interesting directions. Before that point you have to follow the schedule, have you ticked the boxes in the right journals? You've got your monograph, you've got your PhD, you've got your American Political Science Review, or whatever, you've got your big papers, you get your tenure and you're through. And then you can start to take risks and be adventurous.
>
> (Blackmore and Kandiko, 2011, 130)

This offers a very clear account of the building of an academic identity that fits neatly into the expectations of others. In addition, ideas of the generation of academic artefacts, that can be thought of as capital, can be seen throughout this account. A sense of identity will be maintained and developed through the possession of or association with various forms of capital, discussed below. These may range from the highly tangible, such as respected academic outputs or the achievement of grants from prestigious funding bodies, to the more nebulous, such as the cultural capital of the membership of a network. The relationship between capital and identity may be seen as two-way. Social identity requires the holding of capital of various kinds. The creation or gaining of capital generates the potential for identity. The idea of a prestige economy thus provides a means of illuminating the interaction between the individual and their social context as identities are developed and confirmed through the generation and acquisition of items of capital.

In the academy, the knowledge that is valued, the ways in which it is researched and shared, the form in which it is taught, and the standard to be attained when it is assessed, are highly sensitive areas of tension and dispute, not only because control of them may bring power and influence, but because of their relationship with identity. The conferment and recognition of prestige offers a means by which an individual's sense of self-worth can be bolstered through a close relationship with things that are deemed to have high value. There is a related incentive to value what one has and to seek to convince others that they should value it too.

Individuals and groups may also define themselves in part by the differences they perceive between themselves and other people, in a process of 'othering' (Becker, 1990). Part of the purpose of this is to increase the sense of identity and of status of the preferred individual or group. The differences may occur 'bottom-up' and be generated quite informally, or else be institutionalised through differing conditions of service, accommodation, expectations of dress and so on. A sense of distinctiveness may bolster pride in and commitment to a particular team or enterprise. It may prompt unproductive boundary disputes, lack of co-ordination and social practices that are unjustifiably and inequitably excluding.

This raises questions, explored later, about how groups come to see themselves as such, and about the nature of boundaries. One major concern for organisations that this book points to is the need to consider where difference is helpful and where it is not, and whether or not, and how, intervention might be appropriate.

The individual in the organisation

The role of individual agency has been reasserted robustly in recent years (Archer, 2000). Individuals are taken to have some freedom to act, to a greater or lesser degree, and those actions help to influence the local and to an extent the wider context. Thus individuals and groups can shape structures but are also shaped by them, an idea that has been expressed as 'structuration' (Giddens, 1984). An individual's self-placing and their responsiveness to a stimulus for change will be influenced by the relative strength of their identification with particular settings which may be either close to home or further away, and with what is held to be prestigious in those places. Prestige economies in academic life do not always respect institutional boundaries and are not always related to the source of financial payment. Loyalty to an organisational group does not necessarily imply loyalty to the organisation as a whole. It has on many occasions been observed that academic loyalty tends to be to a discipline or department rather than to the larger organisation (Jenkins, 1996). Thus department and discipline offer a fruitful level at which to examine more collectivist enactments of prestige. The highest quality research is usually defined as having international importance, so discipline has an external dimension. An ambitious academic is likely therefore to spend considerable time cultivating an international profile, and developing a wide network of colleagues in the discipline.

Global trends increasingly affect the local level. In particular, the more direct and interventionist approaches to management that tend to come at times of greater competitive challenge may seem to erode traditional academic autonomy. However, the same processes of globalisation open up opportunities by challenging many traditional boundaries. So as universities continue to grow in size and to be more actively managed, it may be that there will be a more obvious incentive for staff to engage in institution-level concerns, but it may also be that allegiance to individual institutions will continue to weaken, especially among academic staff, depending on the relative attractiveness of the two levels and the opportunities that are available to be connected elsewhere. Differences of view on the space available for agency can be seen in commentaries on academic life. A strand of thinking already mentioned asserts that individual academics have lost autonomy, through increasing external control of academic work, both teaching and research. A long tradition has asserted that autonomy is threatened by managerialism (Halsey, 1995; Trow, 1994), illiberal views of higher education (Barnett, 1994,1997), proletarianisation (Hyland, 1994) and McDonaldisation (Ritzer, 2004; Hayes and Wynyard, 2002). Others, however, assert that individuals may act to increase their own prestige: status is not necessarily a given.

At a system level, the term 'academic capitalism' is, for some writers (Slaughter and Leslie, 1997), a counter-response to the idea that staff in universities are helpless cogs in a machine. Instead, they recognise the new and greater opportunities that some academic staff have, through 'new structures, incentives and rewards' (1997, 1) to manage their academic career.

A wider range of opportunities is now available to many academic staff, through globalisation and the growth of communications technologies. When it is as easy to work with a colleague in Australia or Singapore as in one's own institution, and when staff and students can move readily from one national system to another, this opens up new possibilities for connections and affiliations, challenging the influence of local structures. The trend is not new: a distinction between a 'local' and a 'cosmopolitan' worker has long been noted (Merton, 1968). However, it has become much more significant and provides different opportunities for prestige-gaining. On the one hand a staff member may develop prestige locally, by taking up a senior role in an institution, gaining access to decision-making over strategic direction, budgets and human resources. This might be termed structural or positional or perhaps bureaucratised prestige, depending on the formal position in an organisation. On the other hand, cosmopolitan academics have a reputation that transcends their institution. They are in effect academic 'stars', who may be able to claim substantial consultancy and speaking fees in addition to their salary. The cosmopolitan and the local are generally related. Whilst disciplines are of course international by nature, with the highest quality research being that which is deemed to be of international significance, even such cosmopolitan prestige is usually underpinned by an individual's association with a prestigious home institution. In fact, these categories may not be entirely distinct: one person may have both positional and cosmopolitan-based prestige, and the balance between them may shift at various stages of a career. The same distinction between the local and cosmopolitan may be applied collectively. Prestigious business schools rarely have much influence on their host institution's strategic direction: they generally focus their attention elsewhere.

Prestige roles

A prestige economy consists of far more than those within it who have prestige. The people involved in a prestige economy may be in a range of roles. There are those who have and those who seek prestige. The members of an academic department, for example, or those who are active in a discipline, may either be seeking prestige or may perhaps be generating it simply by doing their work, or else be in an environment where they are aware that others are actively seeking it. There are some who manage prestige, who may be in a position of power or patronage and who can thus influence the environment and the explicit or implicit rules relating to prestige. This would include an ability to allocate resources or to change the ways in which reward and recognition are organised. They may themselves be seeking prestige. There are also others outside the prestige economy, with whom those inside it may or may not interact. There are also those who are seen to be outside a group, who may perform the function of being a foil for it, either by actually being different from group norms or by being perceived to be so. Thus the broad categories are of those who have it, seek it, acknowledge it, broker or manage it or are outsiders, by choice or otherwise.

Capital

The term 'capital' has already been used to describe the currency of a prestige economy. Some examples of capital are obvious, as is their value. An academic curriculum vitae is a list of prestige items: schooling and higher education, qualifications gained, places of employment, professional connections, grants and contracts, publications and referees. Publications are likely to be ranked, with single-authored books taking precedence over jointly-authored ones, followed by edited collections. Single-authored journal articles are preferred to jointly-authored. Articles in refereed journals have higher standing than those in non-refereed journals, or reports or newspaper articles. The order may change slightly from one discipline to another, but within any disciplinary group it is well understood. These are clearly prestige items and the ways they are generated, evaluated and used are fairly apparent.

Prestige is not always so neatly labelled, and may be hidden in a context, signalled by what a person does or does not do. If a book is finished and awaits publication, the publisher may ask the writer for a quote from an eminent person in the field, someone who will give the book weight and credibility. A well-networked writer will have taken care to cultivate colleagues worldwide. The writer may be faced with a choice between one highly prestigious colleague who would add lustre but whose ideas have been robustly critiqued in the book, and another who is of lesser stature but whose work has escaped interrogation. Prestige is at the centre of the writer's conundrum. Whose should be borrowed, what would it be worth and how willingly would it be lent? It may also be in the mind of the prestige lender. Is this book good enough for the reviewer to back it? Do the writer's ideas, reputation and institution feel a comfortable fit for the reviewer?

Prestige questions occur with relationships beyond the academy too. Government departments commission research from universities. The member of faculty involved may suspect that the department will not act on the research, as the government is not known for evidence-informed policy. Perhaps, the member of faculty may think, the department wants an association with a university, as a talisman against future attacks on its policy. A further prestige problem is that faculty may be required to sign away the right to publish independently, as a condition of a grant. So the work brings money and possibly connections but not publishable research outcomes, and seems to have no likely impact on policy. Both parties may have concerns about prestige in mind here, and it is possible that neither will say this to the other.

Clearly prestige comes in many forms, through associations that are quite diverse. In the examples above, prestige items may be artefacts, such as the outputs of academic work. These may be in a range of media, although universities tend to prefer words and numbers, for ease of assessment. However, tangible items are only a part of the prestige picture. Prestige comes through cultural association, by gaining the approval of a particular community that is influential in matters of taste in a particular field. As in the example above, a connection with a leader of opinion in a domain helps with cultural placing. That cultural approval can be seen as a kind of resource, an intangible one, although its effects may be real. Thus prestige also has a social component. Who we know matters, and many people spend a good deal of time networking, in the hope of future advantage. Again, the network is a resource, and access to it may itself be prestigious and may enable the generation of prestige. Importantly, prestige-generating activity of this kind may be hidden, or not recognised as such. As has already been noted, attitudes to prestige-seeking are often equivocal, so individuals may claim not to be seeking prestige, whether or not they are.

Thus prestige may be related to a physical possession or to an intellectual accomplishment or else to knowing somebody. It may be reflected in titles, salaries, rooms, laboratories, furnishings, research assistants and a range of other visible signs of status. All of these can be referred to by the single term 'capital'. The concept of capital is potentially valuable, partly because it is immediately recognisable and can readily be imagined, and partly also because it is an elastic term. In the field of human identity and interaction, capitals of many kinds can be imagined, and have been. Accounts of capital in sociology are dominated by the work of Pierre Bourdieu. A central figure in contemporary analyses of identity and role, whose main influence has been felt over the last thirty years, Bourdieu writes of cultural, social, symbolic, academic and economic capital. He also refers to a *field*, where various forms of capital are generated, valued and exchanged or otherwise used.

The term is in some ways a difficult one, partly because of its universal appeal and application. Almost anything can be labelled capital, if the term refers to something that is relatively scarce, or at least not possessed in great quantity by all, and which has a value of some kind. Business experts wishing to maximise company productivity deal with intellectual capital (Stewart, 1991), referring to the collectivity of assets that are not financial or physical. In teacher education, Fullan and Hargreaves (2012) write of professional capital; in the sociology of music, Cottrell (2002) speaks of musical capital. The elasticity of the term is valuable, because the idea of capital can be applied to all kinds of situations, and new capitals can readily be invented. However, some of these terms are quite hard to operationalise, in that it is not always easy to estimate the presence or possession of capitals that are not material.

In much discussion about capital, human ability is a striking omission. The focus is usually on the products of expertness or on social or cultural context. Aspects of expertise are often expressed indirectly in terms of capital, at an individual as well as an organisational level. Thus, a violin soloist's ability to play well may generate social capital by facilitating connections with others of high standing in the field, or enable participation in performances that have cultural capital, or generate income that is economic capital. Indeed, a full account in terms of capital of an expert violinist's career or even a single public performance would need to include all of these aspects. However, exploration of these various significant concerns may distract attention from the expertise itself. Such an analysis is rather like an account of an economy that concentrates on markets, banks, companies and consumers, whilst ignoring the fact that all of these structures and activities rest on work being done, expertly, by individuals.

Bourdieu pays relatively little attention to expertness, as such. However, Bailey writes of power and influence arising from being expert (1988, 9). Another strand of writing on intellectual capital also does, recognising that one of a company's main assets at a collective level is the skill of those who work in it (Stewart, 1991). In fact the nature of a skill, and the conditions under which it is exercised, are highly relevant to an understanding of the ways in which capital is generated, recognised and transacted. For example, the length of time that it takes to learn a skill to a required level and the number of people who possess that skill may both make a considerable difference to its value, in social and cultural as well as economic terms. However, the relationship is not direct and there are many other intervening factors. In addition, whether the skill is exercised in isolation or as part of a team may also make a difference to its prestige potential.

Further difficulties in defining what counts as capital spring from the ability of some individuals and groups to define the nature of capital, so that it is in alignment with what they possess. Thus, those with power are well positioned to define what counts as capital and, reciprocally, those who have that capital gain power by having it. This can certainly be seen in the creative arts, which is classically a prestige field, in that it is highly subjective and may be strongly practitioner- and broker-influenced. Veblen was an early commentator on the social misuse of prestige. In *The Theory of the Leisure Class* (1899) he developed ideas about the ways in which those in privileged positions separate themselves from those who labour, by preferring things that have an ostentatious value. In this there are similarities with the ways in which Bourdieu saw taste as a means by which social distinctions were made and maintained (Bourdieu, 1984). Veblen's was a dystopian view, critical of what he saw as the prevalent valuing of anything that did not have economic use.

Whilst the use of the term 'economy' is intended to denote only the ways in which goods and services are produced and exchanged in a community, to use that term in association with Bourdieu and to use the term 'capital' to denote everything that is valued appears to stress the inherently competitive nature of organisational life and to foreground the individual interest. Whilst such an analysis has face validity, in that universities are in many respects competitive places where individuals pursue excellence that gives them prestige, thinking in terms of capital in an economy may mean that individual competitiveness is emphasised on the one hand, whilst altruism and generosity are neglected on the other.

A strong tradition of collegiality in academic life can be seen in the enduring appeal of peer review, through which grant applications, journal articles and conference paper proposals pass, as a way of upholding the standards of a group, usually with little or no financial benefit to those undertaking the work. Many other academic activities are undertaken for token payment, such as the external examining of the quality of academic programmes in the UK system. A previous model of an academic prestige economy, drawing on the views of UK and Australian academic staff, has stressed the intrinsic component of strong interest in the discipline itself and in the development of new knowledge (Blackmore and Kandiko, 2011). These suggest that actions are not all motivated by individual self-interest. Attention should therefore be given to how individuals work with others to create communities that sustain a valued activity or way of life, as well as providing individual benefit. This may entail loyalty to a discipline or professional group, a department or an institution. It requires recognition of prestige at levels beyond the individual. This is not to be naively apolitical. Association at work and elsewhere can exist for both altruistic and selfish ends. Institutions and departments may seek competitive advantage. Professions can be seen as a conspiracy against the public interest. The interplay of the individual and the collective interest is politically significant. For example, depicting something that is in the interests of an individual or a small group as being in the interests of the whole is a widely recognised political stratagem. However, there remains a place within discussion on prestige for altruism, solidarity and public service, and of the idea of the disinterested autonomous professional (Parsons, 1939). It draws on the conception considered below of social capital being potentially held at a societal level, rather than only individually.

When exploring a prestige economy, key questions about capital may include: the forms of capital that are present; how capital is generated, by whom and for what purpose; who holds capital; and how capital is exchanged, borrowed, deployed and depleted. The term 'capital' brings difficulties with it, of ideological baggage, of imprecision and of an over-concentration on product over process. However, it is an essential concept in examining prestige, so its use is continued here, but with a strong awareness of the conceptual and operational issues it brings with it.

Social capital

Perhaps the richest exploration of capital in recent years has been that of social capital. The concept has been developed largely since the 1980s, with major contributions from Bourdieu, Coleman and Putnam, who have all explored social capital as a resource involving networks and relationships. Field (2008) offers a straightforward definition: 'People connect through a series of networks and they tend to share common values with other members of these networks; to the extent that these networks constitute a resource, they may be seen as forming a kind of capital' (2008, 1). However, emphases have varied widely. Bourdieu's focus was on ways in which an elite group maintained its position, with capital that was held by individuals. Coleman has taken a less elitist view, suggesting that all members of a society can have social capital, whilst Putnam has seen social capital as existing at the level of a society, a collective resource. Two aspects are of particular interest in a study of prestige. First is the idea that social capital might be either excluding or enabling in its effects, in ways that are related to the power of those involved, and second that social capital can function beyond the level of the individual.

The vocabulary of social capital offers terms that assist in the exploration of prestige, particularly in relation to the distribution of opportunity and exclusion. It can be used to distinguish between the different ways in which capital may work in relation to social level. Thus bonding capital binds a relatively homogeneous group together and can be excluding in its effect, while bridging capital works across social divisions and tends to be inclusive (Putnam, 2000). Woolcock uses the term 'linking social capital' for connections between 'unlike people in dissimilar situations' (2001, 13–14). One useful outcome of these distinctions is the recognition that some forms of social capital may tend to anchor a person within a particular social context, whereas others will provide access to a wider audience and potential resources. Both have their use and value. It may be that prestige could also be differentiated, in terms of its sphere or level of effect, since social capital is a major component of prestige. One might think of bonding prestige that describes the approbation of a homogeneous community, with bridging or linking prestige that works across social levels. Field suggests that the different forms of social capital may be necessary at different stages of one's life. This is perhaps of use in considering an academic career, where an induction phase of bonding is supplemented by bridging and linking, as the individual becomes established in an academic community. A perverse effect of bonding capital may be of reducing aspirations to the level accepted by the dominant group, so that an individual who wants to do something different may have to give up that ambition or leave the group to do so. This aspect can weaken the group, because those who remain with their bonding group and do not participate in wider organisations are not likely to further the interests of their group in that wider community.

Linked with this are the concepts of 'strong ties' and 'weak ties'. Strong ties amongst a close-knit group can be very supportive, but can be conservative and can work against innovation because the people in the group tend to have access to the same knowledge and social contacts. Weak ties, where an individual has a contact beyond his or her group, may be most useful in accessing information that many others nearby may not have, and this is perhaps analogous to the idea of structural holes in networks, considered later. Strong disciplinary ties may cause difficulty in a university if there is a need to recruit senior leaders from within the academy. A strong, disciplinary, research-oriented culture may make it less likely that a member of academic staff would choose to move away and into another area of work.

Social capital tends to be held by individuals and groups, and inevitably confers potential advantage of some kind, and may even positively disadvantage others. The possibly negative aspects of social capital include the inequalities that can come about because the capital is unevenly distributed, coupled with the extent to which the benefit derived is a public or a private good. If the advantage is felt only by the individual or the group, it is unequal in its effects, as compared with a benefit that is shared by a whole community. An example of this might be the existence of freemasonry within an occupational group, though which, according to Field, 'corrupt exchanges are facilitated' (2008, 93). Closure (Coleman, 1994) is also a potentially useful term in mapping prestige, because it has to do with the strength of the boundary of the community and therefore its inner coherence and the ease with which interrelationships and reciprocity can be built up. This may be both positive and negative, in that it may develop a sense of community but also contribute to exclusion.

Another potentially transferable distinction is that social capital can be viewed as an attribute either of an individual or of a group. Similarly, in universities prestige may relate to an individual and can also be held collectively by the institution or a group within it. Prestige may be borrowed, by association with that which is prestigious. Thus a perception that a university is 'world class' may be of benefit to all those who are associated with it, who would share a common interest in maintaining that perception in the eyes of others. Similarly, staff in one academic department or research team may work cohesively together, in competition with another department or team. One might argue that a more socially cohesive and intersupportive culture is likely to result if prestige-seeking occurs principally at a group rather than an individual level. This may offer a useful way of dealing with prestige in universities, and its application is considered in the conclusion.

Prestige economy

Discussion thus far has focused on the broad organisational context and the where, who and what of prestige – the setting, those who are involved and the capital that is valued. Here, issues relating to the idea of a prestige economy are explored, beginning with an attempt to define or at least illuminate what a prestige economy might be. This leads into a discussion on boundaries and from there into questions of organisational level. Finally, some of the ideological problems of an approach based on capital are explored.

A central proposition of this book, drawing on a range of work by other writers, is that an area of organisational life can be identified that has broadly shared beliefs and values and that engages in social practices that have some coherence and continuity over time. Essentially, the term refers to a group of people who tend to value the same things, and often have common behaviours. However, the act of carving out a prestige economy entails separating it from what then becomes its external context. There are consequences in thus identifying a particular organisational area, whether it is an individual department or a research team, or a faculty, an institution or a national system. A prestige economy can be imagined at any and all of these levels, requiring decisions about where one draws the boundary of a prestige economy, what is within and what beyond the boundary and how activity that crosses boundaries takes place, or does not. How are any boundaries spanned and by whom? Are there 'trading zones', between and among settled prestige economies, where ideas and resources may be negotiated?

Some recent work on academic prestige has taken the academic department (Blackmore and Kandiko, 2011) or the research centre (Blackmore and Kandiko, 2010) to be the significant social entity to explore. This is perhaps a reasonable starting point. Studying a department as a prestige economy is convenient and neat. In some ways, the boundaries of the department are obvious. There is a clear cohering activity – the subject itself and the teaching and researching of it, and faculty are strongly socialised into disciplines. It is through the profession of a discipline that faculty gain academic credibility and standing. It is still the case that research excellence is the strongest feature in promotion, and high-quality research continues to be organised on a disciplinary basis, despite the growth of interdisciplinary research and of calls for it to be undertaken. However, it has been claimed that disciplinary groups are much less clearly defined than was previously the case (Becher and Trowler, 2001) and it could be argued that viewing a university as if it were a collection of discrete disciplines is outdated. Many parts of universities are increasingly organised around professional areas or into broad fields of study rather than tight disciplines, with much weaker classification and framing (Bernstein, 1971). Despite this trend, later it will be argued that disciplines still have some power to illuminate some of what happens in universities, and a number of the difficulties in encouraging interdisciplinary and interprofessional work arise from the tensions that accompany differing discipline-related patterns of prestige being brought together.

A focus on the department is a huge simplification in a number of ways. Within any department there will be a range of views on many matters. Physicists, for example, do not always take the same view as one another on every issue. Whilst individuals are certainly socialised into their principal organisational structure, they are also human beings with other affiliations: they may have strong political or religious beliefs; they are of a particular ethnic origin, gender, age and stage of career. Thus the members of the economy are not homogeneous. The prestige economy argument is that there is sufficient commonality to generate a tendency for particular beliefs, values and behaviours, and indeed, it is at the level where sufficiency is reached that one might be able to say that the entity could be considered to be a prestige economy.

A basis for boundaries

The idea of a prestige economy, as it is being discussed here, suggests an area where certain beliefs, values and activities tend to be the norm. The idea of an area necessarily suggests that it is bounded in some way and raises a number of questions:

- What does it cohere around?
- What is the size and boundary of the domain?
- Who is in and who is out, and on what basis?
- What are the consequences of such decisions?

These questions may be linked with the metaphors of organisation discussed earlier. An obvious distinguishing aspect of an academic prestige economy is epistemological, on the grounds that subject knowledge in universities is complex and, in research and higher levels of teaching, highly specialised. It might be argued that the nature of knowledge and an individual's relationship with it differ across disciplines, so the issue is also an ontological one. These questions are returned to in a later discussion of interdisciplinarity, including the idea that some disciplinary boundaries are more permeable than others. A second basis, related to the first, is organisational. When roles are distributed and resources allocated in particular ways in an institution, power is distributed too, and some people will have more influence than others and will in effect be able to decide what is valued, at least financially. Functional analysis in workplaces produces detailed role descriptions of responsibilities and permissions for each individual. By these means, organisational boundaries are established, producing silos and making it hard for ideas and activities to flow freely across the organisation. Some forms of activity will be easier and others harder. Some will be rewarded more and others less so. Again the idea of permeability is relevant. Strong boundaries will privilege those who are within the prestige economy. A third and related basis is political, and often has to do with access to resources, including prestige. Boundaries mean that some people are on the inside and others on the outside. For those on the inside, there may be a tendency to emphasise the unity, similarity and virtue of those inside, appropriating to the insiders a range of desirable attributes that outsiders are deemed not to have. This raises a major issue of vested interest. In any field where financial and other advantage is to be gained through a monopoly position on an aspect of practice, for example where a professional body is seeking to establish its particular claim to expertness, there is a strong motivation to emphasise the extensiveness of the required knowledge base, the time needed to master it, the difficulties of making independent professional judgements and the necessity of doing so. Thus a professional body will establish a claim to control of practice, and by doing so will attract prestige both to itself and to those members it serves. Boundaries also offer a source of power and influence to those who can span them.

Discussion of boundaries implies a conventional view of organisations, consisting of discrete, immediately identifiable components. Thinking in terms of boundaries remains useful for focusing on a particular area where a group of people seem to have common values and practices. However, all prestige economies will be to some extent permeable, and will intersect with others, both horizontally and vertically, in organisational terms. Even colleagues who are geographically close may have very different patterns of association with others. For reasons that are explored later in discussions on globalisation, such a metaphor is no longer always the most appropriate to describe how relationships are developed and maintained. A network metaphor might have more power to explain complex interconnections, where the idea of a fixed identity and a set community becomes less attractive. Indeed, the whole idea of a particular boundary may be an individual or group perception that may not be shared by others. So, although a bounded economy offers clarity and simplicity for analysis, it may in some circumstances be more useful to think in terms of prestige existing in complex networks with an infinite number of interconnections, with individuals and groups acting in a variety of ways that are related to the many contacts that they have and the concern and activity of the moment. On the other hand, human social identity is not in total flux. There is some continuity, and there is usually physical positioning and management. Most departments are in a specific physical location, and indeed may need specialist space because of what they do. Some functions require groups to meet frequently – to plan and review teaching, for example. The line management principle means that formally all staff in an institution have a person to whom they report, and this inevitably produces clusters. Taken together, these make some aspects of organisational life less network-like.

Prestige arenas and brokers

There are obvious points at which prestige may formally be recognised, and which may have been established for the specific purpose of recognising merit or status. They are in some ways similar to the arenas described by Bailey who, writing of power in organisations, defines an arena as 'sets of rules which lay down how competition should be conducted' (1977, 13). These include promotion rounds and honorary doctorate ceremonies. The former are marked out by large committees of senior staff and copious amounts of paper and the latter through the rituals of academic dress and procession. At others, prestige is conferred as a by-product of the activity. For example, conference keynotes, the inclusion of articles in publications and the awarding of a grant are all points where prestige is generated, and will be captured in an individual's curriculum vitae. Other points at which prestige can be 'read' may include the physical positioning and quality of accommodation, whether in glossy premises or near to those with positional power. Other points of recognition may be much more local, embedded in day-to-day business. It would include the right or expectation to chair or be a member of a committee, and the expectation of the nature and extent of participation in meetings. There are also places of prestige generation and allocation at national level. English (2005) explored this in his study of literary prizes. These he saw as a deliberate attempt to generate and allocate prestige. In UK higher education, the Research Excellence Framework (REF) for assessing the quality of research confers immense prestige on institutions, departments and individual academic staff, withholding it from others. Teaching competitions, such as National Teaching Fellowships in the UK, University Grants Committee teaching excellence awards in Hong Kong, Australian Learning and Teaching Fellowships and others elsewhere are also places of prestige generation. University league tables are further prestige sites.

Places where decisions are made require individuals to make those decisions or else to manage the process or the climate that will lead to the bestowal of prestige. The set-piece events above clearly require people to make and to look after the rules when awards are made. In the construction and publication of league tables in particular one can see prestige brokering at work. It is in the interests of the newspapers and journals that publish the results of such exercises that there should be a competition, and that there should be winners and losers. Prestige is newsworthy. Disciplines and professions require rules, too, which are established and maintained by their societies and associations. Many academic staff give a great deal of time to such commitments, thus acting as brokers, influencing the climate in which they and their colleagues work. Part of the ongoing sensitivity over decision-making in universities is a preference among many academic staff that decisions that are academic in nature, such as the quality of a piece of research or of teaching, should be made by those who are in academic positions – hence the strong tradition of peer review. Bailey, and others, use an acting metaphor to stress that negotiation may be conducted frontstage or backstage (Bailey, 1977). The latter is particularly important in prestige discussions, such as which institutions are included in a particular mission group, or the kind of institution from which external examiners will be sought. Backstage may be where a university decides who will be offered honorary degrees, or who will be invited to give their name to a new building.

The presentation of self

An inclusive view of prestige would assume that all individuals have the potential for prestige, enacted at an individual level, in everyday relationships and behaviours. Erving Goffman offered an influential and long-lived account of how individual prestige is managed, mainly at the level of the individual, by everybody, through processes of social interaction. Goffman's principal metaphor is that of the stage, emphasising the idea of performance and audience. Writing about what people actually do in negotiating relationships, he discusses the relational issues that arise and the repertoire of activities that are involved in the negotiation. At the centre is the need in human interaction for participants to come together with mutual respect for each other's stories, meaning the conception that they have of themselves, that they are inviting the other person to take at face value. This may occur only for the time that the two sides are in contact with each other, but it is essential that it should, to create a comfortable space. He describes a shared definition of the situation as a factor that has to be sustained 'in the face of a multitude of possible disruptions' (1990, 246). Discomfort is to be avoided, and many social activities are to do with the development and protection of a sustained view, requiring overt consensus and tact. There must be smoothness and this means that the human spirit has to be 'bureaucratised', in that difficult emotions and views have to be suppressed in the interests of harmony. When agreement breaks down, there may be problems at three levels: social interaction may be impeded, with a sense of uncertainty and lack of direction; a person may find their place in the social structure jeopardised; and a person's sense of their own personality may be disrupted. So consensus is valued and worked for, because it is both psychologically and socially valuable.

Social status plays a major part in the ways in which people interact. People are categorised and segmented, often for ease of handling, so that stock responses or clusters of permissions can be used. In some places Goffman takes a functionalist view, in that some roles carry with them standard permissions, but the general thrust of his work is interactionist, where relationships are constructed moment by moment. People are also kept at a distance, sometimes through the use of professionalism, and the permissions that tend to come with it. Despite the principal focus being on the presentation of the self, Goffman also notes that many relationships are about teams rather than individuals.

Goffman uses the term 'social establishment', by which he seems to mean a closed social system. This may perhaps be analogous to a prestige economy. He suggests that one can view a social establishment technically, politically, structurally and culturally and that all of these are related to a fifth area, dramaturgy. Thus he emphasises the importance of what happens, including the objects in the space. Teams require a certain amount of idealisation and illusion if they are able to achieve their ends by convincing those outside the team that the team is competent. Thus secrecy is a feature of teams. There are several kinds of secret, some of which are 'dark' and disreputable, others 'strategic' in that they may have to do with business intentions. The most powerful idea is that of a latent secret, which is something the potential facts of which might make it too uncomfortable to be investigated.

Goffman is very sensitive to the nuances of human interaction and so makes a major contribution to the study of prestige, in that he offers a highly developed analytical account of how prestige, in its broadest sense, is claimed and maintained and lost, at the level of individuals and groups involved in events. In using the metaphor of the stage he emphasises performance, which is valuable, since prestige has to be negotiated and enacted in social spaces.

Language and prestige

In universities the power of one language in relation to another can be seen in the dominance of English as an international academic language, meaning that those who write in other languages may be systematically disadvantaged (van Raan et al., 2010), unless they are published in translation. Often literacy has been seen as a set of generic skills, but it can also be viewed as a social practice that takes place in a context, influenced by prevailing values and having a relationship with identity and power. If one takes this 'ideological' view (Street 1984, 1995), then even within a single language there are infinite opportunities to claim status through language. Indeed, one of the main social functions of language will be to confer or deny social status. Thus, even in a national setting with a strongly dominant language, one of the main ways in which prestige is negotiated and recognised is through spoken and written language and through spoken dialect, meaning here variants within a language.

There need not be a single language or dialect that is a dominant form and is universally respected the most. In the academy it can be argued that the distinctive ways in which disciplines and professional groups express themselves both formally and informally are in effect a range of dialects, so that there is no single shared academic language. This opens the possibility that some dialects may have a higher status than others. It is often claimed that there is a 'pecking order' among disciplines, and this may find expression in the kinds of language that are valued in particular circumstances. Each group maintains its own expectations, conformity with which is a prerequisite for prestige to be accorded within the group. Only a relatively confident few can expect to stand out against such norms and be accorded high prestige as mavericks who feel sufficiently secure not to follow their group's language norms.

Variation in the ways in which language is used may reflect underlying epistemological differences in the nature of knowledge and also of ontological variation, about the nature of being in a field, in particular the relationship between the knower and what it means to know. Bernstein's work has been extended by others as a way of mapping difference of these kinds. Legitimation code theory (Maton, 2000, 2013) takes the work of Bernstein, Bourdieu and others and argues that knowledge gains its status from its relationship with a number of features: autonomy, density, specialisation, semantics and temporality. Epistemic relations refers to the extent to which academic knowledge is formal, and bounded from the everyday. Social relations refers to the roles of personal experience and opinion in knowledge. Each may be stronger or weaker. Where both are strong, an elite code exists, such as in architecture, and where each is weak there is relativist code. Strong epistemic and weak social relations produce a knowledge code, such as in mathematics, and strong social relations and weak epistemic produce a knower code, for example in English. Further, knowledge structures may be horizontal, such as in social sciences and humanities, consisting of many groups with differing uses of language and diverse sets of values and assumptions, or hierarchical, as in the sciences, with a more unified set of organising principles.

These different ways of organising and valuing knowledge and conceptualising the knower play out in a number of ways in universities. There may be difficulties in the formation of interdisciplinary academic research groups, where ideas of what constitutes valid knowledge may be diverse, and in achieving publication of interdisciplinary work when the majority of the most prestigious journals are monodisciplinary. Students who are taught in more than one discipline often report variation in the kinds of writing that are expected, such as the use of the first person or the extent to which a discursive treatment is encouraged.

Alongside diversity in academic dialect, there are system-level pressures towards greater homogeneity of language, in large part through the introduction of standard administrative procedures. Thus the growth of explicit planning for teaching quality assurance as a formal activity in universities has led to the universal adoption of terms such as aims; objectives, both teaching and learning; learning outcomes; key, core or transferable skills; formative and summative assessment and many more. Whether those terms actually mean the same thing across a university is a question that is only noted here. However, the universal adoption of a quality assurance dialect does not necessarily mean that its use confers prestige on the user. It may be that access to senior roles in the institution requires an ability to deploy such language, whereas prestige in some parts of the university that are less close to the central administration may lie in rejecting such terms, by treating them ironically or paying only lip service to them.

Towards the psychology of prestige

This chapter has outlined some aspects of prestige: some of the ways in which organisations can be viewed and the kinds of capital associated with them; the organisational levels at which prestige may be said to work; the relationship between identity and capital; various kinds of capital, including social capital, and the possibilities of holding capital in common. Arenas for prestige generation, exchange and display have been noted as has the role of language in negotiating and expressing prestige. Prestige is also and fundamentally a process, involving the interaction of people, through which prestige is developed, recognised, gained, traded, depleted and lost. This may include some fairly subtle social activities, such as: permission to participate in meetings; a tendency to express, or not, praise and blame; approval or tolerance of prestige-seeking behaviour; and attitudes to success. Distinctions may be quite subtle, and not at all overt. Prestige can also be explored from a psychological perspective. Prestige influences how individuals perceive the world, how they take decisions and how they decide whom they relate to and want to work with. Chapter 3 therefore considers the psychology of prestige.

References

Archer, M. (2000) *Being human: The problem of agency*. Cambridge: Cambridge University Press.
Bailey, F. (1977) *Morality and expediency: The folklore of academic politics*. New Brunswick, NJ: Aldine Transaction.
Bailey, F. (1988) *Humbuggery and manipulation: The art of leadership*. Ithaca, NY: Cornell University Press.
Barnett, R. (1994) *The limits of competence*. Buckingham: Society for Research into Higher Education/Open University Press.
Barnett, R. (1997) *Higher education: A critical business*. Buckingham: Society for Research into Higher Education/Open University Press.
Becher, T. and Trowler, P.R. (2001) *Academic tribes and territories*, 2nd edition. Buckingham: Society for Research into Higher Education/Open University Press.
Becker, H.S. (1990) Generalizing from case studies, in E. Eisner and A. Pecking (eds), *Qualitative inquiry in education: The continuing debate* (pp. 233–45). New York and London: Teacher's College Press.
Bernstein, B. (1971) *Class, code and control: Volume 1: Theoretical studies towards a sociology of language*. London and Boston: Routledge and Kegan Paul.
Blackmore, P. and Kandiko, C.B. (2010) Interdisciplinary leadership and learning, in M. Davies, M. Devlin and M. Tight (eds), *Interdisciplinary Higher Education: International Perspectives on Higher Education Research*, Vol. 5: 55–74. Amsterdam: Emerald Group; New York: JAI Elsevier Press.
Blackmore, P. and Kandiko, C.B. (2011) Motivation in academic life: A prestige economy, in *Research in Post-Compulsory Education* 16, 4: 399–411.
Bourdieu, P. (1984) *Distinction: A social critique of the judgment of taste*, trans. Richard Nice. Cambridge, MA: Harvard University Press.
Bruner, J. (1991) The narrative construction of reality, in *Critical Inquiry*, 18, 1: 1–21.
Coleman, J.S. (1994) *Foundations of social theory*. Cambridge, MA: Belknap Press.
Cottrell, S. (2002) Music as capital: Deputizing among London's freelance musicians, in *British Journal of Ethnomusicology* 11, 2: 61–80.
English, J.F. (2005) *The economy of prestige*. Cambridge, MA: Harvard University Press.
Field, J. (2008) *Social capital*. Abingdon: Routledge.
Fullan, M. and Hargreaves, A. (2012) *Professional capital: Transforming teaching in every school*. New York: Routledge.
Giddens, A. (1984) *The constitution of society: Outline of the theory of structuration*. Cambridge: Polity Press.
Giddens, A. (1991) *Modernity and self-identity: Self and society in the late Modern Age*. Cambridge: Polity.
Goffman, E. (1990) *The presentation of self in everyday life*. London: Penguin.
Halsey, A. (1995) *Decline of donnish dominion*. Oxford: Oxford University Press.
Hayes, D. and Wynyard, R. (2002) *The McDonaldization of higher education*. Westport, CT: Bergin and Garvey.
Henkel, M. (2000) *Academic identities and policy change in higher education*. London: Jessica Kingsley.
Hyland, T. (1994) *Competence, education and NVQs*. London: Cassell.
Jenkins, A. (1996) Discipline-based educational development, in *International Journal for Academic Development* 1, 1: 50–62.

Maton, K. (2000) Languages of legitimation: The structuring significance for intellectual fields of strategic knowledge claims, in *British Journal of Sociology of Education*, 20, 2: 189–206.
Maton, K. (2013) *Knowledge and knowers: Towards a realist sociology of education*. London: Routledge.
Merton, R. (1968) The Matthew effect in science, in *Science* 159, 3810: 56–63.
Parsons, T. (1939) The professions and social structure, in *Essays in Sociological Theory*, revised edition: 34–49. Chicago, IL: Glencoe.
Putnam, R. (2000) *Bowling alone: The collapse and revival of American community*. New York: Simon and Schuster.
Ritzer, G. (2000) *The McDonaldization of society*. Thousand Oaks, CA: Pine Forge Press.
Slaughter, S. and Leslie, L.L. (1997) *Academic capitalism: Politics, policies, and the entrepreneurial university*. Baltimore, MD: Johns Hopkins University Press.
Stewart, T. (1991) Brainpower: How intellectual capital is becoming America's most valuable asset, in *Fortune* 2: 44–60.
Street, B. (1984) *Literacy in theory and practice*. New York: Cambridge University Press.
Street, B. (1995) *Social literacies: Critical approaches to literacy in development, ethnography and education*. London: Longman.
Trow, M. (1994) Managerialism and the academic profession: The case of England, in *Higher Education Policy* 7, 2: 11–18.
van Raan, A.F.J., van Leeuwen T.N. and Visser, M. (2010) Germany and France are wronged in citation-based rankings, http://www.cwts.nl/pdf/LanguageRanking 22122010.pdf, accessed 1 January 2014.
Veblen, T. (1899) *The theory of the leisure class: An economic study of institutions*. New York: MacMillan.
Woolcock, M. (2001) The place of social capital in understanding social and economic outcomes, in *Isuma: Canadian Journal of Policy Research* 2, 1: 11–17.

Chapter 3

Psychology of prestige

A shared sense of what is most prestigious can be found in many aspects of life. Universities, with their roles in the creation and sharing of knowledge, are inherently prestige-generating both in terms of academic careers and students' life chances. Institutions, as discussed later in the book, are thought of as more or less prestigious, and are ranked in league tables that signal their relative standing. Disciplines and professional groups have greater or lesser prestige than one another. The presence of a discipline or profession in universities confers prestige on it. Basic research is, for many, valued more highly than applied research, and research of almost any kind tends to be valued over most teaching. Postgraduate teaching tends to be more prestigious than undergraduate teaching. Thus an understanding of what happens or does not happen in universities can be assisted by paying attention to the working of prestige. Chapter 2 explored the organisational context of universities, considering those who are involved in prestige-gaining and recognition, the kinds of things that can be prestigious and some of the processes of prestige. These are largely sociologically informed issues, external to the individual although often considered at an individual level. It is obvious that prestige is a deeply rooted and enduring feature of human social existence. However, prestige also raises psychological questions. Why do we appear to need prestige? Why are we so inclined to attribute more worth to some things than others? What function does this serve and how does it work? To what extent are we conscious of mental processes that relate to prestige?

Some prestige items are relatively explicit, in that they exist tangibly in the world. These might include formal rank, job titles, awards and salaries. They are public, and quite often deliberately intended to be so, as ways of signalling a person's position and worth within a society or an organisation. Beyond this are implicit aspects of prestige, less tangible and less openly acknowledged. These might include quite nuanced behaviours and attitudes, such as senses of relative social positioning between the individual and others. Much of the culture of an organisation – 'the way we do things here' – is never written down, but is widely shared and tends to guide attitudes and actions. Although implicit, these aspects of prestige can be the subject of conscious thought, open to reflection. However, some mental states and processes that have a bearing on prestige are not directly available for reflection, because they are not consciously held. This chapter deals with both the implicit and the unconscious, aiming to explore some of the insights that psychology offers into prestige at work. Firstly, a review of some themes in the study of academic motivation aims to help outline human drives, emphasising some of the literature on academic motivation to draw out the relevance of these issues in academic life. Secondly, the role of prestige in cognitive processing and decision-making is explored, one that is not always visible or available for reflection.

A motivation backdrop

Academic motivation requires new attention, because so much is being required of universities, with rapid and complex changes in the cause of increased output in teaching, research and other activities. A mismatch between management intention and the degree of engagement of staff in the organisation can be costly, in terms both of efficiency and goodwill. McInnis, drawing on extensive studies of academic and administrative staff in universities over many years, comments that institutions can 'undermine academic productivity and lose faculty by failing to address the values and work preferences of individuals that attract them ... in the first place' (McInnis, 2012, 162).

A number of models, the rational economic, the social, the self-actualising and the complex, provide a basis for analysing staff motivation in higher education (Rowley, 1996). The first three are content models, having to do with explanations of the factors within the person. A rational economic model (Taylor, 1947) puts economic self-interest at the centre, and assumes that people want to maximise financial and material reward. In such a model, the offering of a financial reward is a way of stimulating motivation. A social model (Mayo, 1975) focuses on social needs and relationships with people. Social relationships are held to become relatively more important when work that has been routinised becomes less attractive. Immediate social relationships may be so influential that a desire for peer-group approbation may be more sought after than that of more distant leaders and managers. Effective management therefore takes note of people's need for belonging and identity. Self-actualisation is best exemplified by Maslow (1997), who proposed a hierarchy of human needs. Once basic safety needs are met, higher needs of self-actualisation are required to be satisfied, in which the individual gains personal growth and self-fulfilment. Social and self-actualisation models make the assumption that humans are self-motivated. A complex model, presented by Schein (1980), suggests that humans vary greatly in their needs and motivation, according to their situation and their experience and other factors. So, effective leadership requires an awareness of motivational differences among people and an ability to work flexibly, in ways that are most likely to achieve high levels of motivation in others.

Motivation is often held to be intrinsic, or extrinsic, or a blend of the two. Intrinsic motivation includes achievement, recognition, advancement, responsibility and personal engagement and growth, which are believed to be strong motivators in work. In this field, Ryan and Deci (2013) reviewed much of the research that draws on self-determination theory, which suggests that competence, autonomy and relatedness are needs, the meeting of which leads to individual wellbeing. Feldman and Paulsen (1999), writing of academic motivation, list a number of internal motivators: enjoying open-ended problem-solving; being helpful; making a difference, including helping students to grow; satisfactory student interaction; feeling competently skilled and knowledgeable; having an opportunity to learn; and having autonomy. Writing of needs in organisations, Alderfer (1973) listed existence, relatedness and growth. Extrinsic motivators include salaries, relations with other workers and working conditions. Feldman and Paulsen list external motivators that include the granting of a permanent position, promotion, merit pay, travel, expenses and clerical support. Hertzberg (1966) differentiates between intrinsic motivators and extrinsic or hygiene factors, the latter of which do not strongly satisfy but are needed to reduce dissatisfaction. However, Rowley (1996, 15) points out that satisfaction and motivation are not necessarily interchangeable, and that an increase in satisfaction will not necessarily lead to an increase in motivation. Thus, many academic staff are already strongly motivated, so that the main job of management is not to provide motivators but to reduce dissatisfiers.

Job satisfaction has often been measured in large studies. Capelleras (2005) took a broad view, including context, intrinsic and extrinsic factors, in finding that there were four aspects that were the most important sources of satisfaction: inner rewards; role conflict and balance; economic compensation and security; and support and recognition. Job security has been an important feature of academic life, and it has been claimed that systems that have historically provided the most security for faculty, such as the US system of tenure, encourage complacency and discourage motivation. Bess (1998, 4) claims that tenure does not reduce faculty motivation, as is sometimes supposed. Instead, it is the absence of other factors that would produce strong motivation.

From a prestige perspective, perhaps the more significant aspects of ideas about motivation include the desire for approbation through strong personal relationships and the wish for self-actualisation. The first suggests that the approbation of the group with which the person principally identifies will be the most sought after, a tendency that may underlie the idea of a prestige economy. Self-actualisation for many members of faculty is highly likely to be based around research achievement, emphasised by the kinds of capability that are both required on appointment and recognised through promotion. Rowley makes the point strongly that staff are immensely diverse in many ways, and so they are likely to be motivated by different factors. However, recognition and reward tend to be dealt with across an institution uniformly. This may not be the most effective way of proceeding, although there is an obvious requirement for staff to be treated equitably.

There may be a mismatch between what an employer believes an employee will find to be motivational and what the employee actually does find to be so. Thus in signalling that priority is being applied to a particular motivator, such as financial reward, an employer might actually forfeit the respect of the employee who does not believe that finance should be such a strong motivator in academic life. A major area of mismatch may lie in the differences between striving for reputation and for prestige. As already discussed, universities are likely to be principally prestige-driven or reputation-driven, or be aiming at becoming prestige-driven. Almost all activities will achieve either prestige or reputation or neither. Therefore, many tensions in work allocation and the availability of opportunities will be in effect a tussle between the competing claims of prestige and reputation. Thus an appraisal meeting can be a site of disagreement over what is valued. An example might be to compare the respective motivations to teach and to research. The achievement of high levels of student satisfaction or engagement, as measured by a student survey, is a reputational issue. As explored earlier, reputation is generally earned by satisfying the wishes of external stakeholders, often by providing a reliable service within a defined cost. A prestige-related activity is more likely to be curiosity- and academically driven, and will often be undertaken without being fully funded for its costs. Much academic research would be of this kind.

Disagreement between a member of staff and an organisation over expectations can be explored through the idea of the psychological contract, first used by Argyris in 1960, and developed extensively from the late 1980s onwards. Schein defined it as: 'A set of unwritten reciprocal expectations between an individual employee and the organisation' (Schein, 1980). It is considered here, because it bears some relationship to prestige. The idea has its critics, Guest describing it as neither a theory nor a measure but a hypothetical construct, and one that is rather hard to pin down. He comments that it 'is concerned with the interaction between one specific and another nebulous party. The contract resides in the interaction rather than in the individual or the organisation' (1999, 650). Despite reservations, he finds three reasons for taking psychological contract seriously. Firstly, that it 'captures the spirit of the times' by reflecting an increasingly individualised employment relationship. Secondly, he claims that there is increasing inequality in power relationships between the individual worker and a large organisation, and so the concept of the psychological contract is one way of drawing attention to the costs of such inequality. Finally, Guest believes that, with further work, psychological contract can be used to integrate some important organisational concepts. He believes its value is in giving some voice to the idea of trust in human interaction, as against conventional economics which assumes self-interest. The idea of a psychological contract may be valuable as universities come to be more actively managed and responsive to external stakeholders, so that previous implicit understandings of what was valued may come into question, often when financial concerns lead to a decrease in academic autonomy and the replacement of prestige by reputational goals.

In summary, then, motivation is a complex field. Individuals are moved variously by a range of intrinsic and extrinsic factors. In academic work, as in many other occupations, intrinsic motivation is often extremely strong. Where there is a mismatch between what an employee wants to do and what an institution requires, the resulting clash of expectations may lead to work dissatisfaction. This is very relevant to prestige, in that one can expect significant tensions when academically led and curiosity-driven work is valued most highly, by an individual and also perhaps in the working environment, but the institutional drive is to meet reputational goals, externally defined.

The role of prestige in cognitive processing and decision-making

In both organisational and personal life, individuals have to make countless decisions in limited time, usually with imperfect information. Such decisions often require the person to decide what it is best to do, taking into account the attitudes, wishes and needs of others. This may entail taking a view on what or who is the pre-eminent person, product or idea in a particular field, the sense of esteem for whom, or which, would be widely shared. Prestige and reputation thus have a highly practical psychological function, in that they can speed up decision-making and reduce the possibilities of conflict and of failure, or at least reduce the level of anxiety about them. A preference for the proven and need to economise on thinking time extend through most of our complex thought processes.

Cognitive efficiency

A long tradition about decision-making, particularly in economics, suggests that people make rational choices in the light of evidence. Such a view can be seen in the recent proliferation of university league tables and other data and advice on how to interpret them, discussed in a later chapter. However, this does not match with the reality of much decision-making. Decisions tend to be taken without full information and in limited time. This tendency to make the best use of limited information and indeed of mental capacity has been termed 'bounded rationality' (Simon, 1991) and 'satisficing' (Simon, 1956) and may also involve reducing available choices before applying rationality to make a choice or using heuristics as a guide. So, the complexities of life make full rationality impossible to achieve and require us to cut cognitive corners, often by emulating others.

Studies of the ways in which experts work have long shown that expertness functions differently from novice or competence levels of performance (Dreyfus and Dreyfus, 1986). The sheer quantity of data to which an expert has access is potentially a problem for rapid decision-making. In any field, a world-class expert will have 50,000 items of information in memory (Simon, 1991, 129). Experts are not simply thinking in the same way as competent people, but faster. They think in different ways, avoiding the need to take logical steps by referring to stories or schemata that 'place' a problem. Indeed, experienced decision makers who are working under pressure tend not to consider options, because only one approach comes to mind (Klein, 1998). Paradoxically, then, the more expert a person is, the fewer mental processes are performed, and the less aware is the expert of the basis of the expertise or the process by which it has been brought to bear on a problem.

However, it is not only experts who appear to be on automatic pilot. Many life processes take place for individuals with very little or no conscious thought guiding them. A distinction between intuitive and deliberate thought is proposed by Kahneman, who outlines a 'two-system view' of intuition and reasoning. Operations in system 1 are 'fast, automatic, effortless, associated, implicit (not available to introspection), and often emotionally charged'. They tend to be habitual and so are difficult to change without deliberate thought. System 2 is 'slower, serial, effortful, more likely to be consciously monitored and deliberately controlled'. It is also more flexible and capable of being controlled. However, it is a light control system and misses things. It can be influenced by time pressure, concurrent involvement in another cognitive task, by time of day and by mood (Kahneman, 2003, 711). System 1 tasks can run in parallel without affecting each other. System 2 tasks require thought and therefore parallel processing is difficult. Kahneman concludes that system 1 produces impressions that control our judgements, unless system 2 modifies or overrides them. Decisions on moral worth and other matters are often taken swiftly: 'The assessment of whether objects are good (and should be approached) or bad (and should be avoided) is carried out quickly and efficiently by specialised neural circuitry' (2003, 700). The brain in relation to moral issues has been likened to a dual mode camera (Greene, 2014, 15), suggesting that automatic decisions are taken quickly but inflexibly, whilst 'manual mode' decisions are more flexible but take longer. It is claimed that emotions are automatic processes that act as a guide for what to do, producing efficiency in behaviour, and based in part on lessons learned from past experience. Schneider makes a similar point about cognitive efficiency when he discusses stereotyping, claiming that this is an entirely normal cognitive activity that trades 'somewhat impoverished experiences for safety and mental calm' (2005, 28).

A number of mental processes that enable us to take short cuts with thinking pre-dispose us to be in favour of that which is prestigious. For example, the context in which we meet a problem influences the way we engage with it. Thus we may not make use of available knowledge that is potentially useful in problem-solving unless the possibility that it might do so is made obvious to us. We are more likely to apply particular heuristics if we are primed and reminded that they exist prior to the decision. So the extent to which a thought can be accessed is related both to the cognitive mechanisms that produce it and to the characteristics of what is being considered. If we find a stimulus to be motivational and it arouses our emotions, we are likely to pay it attention and in so doing, to pay less attention to other thoughts. If we are familiar with a social category then the traits connected with it will be brought more strongly to mind. The way something is framed, meaning the parts of it that are readily accessible, makes a difference to what we attend to and what we decide. With framing effects, we sometimes take decisions on the basis of irrelevant information. For example, we may choose something because we know more about it (Kahneman, 2003, 783). People will tend not to reformulate the information they are given 'but will adopt the representation that constitutes the most straightforward translation' (Simon and Hayes, 1976, 183). This suggests that those who can generate a strong identity or idea are likely to influence the amount of attention they receive and, of course, the amount that is left over for competitors.

Some have suggested that we have a general disposition towards evaluation. Thus Slovic et al. (2002) have proposed an 'affective evaluation', suggesting that all stimuli produce such an evaluation that tends to contain particular assumptions and to be from a particular perspective, and that this may not be a conscious action, but may be influential in evaluating a wide range of complex issues. Kahneman's work supports this, suggesting that 'an automatic affective valuation – the emotional core of attitude – is the main determinant of many judgements and behaviours' (2003, 710).

All of the above suggests that if something is thought to be prestigious, then it is more likely to be brought to mind. A further step in the field of aesthetic judgement has proposed that prestige is influential in initial sense-making. Hargreaves notes that aesthetic judgements about music among experienced musicians are influenced by prestige and propaganda factors such as the perceived 'seriousness' of the composer (1986, 198). Thus, such an audience would, on hearing a piece of music that they had been told was composed by Mozart, invest it with more artistic merit than if they had been told that a young and unknown composer had written it. He cites earlier work by Asch (1948), suggesting that there is 'complex conceptual reorganisation'. That is to say, prestige perceptions influence what is actually understood. If that is so, then according prestige to something becomes part of the process of making sense of it. We see positive qualities in something because it is prestigious. This moves beyond the idea of prestige and an object as separate items. Prestige changes the item in an individual's perception. This may perhaps be an example of priming, in which an audience, having been led to expect something of a particular quality, draws on conceptions that are connected. For example, a composer's emotional restraint might be interpreted either as a sign of maturity or as an inability to express emotion, depending on an initial perception of the level of a composition's quality.

Reducing conflict

The adoption of an agreed standard by a community has a further benefit in that it can reduce the possibility of conflict. When a prestige object, an entity which is held to have high status, has been identified, it becomes possible to adapt beliefs and behaviours in order to associate with that which has a high value. By aligning with others who accord prestige in similar ways, the individual can join a community of the like-minded, and benefit from this further form of association.

Such a phenomenon is contained in Bourdieu's (1984) proposal that judgements of aesthetic taste offer ways in which a person can gain social standing.

However, a more fundamental need for agreement with others has been claimed. Drawing on developments in neural science, Lieberman argues that Maslow's depiction of the hierarchy of human need was inaccurate, and that being socially connected is the most important human need. A 'thirst for connection' (2013, 43) helps to assure health and long life, and the human brain has evolved to cope with being social, managing many relationships by continually working out what people think and mean. When the brain is doing nothing else it is dealing with social matters as its preferred activity. Thus abstract reasoning is not the most vital ability, but our ability to think about social matters. Much of our thinking, it is maintained, is not for the purpose of having novel and individual thoughts but instead to be convergent with the thinking of others: 'Our brains are designed to be influenced by others ... to ensure that we will come to hold the beliefs and values of those around us' (2013, 8). Our ideas of who we are, he suggests, are inaccurately attributed, because rather than developing our own beliefs, values and views, we tend to spend much of our time interpreting the meanings of others, so that we can adapt, develop bonds and fit in with them. Humans spend a great deal of time thinking about the intentions and actions of others and interpreting them to understand their motivations. Thus we tend to be strongly influenced by group beliefs and values, which become more influential than others we may have developed. We tend to think that our 'foundational world views' are our own, and defend them. However, they have been learnt by imitating others and they are the values of the wider society. We are, in a sense, made by outside influences that we feel we are dealing with. This is essential so that people can live socially together. Indeed, he argues that the self exists primarily as a conduit to let the social groups we are immersed in (that is, our family, our school, our country) supplement our natural impulses with socially derived impulses. Thus a common set of values in society is assured. Where humans are together in numbers, there is inevitable competition for resources and relationships, and social skills can enable friendships and alliances to develop. The negative aspect of this is that rejection from a group is painful. We have a lifelong attachment system, and rejection by one implies rejection by all, so standing aside from a group is difficult, and generally will be avoided.

How prestige operates

Prestige is a social phenomenon, requiring interaction with others for its generation, acknowledgement and display. A great deal of research has examined the ways in which individuals and groups develop and maintain their standing in a field. Here, the tendency to impress through display is explored, together with the roles of altruism and reciprocity. Whilst many aspects of organisational life may appear competitive, a very high level of collaboration is needed if complex tasks are to be achieved. This requires trust and also a form of altruism, in that some tasks must be done on behalf of others. Reciprocal altruism happens when a person performs an action in the expectation that an equivalent benefit will be received in return (Greene, 2014, 32). However, reciprocity extends beyond those we know. Indirect reciprocity occurs when we punish unco-operative behaviour even though it is not to us, on the grounds that it makes it more likely that somebody else will behave in ways we do not want and that this might affect us. We are very interested in whether people get their just deserts. A great deal of fiction is about exactly this.

The role of co-operation

One way of achieving and maintaining prestige is through display, by showing that one has an attribute that others do not. This is termed 'costly signalling' (Whitfield, 2012, 30). Answering the question of why people do apparently generous things, he introduces the idea of 'conspicuous production' (2012, 32), a variant of 'conspicuous consumption' (Veblen, 1899), where people in many walks of life offer goods and services freely to the community. Such generosity does not expect immediate repayment, but is an investment in reputation. Part of the value of this is that it publicises one's abilities and also demonstrates that one has resources that one can afford to give away. There have been many tests of the idea that people will choose to live with those who are the most generous, and investigations of the circumstances in which that generosity takes place. There is evidence that 'the most public spirited people eventually generate private wealth with one another' (Whitfield, 2012, 34). Whitfield claims that many good deeds can be explained through competitive altruism. This proposes that people do altruistic things that lead to an increase in their reputation so that they are inclined to be trusted and others want to work with them. This is not to claim necessarily that good deeds are fuelled by self-interest, because the motivations for an act are not the same as the force that caused the evolution of the behaviour, but the result is the same. It may not be done for reward, but there still is reward. It is incidentally important not to make it obvious that one is being altruistic for reward, as this can have a negative effect.

Reciprocal altruism occurs when a favourable deed is repaid by the beneficiary. This will work most effectively if it is possible to see how another person has previously responded to similar situations, in order to be generous with the person who is generous. So some access to another's previous decision-making is helpful. There are many examples of tests where people will choose to work with others whom they perceive to be generous. We wish to gain advantage and to avoid being exploited. People's interests are in general in partial alignment, and the skilful management of these coincidences and conflicts of interest occupy much of our thought. We also co-operate within groups in order to compete better with others. Network reciprocity (Ohtsuki et al., 2006) refers to this tendency to work together in groups.

We are not only concerned with how people behave towards us, but how they behave towards others, as this may be some indicator of their likely behaviour towards us if this becomes an issue. This moves us into the field of indirect reciprocity, covered by the biblical injunction 'do unto others as you would be done by', a maxim common to a number of religions. Whitfield cites a number of examples of experiments in which those who are generous with others are thought to be good to work with. Frequently a person will decide whether to help another person on the basis of how the other person has treated a third person. Thus, reputation influences who we work with, even at a distance from an act that produced reputation or its reverse. However, mapping decision-making of this kind is very difficult. One of the problems is that we judge not only what people do but also their intentions. There is a role for forgiveness, too, where a single good deed may restore a good reputation. Sometimes people deal with others who have a bad reputation, which makes the situation more complex yet. Those in particularly good standing can afford to do this. Gossip is generally believed, and drives indirect reciprocity. Our reputation is not entirely in our hands, as it relies so much on what others say of us, whether it is true or not. We tend to pass on good gossip about people we like and bad gossip about people we dislike. We 'filter and spin in the way that we think will best serve our own interests' (Whitfield, 2012, 70) and can use gossip to drive someone from a group if we do not find them acceptable.

Lieberman (2013) notes that humans co-operate more than any other species and will work hard for something that they identify with and believe in. He cites the principle of reciprocity as a strong social norm and criticises the long tradition of people believing that humans are always self-interested. In addition to being selfish, he claims, we are also interested in the welfare of others for its own sake. Pleasure in altruism is associated with heightened levels of oxytocin. He notes that socially we find it difficult to say that we are being unselfish, so we sometimes claim to be even if we are not. If we do indeed have such a strong wish to fit in and to contribute to a general good, that may be a psychological basis for prestige that is held at a group level, existing side by side with the desire for individually held prestige. Group solidarity has value for individuals, if all are united in admiration of a particular item of capital. The benefit is felt by all, through a sense of connection and unity. Individually held prestige serves the function of securing the approbation of a group, for status becomes an end in itself, desired because it signifies that others value us, that we have a place of importance in the group and therefore are connected to the group.

Sources of bias

As already noted, judgements have to be made, often very quickly. Here some of the factors are considered that may lead to rapid but not necessarily accurate judgement. A number of aspects of biased decision-making have been identified, each an example of a way in which data have been used wrongly to emphasise or detract from the worth of someone or something. Perhaps the foremost is the role of stereotyping, but there are also halo, Matthew and spill-over effects.

The idea of stereotyping is contentious, in that it has been associated with uncomplimentary and inaccurate generalisations about groups of people, so that it is on the whole used as a pejorative term, but Schneider has attempted to rescue it from such criticism, arguing strongly for its importance when it is understood to refer simply to qualities or characteristics that tend to be applied to groups of people. He argues that this is another example of efficient decision-making on the basis of accumulated other experience. He claims that if we did not use stereotypes then we would not be able to generalise, and that this would be an unacceptable exchange, for generalisation is 'a central, primitive, hardwired cognitive activity' (Schneider, 1992, 8).

The halo effect (Thorndike, 1920) has long been recognised as a feature of human judgement. Positive views in one domain can influence judgements elsewhere. Classically, physically attractive people have repeatedly been found to be rated more highly in a number of other attributes. There is clearly a potential external prestige benefit to an individual if their success in one field gives them social permissions in others. The psychological benefit may be to reduce a sense of uncertainty and the number of judgements that have to be made and to speed up decision-making. This raises the question of what might be the aspects of the situation, the prestige cues, that are likely to be attended to and to influence the status of the object of attention.

A related phenomenon is the Matthew effect, first proposed by Merton (1968), meaning that success tends to attract further success. An example would be the findings that for a given quantity and quality of research, an eminent researcher receives more recognition, in the form of citations, than does a little-known researcher, and that female researchers benefit from the introduction of double-blind refereeing of journal articles (Budden et al., 2007). Researchers concerned with enterprising universities have also noted a Matthew effect in relation to an institution's ability to generate patents (Sine et al., 2003).

A further source of bias is in spill-over effects, in that when we see success in one area, we are more likely to follow the person in other areas. Thus an expert in one field is likely to be given more of a hearing in an area about which they have no obvious expertise. It may be that we have this generalist approach to expertise because it is hard to decide what it is that has produced the excellence, and so we tend to accept the broad spectrum of attributes and behaviours in the belief that somewhere in there is the basis of the excellence.

Avoiding mistakes

Making decisions is a centrally important part of living. One easy way of making a decision is to copy what others do. If what is excellent in a context has already been defined, this can be taken as a given, which removes the possibility of making mistaken choices. This is especially so where one does not have first-hand experience as a guide, so that social learning becomes valuable, when one tends to copy those who have been successful, on the grounds that they are likely to have made correct decisions. Rather than trial and error, learning from others offers 'access to vast quantities of knowledge and expertise that no individual would be able to discover independently' (Whitfield, 2012, 15). Whitfield claims that the tendency to copy apparently successful higher-status individuals is based on the assumption that the person is doing something right. An additional benefit of decision-making by copying was captured by the apocryphal and often used comment that 'Nobody ever got fired for choosing IBM', meaning that subsequent failure would not be blamed on the person taking the decision, provided it was the decision that most people would be inclined to make.

A further source of bias is in the views that we already hold. Greene points out that 'which side of the dispute you're on unconsciously changes your thinking about what's fair' (2014, 85). Thus we pay far more attention to evidence that fits with the views that we already hold. This tendency applies even among the most educated. He cites the environment as an issue about which the scientifically literate 'rather than gravitating towards the truth, will simply be more adept at defending their tribe's position, whatever it happens to be'. He suggests that we are so inclined to be biased in our fairness that it may be better for us to think selfishly and admit that we are doing so rather than attempt to be moral.

Conclusions

Individuals usually have a strong sense of a personally derived set of beliefs and values, socially acquired, and reinforced by association with a group that has similar beliefs and values. Thus relationships between the individual and their principal sources of socialisation are significant. A main reference group may be the university, but it is more likely to be the department, discipline, research or teaching group, or a more abstract sense of the values of an academic community. It is highly desirable for there to be a match between institutional aspirations and the values of those who work in the institution. Whilst the sum of the work desires of those in the university may not amount to something that would sustain the university financially, the opposite position is not tenable either, where there is little relationship between staff and institutional values and aspirations. Clearly, the closer the match, the better. Psychological contract highlights expectations that are met or otherwise, or that move out of alignment over time. In particular, staff appointed in one era may find that expectations of them and of the nature of their work change substantially. A sense of psychological contract is in the end an understanding developed by an individual that may or may not reflect reality. Thus, a golden age of academia may be largely mythical, but may nevertheless fuel a preference for an unrealistic degree of autonomy and freedom from financial facts of life, thus increasing dissatisfaction.

The speed and complexity of change in institutions and departments can compound the problem of motivation. Many influences will be acting on any system at once, and at any time there will be a range of initiatives that may be in tension with one another. Thus a new plan is likely to be overtaken by the next strategic imperative. The rapid turnover of staff in departments is also a challenge to the continuity of service and of culture. A 20 per cent turnover of staff means that the department is renewed every five years, yet planning for teaching and high-level research has to have long timescales. In many national systems an increase in part-time and short-term working has been reported, reducing shared understandings and sense of commitment further. There are also many situations where higher education is taking place in new or radically reconfigured situations, such as in new private provision, in further education or where major mergers have taken place. Some of the issues that have been considered here suggest that to concentrate on structures and funding and to neglect cultural understandings as a component of motivation is to neglect a crucially important component.

Claims that humans are far more communally minded than is often supposed are relevant to the practice of aiming for corporate objectives through the performance management of individuals, with financial incentives sometimes attached to specific requests for performance. As already mentioned, the attachment of financial incentives itself may have a negative effect, if it signals a valuing of financial reward that is not shared by the individual. Further, if an individual feels no sense of connection with an institution, but has an investment in community at a lower organisational level, the attainment of corporate objectives may not be motivating, unless there is a clear link between benefits at the corporate and the more local levels. Finally, an emphasis on individual recognition and reward may be counter-productive, where there is a strong collectivist ethos, as is sometimes held to be the case in many teaching environments.

The extent to which judgement is unconscious is also a challenge. A community of scholars will be strong where it has shared values and approaches. However, those often unconscious agreements may cause difficulty when there is a need for change, or to collaborate with other communities. The tendency to reinforce a view one already holds rather than objectively considering evidence also has implications for approaches to change. It suggests that constantly appealing to what Oscar Wilde referred to as 'brute reason' may be less effective in winning an argument than would long-term efforts to generate a culture that is likely to support desired ends.

The difference between an institution that seeks prestige and one that wishes for reputation is an important one. It can drive academic preferences for basic research over applied research and consultancy, and for research rather than teaching, particularly when the institution is more inclined to reward prestige than reputation through its recognition and reward systems. Thus, in promotion decisions, a strong emphasis on research outputs and cursory attention to good citizenship in the institution sends clear signals about what is valued. An emphasis on prestige may also produce an unhelpful division between the academy and the administration, if the academy is focused on academic outputs and the administration on the management of costs. Development provision in universities can also fall victim to prestige concerns. To offer support in areas that it is plain that an institution does not value is likely to be a thankless task.

The idea that perceptions of value are influenced by the prestige that attaches to something demonstrates the advantages that accrue to institutions, groups and individuals who can develop a prestigious position. To be perceived to be prestigious is itself a resource, tending to validate everything that one does. A university can benefit by acting in a philanthropic way. Costly signalling, generosity with resources and community mindedness, whether based in altruism or self-interest, is likely to yield a more prestigious image and similar responses in return. The tendency for judgements to be influenced by perceptions of existing prestige and expertise in other areas, and the prevalence of stereotyping as a feature of much thought points to an area of high risk in the academy, where so many judgements are made in relatively small communities where many of the members are known to one another.

A principal conclusion must be that motivation is a critically important matter in any organisation and the distinction between prestige and reputation is a particularly important one in academic life. Staff have highly developed and often unconscious sets of beliefs and values, that can often be reinforced, for good and ill, by recognition and reward practices.

References

Alderfer. C. (1973) *Existence, relatedness, and growth: Human needs in organizational settings.* New York: Free Press.

Argyris, C. (1960) *Understanding organisational behaviour.* Homewood, IL: Dorsey Press.

Asch, S. (1948) The doctrine of suggestion, prestige and imitation in social psychology, in *Psychological Review* 55: 250–76.

Bess, J.L. (1998) Contract systems, bureaucracies, and faculty motivation: The probable effects of a no-tenure policy, in *Journal of Higher Education* 69, 1: 1–22.

Bourdieu, P. (1984) *Distinction: A social critique of the judgment of taste,* trans. Richard Nice. Cambridge, MA: Harvard University Press.

Budden, A., Tregenza, T., Aarssen, L., Koricheva, J., Leimu, R. and Lortie, C. (2007) Double-blind review favours increased representation of female authors, in *Trends in Ecology and Evolution* 23, 1: 4–6.

Capelleras, J. (2005) Attitudes of academic staff towards their job and organization: An empirical assessment, in *Tertiary Education and Management* 11: 147–66.

Dreyfus, H. and Dreyfus, S. (1986) *Mind over machine: The power of human intuition and expertise in the era of the computer.* Oxford: Blackwell.

Feldman, K. and Paulsen, M. (1999) Faculty motivation: The role of a supportive teaching culture, in *New Directions in Teaching and Learning* 78: 71–8.

Greene, J. (2014) *Moral tribes: Emotion, reason, and the gap between us and them.* London: Atlantic Books.

Guest, D. (1999) Is the psychological contract worth taking seriously?, in *Journal of Organizational Behavior* 19: 649–64.
Hargreaves, D. (1986) *The developmental psychology of music.* Cambridge: Cambridge University Press.
Herzberg, F. (1966) *Work and the nature of man.* Cleveland, OH: World Publishing.
Kahneman, D. (2003) A perspective on judgment and choice: Mapping bounded rationality, in *American Psychologist* 58, 9: 697–720.
Klein, G. (1998) *Sources of power: How people make decisions.* Cambridge, MA: MIT Press.
Lieberman, M. (2013) *Social: Why our brains are wired to connect.* Oxford: Oxford University Press.
Maslow, A. (1997) *Motivation and personality*, 3rd edition. New York: Harper and Row.
Mayo, F. (1975) *The social problems of an industrial civilisation.* London: Routledge and Kegan Paul.
Merton, R. (1968) The Matthew effect in science, in *Science* 159, 3810: 56–63.
McInnis, C. (2012) Traditions of academic professionalism and shifting academic identities, in G. Gordon and C. Whitchurch (eds), *Academic and professional identities in higher education: The challenges of a diversifying workforce.* London: Routledge.
Ohtsuki, H., Hauert, C., Lieberman, E. and Nowak, M. (2006) A simple rule for the evolution of cooperation on graphs, in *Nature* 441, 7092: 502–5.
Rowley, J. (1996) Motivation and academic staff in higher education, in *Quality Assurance in Education* 4, 3: 11–16.
Ryan, R. and Deci, E. (2013) Overview of self-determination theory: An organismic dialectical perspective, in R. Ryan and E. Deci (eds), *Handbook of self-determination research* (pp. 3–35). Rochester, NY: University of Rochester Press.
Schein, E. (1980) *Organisational psychology.* Englewood Cliffs, NJ: Prentice-Hall.
Schneider, J. (1992) *The psychology of stereotyping.* New York: Guilford Press.
Schneider, D. (2005) *The psychology of stereotyping.* New York: Guilford Press.
Simon, H.A. (1956) Rational choice and the structure of the environment, in *Psychological Review* 63, 2: 129–38.
Simon, H. (1991) Bounded rationality and organisational learning, in *Organization Science* 2, 1: 125–34.
Simon, H. and Hayes, J. (1976) The understanding process: Problem isomorphs, in *Cognitive Psychology* 8: 165–90.
Sine, W., Shane, S. and Gregorio, D. (2003) The halo effect and technology licensing: The influence of institutional prestige on the licensing of university inventions, in *Management Science* 49, 4: 478–96.
Slovic, P., Finucane, M., Peters, E. and MacGregor, D. (2002) The affect heuristic, in T. Gilovich, D. Griffin and D. Kahneman (eds), *Heuristics and biases: The psychology of intuitive judgment*: 397–420. New York: Cambridge University Press.
Taylor, F. (1947) *Scientific management.* New York: Harper and Row.
Thorndike, E. (1920) A constant error in psychological ratings, in *Journal of Applied Psychology* 4,1: 25–9.
Veblen, T. (1899) *The theory of the leisure class: An economic study of institutions.* New York: MacMillan.
Whitfield, J. (2012) *The surprising science of reputation.* Hoboken, NJ: Wiley.

Chapter 4

Globalisation and national systems

Introduction

The development of a global market in higher education has led to an increase in competition among a number of institutions and a need for them to signal excellence in a very obvious arena of prestige-seeking. National systems are also in competition, with governments increasingly concerned to demonstrate and safeguard the quality of their higher education provision. The greatest attention has been focused on the presence or otherwise of 'world-class' institutions in national systems, and on a need perceived by many governments to enhance national performance in the global competition.

In this chapter I briefly explore the international aspect of universities and the increase in competition globally, both at the level of the nation state and the individual institution, as a setting for later discussion of global hubs and global league tables. I will suggest that global competition has increased interest in comparisons among national systems, particularly in those countries that do not show up well in international league tables, but also in those that do. Comparison of this kind is useful for a study of prestige because it helps to characterise the national climate in which institutions exist, and which is likely to influence prestige behaviours and attitudes both beyond and within universities. It may be possible to identify factors that contribute to the motivational climate within universities and in a national system. Prestige behaviours are not all outcomes of deliberate policy or even directly related to universities. Prestige and reputation-seeking are deep-seated social and cultural phenomena. However, it seems likely that aspects of higher education organisation and financing, beyond and within institutions, will have a bearing on patterns of motivation and more specifically on the nature and extent of prestige-seeking and possession. A better appreciation of this may assist in beneficially influencing prestige-related attitudes and behaviours. This chapter explores these issues. A more conjectural conclusion moves beyond what some have termed a neo-liberal conception of globalisation and considers another possible future as radical changes take place in the availability of knowledge in the world. League tables and global hubs are treated separately later.

The international aspect of universities

There has been an international dimension in academic work for many years. It has often been observed that the principal loyalty of the academic is to disciplinary community rather than to employing institution, and that such communities transcend national boundaries (Jenkins, 1996). There is also a tradition of physical mobility. Many members of faculty now have academic training and careers that span a number of countries. National systems have borrowed extensively from one another and, as will be seen, this practice continues, so that some universal forms of organisation and practice can be seen worldwide, alongside local variations. The Humboldtian model, originating in Germany in the nineteenth century and uniting research and teaching through the work of the scholar, was centrally influential in generating the most prestigious model of a university, seen in the establishment of institutions such as Johns Hopkins University in the US and thereafter the most powerful model in Western higher education. The UK, which also absorbed the Humboldtian model in its elite institutions, has been very influential in shaping the systems of many of its former colonies – such as those of South Africa, Australia and Hong Kong. There are characteristic differences. The UK has traditionally preferred a narrowly focused curriculum; the US has a tradition of a broader curriculum for students, particularly at the start of a degree programme. Recent curriculum change in Singapore, with the adoption of a liberal arts model that aims to recognise Singapore's position between East and West (Tsui, 2012), is an example of a move from a British- to a US-influenced model. Universities in these two countries have provided examples that many have followed throughout the twentieth century, and this influence continues today, given highly visible expression through the dominance of US and UK research-intensive universities in international league tables.

The US retains an immensely dominant position in higher education internationally. Any international league table is populated heavily with US institutions. Marginson offers detail on the size of the US lead – for example, in 2003 the US invested seven times as much in tertiary education as the next highest spender, Japan (2010, 214). The US is highly dominant in research publications and citations. Marginson describes the 'soft power' of the US system and its influence on the rest of the world, so that others tend to follow a US lead in the way that universities are thought about, led and managed. Other relatively successful countries in terms of internationally prominent institutions – the UK and Australia – illustrate the shared advantage that these countries have in the English language. The US maintains its strong position partly by being an attractive country in which to do academic work. Marginson describes the US as the 'world's graduate school' (2010, 218), retaining many of those who come for their education to the US, and being less concerned to make a profit from international education than the UK and Australia. Foreign students at doctoral level are strongly subsidised and many remain in the US.

There is in some respects an increasing tendency for policy convergence and for policy in one country to influence policy choices in another, and a risk that policy designed to increase international prestige may have wider and unintended consequences, an issue that is explored later, in a discussion of ranking and league tables. Marginson claims that two kinds of American institution have come to be seen as the norm: 'high status not for profit private research intensive university' and 'the for-profit vocational institution, broad-based training in business studies and possibly also technologies, health and education' (2010, 219). Other universities that do not fit such patterns may come to be marginalised, especially when they are not rewarded by ranking systems.

Whilst this position of strength has existed for many years, it is open to challenge. Demand for higher education is increasing rapidly throughout the world. Many countries have identified higher education as essential to their future prosperity and are rapidly expanding their higher education systems, both to deal with the needs of their own economy and society and to attract students from elsewhere. Some are seeking to position themselves as 'global hubs', attracting both researchers and students, in significant developments that are partly exercises in the development of prestige and that therefore merit separate treatment later in the book. These ambitions are a threat to the prestigious position long enjoyed by a small number of national systems. The scale and direction of student flow says a good deal concerning the international nature of higher education, particularly at postgraduate level, about the comparative prestige of national systems and, perhaps, about the ways in which the balance of power may be beginning to shift. The US, UK, France, Australia and Germany continue to attract the largest numbers of both overseas students and staff. However, with the extent of international interaction now much greater than it has ever been, these countries' share of the total overseas student market has declined from 55 per cent in 2000 to 47 per cent in 2012. The largest exporter of students is China, by far the largest with 694,400 studying abroad, followed by India, the Republic of Korea, Germany and Saudi Arabia (UNESCO, 2014). The incentive for exporting nations to improve the quality and prestige of their own systems is obvious, both to retain their own students and to attract those of other nations. So at the level of nation states, competition has sharpened and comparisons are increasingly made between and among systems. One may reasonably conclude that although its dominance will be challenged increasingly in the coming decade, the US has so many advantages – its existing major strength, the English language and a socio-political environment that accommodates universities as they are currently constituted – that it will be some years before a more pluralist picture emerges. However, this seems likely in due time, in part because of the greater speed and flux brought about through communication technologies and associated changes.

Higher education has, for many universities, become a global issue, with increasing flows of both faculty and students across national boundaries, and a need to project institutional excellence worldwide. A new arena has come into being in which universities can seek and display prestige. International competitiveness is being played out through worldwide university rankings, displayed in an ever increasing number of international league tables, that have led to a drive in some countries to sustain and in others to create prestigious 'world-class' universities. An obvious effect is that international competition is likely to be more keenly felt, stretching universities that might otherwise sit very comfortably as elite institutions in their own national system. However, such comparisons are inherently difficult to make, not only methodologically but also partly because some of the perceived differences may be attributable to the effects of national systems. One of the least desirable consequences is that a particular kind of university comes to be the measure against which all are judged. As mentioned earlier, an institution with a strongly local mission may perform very well but not be engaging in activities that show in such tables. News presentation and interpretation may well miss this more nuanced picture, especially when the winners of such competitions are keen to publicise their achievements. The negative effects of this are noted by some of the heads of institution whose views are reported in chapter 10. International league tables are such an obvious and visible expression of prestige that they are dealt with later.

These prestige stories are interesting in their own right and suggest some important questions. Who will be the leading nation states in the coming years in a global higher education economy? How will nations attempt to assert their standing and status, as whole systems are increasingly evaluated and as faculty and students alike become more able to evaluate practically, by choosing where to study and work, across the world? What will be the effect of global rankings of institutions? Will we see convergence and compliance or increasing differentiation? Will there be more competition or co-operation, or a mix of both? What sorts of competitiveness and alliance-making will institutions engage in, as they look for security and growth? At the level of the individual member of faculty, what opportunities open up with globalisation? In the spaces that appear because knowledge and its communication are less controllable, and structures become inevitably more fluid, is there an opportunity for greater agency? What relationships can be formed? What new kinds of work and prestige are possible? These questions are part of a larger picture, of fundamental changes in knowledge creation and flow, and in the current and future role of the university in what has been termed the knowledge economy.

Comparing prestige in nation states

I intend to argue that nations have very distinctive prestige climates or environments, where through their socio-cultural norms, as well as the ways in which they explicitly organise for higher education and research, they prompt particular prestige behaviours and states. Not all would expect to see international variation in patterns of prestige. A comparative study of occupational prestige across sixty countries argued that prestige patterns are remarkably uniform internationally, and proposed an economic explanation. In a very well-known study that brought together data from a wide range of sources, Treiman found considerable similarity in the esteem enjoyed by various occupations. This study of course dealt with the prestige of occupations rather than of academic institutions or national prestige, but it is perhaps the claimed economic underpinning of prestige and supposed similarities over time and across nations that are of interest here. Treiman claimed that all people have a shared sense of such worth, in what he termed the 'conscious collective' (1977, 1). He argued that such valuations persist over time, and that even when there is technological change, the valuation of the function is retained, even if a job is done in a different way. Treiman's economically driven view of prestige argues strongly for a structural explanation, based on the need for differentiation of labour, leading to stratification on the basis of access to resources, skill, authority and property, which provide power and in turn lead to the possibility of gaining privilege. Power and privilege are said to be universally well regarded, and to provide prestige. Horizontal stratification occurs because of the range of roles, each requiring differing levels of skill. Vertical differences arise from the self-interest of the skilled specialist and the desirability of paying at a high level only for scarce skills, and then using the capacity at the level it can be most effectively used. If such an analysis is applied to universities, one would want to examine institutional differentiation and system stratification. Where these exist, prestige for some institutions will be generated as a consequence.

Analyses of higher education systems are also often made on an economic basis. Clark suggested that the factors that most influence the context for higher education in a country are the relationships between the state, the markets and what he termed the 'academic oligarchy' (1983: 143). McNay takes a related approach, proposing that the two dimensions that can be used to characterise higher education systems are the extent to which they are controlled by the state or by the institution itself, and the extent to which they are regulated (1995). The extent of institutional autonomy from government is variable across nation states, with some countries permitting a high degree of institutional and academic autonomy. In the US system, for example, the most prestigious research-intensive institutions are usually private institutions, largely independent of government control and even direct influence. Many other institutions in the US are more dependent on funding and support and are more accountable at a state (regional) level. In many other countries there is significant state intervention and management at national level, often through an arm's-length body that requires plans, monitors activity and distributes resources. Examples include the funding councils of the UK, Australia and Hong Kong. Almost all of the universities in these countries are public institutions. Western EU countries have maintained largely public institutions, with varying arrangements for accountability at national and regional levels. A number of the newer EU countries have developed a private sector, in addition to the existing public provision. Some countries that are rapidly expanding their higher education sector have encouraged the growth of private institutions, such as in some of the Gulf states, Singapore and South America. Others have encouraged overseas institutions to set up branch campuses

– Malaysia and Singapore are examples. Each of these approaches brings its own governance and cultural issues. However, there seems little evidence that public or private systems as such would necessarily have or not have prestige, nor that in mixed systems either kind of provision would necessarily be the most prestigious. Setting the US and UK systems alongside each other makes that point. Although the UK has now shifted the burden of paying onto the shoulders of students and their parents, through the introduction and increase of tuition fees, for many years the UK has had an almost entirely state-funded public system, some parts of which have enjoyed high prestige, nationally and internationally. Indeed, it has been argued that it is extremely difficult to maintain 'world-class' institutions without high and consistent levels of public funding (Salmi, 2009).

Another major difference in higher education systems, with considerable significance for patterns of prestige, is the extent of differentiation among institutions, since difference almost inevitably brings hierarchy. Governments can set the rules for the kinds of institution and numbers that are permitted to exist, and can encourage specialisation of role through funding. In many countries that have strong vertical stratification, difference is partly historical and partly deliberately maintained by groups of institutions. As examples, the most prestigious research-intensive institutions are marked out as 'Russell Group' in the UK, 'Ivy League' in the US and 'Sandstone' in Australia. The Russell Group emerged from a perception of shared interest among a group of institutions, most of which had medical schools. It has since developed to be a strong brand that is almost synonymous with excellence, to the pleasure of members and chagrin of some of those who are not, as a later chapter notes. Thus stratification may be established and encouraged by government policy, but is also a product of universities themselves.

One of the main differences among national systems is that some maintain an academic and vocational separation. In Holland, for example, there are both universities and technical universities. In the UK, institutions in the former polytechnic sector were granted university status through the 1992 Further and Higher Education Act, although major differences in mission continue to exist within the sector, and 'mission groups' have formed, voluntary associations of institutions that are relatively similar in their nature and aspirations. Some countries have a strongly Humboldtian tradition of preferring research and teaching to take place in the same institution. Others, notably in the French system, with its Grandes Ecoles, have tended to differentiate between institutions that are principally for an elite level of teaching and those that are for more general academic entry and for research. Students gain entry to a Grand Ecole through competitive examination, whereas for most universities, a baccalaureate qualification is sufficient. All of these differing arrangements and institutional missions are likely to have an effect on the prestige of one institution as against another, and of what is valued and rewarded within an institution.

Whilst a public or private label appears not to be critical to the existence of prestige and its distribution, the nature of the governance and funding regime within a nation state clearly makes a difference, although the connection is not straightforward. Some of the national systems that are least managed by government and that pay least attention to quality assurance are also the least well regarded. On the other hand, some systems with a high level of government control are also widely believed to under-perform. Salmi (2009) cites France and Germany as examples, constrained by an academy that is largely governed by civil service rules and with little incentive for enterprise, a problem that Aghion extends to all European universities (Aghion et al., 2007). Universities cannot generally pursue an entirely independent mission if they are applying annually to government for funding, and so governments can influence institutional behaviour and the environment for prestige to some extent. Universities are likely to have to be responsive to shorter-term goals if under financial and competitive pressure. The relationship is characterised by tensions, for government policy requirements, driven by electoral cycles and largely economic concerns, may be not only shorter term in aspiration than are the traditions of an institution, but also have differing intentions. They may also run counter to existing prestige patterns in institutions. Thus governments increasingly invest in higher education in order to stimulate economic growth, but an emphasis on applied research that has economic impact and on students' employability may be at odds with deeply rooted preferences for research and education for their own sake.

The overall proportion of gross domestic product spent on universities and the funding available to individual institutions make a difference to a university's ability to attract the best talent through salaries, a further factor influencing the climate for prestige. Salmi notes that in the US, public institutions lag behind private in that regard. However, levels of salary do not always appear to be related to prestige. For example, the UK retains national pay bargaining so that salaries are relatively even across universities. The US system, however, has greater disparity, both among institutions and among disciplines. Differential funding may be a deliberate aim of national policy. Altbach and Salmi (2011) argue that over-extensive competition from non-university research institutes may harm research universities, by diluting the talent pool and limiting the scale of activity in single institutions. Thus, the opportunity to compete for public research funding may be restricted to public institutions. A similar argument may be applied to the distribution of research among the range of universities: thus the UK's research has become increasingly concentrated in a small number of institutions, as a deliberate national policy, effected through successive rounds of system-wide research assessment.

Changes in the external environment for universities are likely to have a range of consequences as institutions adjust to them, which are particularly significant for a study of prestige, especially where institutions have internal autonomy in such matters as resourcing and staffing. New forms of role, often hybrid and sitting between the academy and the administration (Whitchurch, 2007) complicate staffing structures and relationships. Increased competition for external and internal funding may stimulate initiative (Blackmore, 2013, 6) but may also erode collegiality in universities. Performance management systems may enable an institution to signal its priorities, but an institutional priority is only part of the equation. The relationship is a complex one, as enterprising members of faculty accommodate their own aims within a policy and funding context, often through creative management and through careful attention to their own careers.

A possible prestige driver may perhaps be found in the ways in which government seeks and rewards quality across the range of academic activity. For many years the UK's funding systems for research and teaching have differed in that funding levels for research have generally been related to both the quality and quantity of what an institution produces; teaching funding has tended not to vary on the basis of quality, but has instead been costed on the basis of student numbers and nature of activity, largely because quality is extremely hard to measure. Thus in most institutions, paying attention to research quality could lead to higher levels of funding, but care taken over teaching could not. This is a basic asymmetry that has real effects on attitudes and behaviours. More recent changes, transferring the cost of education to the student and partially removing the national limit on student numbers, do provide financial incentives to concentrate on teaching, provided that fees are set at an attractive level for universities. It could also be argued that the market pressures of student consumers provide a disciplining force on universities. However, as is suggested elsewhere, in the more prestigious institutions, those pressures may be significantly reduced where student choice is governed more by prestige benefit than by conventional measures of quality of provision.

The right to select students is a key prestige factor. In the UK and many other systems, universities seek to attract the most academically able students. However, in much of mainland Europe, for example in Holland and Germany, institutions are required to accept all those students who apply and who have the required grades, except in a limited number of disciplines such as medicine. As a result, particularly in Holland, the university system has less obvious hierarchy of institution. A consequence of university students being of comparable academic quality is that this is not an area for competition among institutions, and so competitiveness migrates to other fields.

One effect of an increasingly performance-conscious environment that develops key indicators against which individuals and groups are assessed may be that prestige will be more overtly sought and claimed. This does not necessarily mean an overall increase in prestige-seeking; it may be only a change in its form and its visibility. Such a change may have benefits: advancement may perhaps tend to be more closely related to performance than to position. This tendency towards public displays of prestige is increased by the opportunities that the internet provides for projecting individual prestige. Websites such as ResearchGate and Academia.Edu offer faculty the opportunity to present their work globally, and are part of a wider pressure on faculty to ensure a positive digital presence. There is little choice but to participate, since absence conveys its own message.

In summary, university life has certain similarities worldwide. Beliefs and values are often anchored strongly in the academy and may be resistant to change. However, government can and does set the stage for prestige in universities. It does so by influencing the numbers and types of institution that are recognised, and through the management of institutions, particularly quality and funding arrangements. A trend towards specialisation and a desire for 'world-class' status are tending to increase differences between institutions that are prestige-seeking and those that are reputation-seeking. The actions of institutions themselves may also contribute to the generation of perceived difference. Individual staff pursue their careers in an environment that increasingly encourages the seeking and more public display of prestige.

University prestige

Globalisation requires universities to project a sense of prestige to anywhere in the world that the institution wishes to be influential. Much of what a university 'produces' is not tangible, and cannot easily be measured. Some of its outcomes are 'credence goods' (Emons, 1997), the value of which can never fully be known by the beneficiary. Marginson suggests that this has produced a vacuum, within which universities have to show their worth continuously, through the public display of virtue (2010, 152). International aspects of universities provide opportunities for competitive display, although some activities lend themselves more to competitive international prestige than others. The need for display inevitably gives primacy to that which can to an extent be measured. Education may not be a beneficiary. Marginson suggests that pastoral care for students is more attractive as a display item than 'pedagogy and the fostering of intellectual growth' (2010, 153).

An important and relatively easy way of demonstrating virtue is through research performance, because it is easier to measure some aspects of it and plausible to suggest that discoveries in basic research will be of benefit, especially in medicine and other applied fields. The link is not as straightforward as has been claimed, an issue returned to later. Research achievement has the added benefit of leading to success in global rankings, which transmits institutional prestige universally and immensely speedily. Marginson points to a tendency to concentrate on research capacity. The desire for research excellence drives a need for strong institutions that can attract the best staff, ally with other strong institutions and manage an effective research strategy, lending credibility to the research outputs of its staff. This produces a major arena for the seeking and display of prestige. The level of competitiveness is likely to grow and, claims Marginson, the number of staff with no particular allegiance will grow too (2010, 158).

A university may gain in prestige by being overtly international in outlook and action. Thus Monash University referred to its 'global footprint' and University College London has described itself as 'London's global university'. Another way of achieving global prestige is through the formation of alliances. These may include joining high-profile groups of peer institutions, and are explored in the chapter on rankings. They may also include memoranda of understanding, which are normally agreed between institutions of equivalent stature, or where there is a clear prestige benefit on both sides. The agreement on a memorandum of understanding may itself be a source of prestige, since it is a visible event, whether or not it leads to any real research or teaching collaboration. Partnerships are seen as good in themselves. Signing ceremonies are sites of prestige and the agreement is symbolic. Many more memoranda of understanding are now signed (Marginson, 2010, 159). The 'top' universities are desired as partners, as prestige can thus be acquired. There is also a prestige benefit for those working within an institution, where international activity can add to individual and group status. Marginson points to the high level of resourcing that is often available to international activities at executive level (2010, 154). The payback is often in prestige rather than in money.

The rhetoric of globalisation can become a means of advancing particular desired policies. Indeed, being seen to be responsive to globalisation may of itself be prestigious. Curriculum is one battleground for prestige perceptions. Many institutions worldwide have reviewed and revised their curricula (Blackmore and Kandiko, 2012). The reasons for doing so are strikingly similar. It is often claimed that a more global world requires citizens who can function effectively internationally, dealing in a creative and flexible way with a range of cultures, working with complex problems that need the contributions of a range of disciplines in their solution (KLI, 2012). On this basis, it can be argued that undergraduate curricula should be international in outlook, research-orientated, so that students can apply the skills of a researcher, and interdisciplinary, with a focus on learning processes to encourage, through student reflection and other means, the growth and application of creativity. These may seem highly desirable attributes both of a curriculum and of a graduate, but they do not sit comfortably with many traditional views of curriculum, which may emphasise extensive single-subject study to a high level before anything broader is attempted, and do not fit with a pedagogic conservatism that values what is learnt more highly than how it is learnt, or is at least suspicious of more student-centred and participative approaches to curriculum. Thus talk of globalisation legitimises particular approaches to curriculum.

Developments in both teaching and research have the long-term potential to decrease the role of the nation state in some universities. As an increasing amount of educational opportunity is 'delivered' at a distance, partly through learning technologies, the influence and social context of physical place may weaken, so that the national base of a programme becomes less relevant to a number of clients. National boundaries are already blurring through cross-border education. There may be an opportunity for the highest prestige to be generated by universities that detach themselves from their parent state and become truly global universities. This is not to argue that all of higher education will become detached from its national roots. There will remain a large national market, retained by a sense of national identity that is attractive to indigenous students and migrants alike, for much of the attractiveness of studying abroad is to gain a sense of other cultures. So it seems quite likely that much of the most prestigious higher education will remain strongly identifiable with a particular country. However, even at this end of the education market the development of overseas campuses may offer students an experience that is a hybrid. There are interesting prestige aspects. When the UK's University of Nottingham opened an overseas campus at Ningbo in China it reproduced a traditional English university building, a projection of the prestige associated with UK higher education. This cultural invocation is not new. When the University of Melbourne was founded in 1853, some of its architecture was borrowed from the Scottish baronial tradition, offering a reassuring northern hemisphere hallmark. Neither is the UK immune from cultural borrowing, its most prestigious institutions often housed in buildings that recall ancient Greece and Rome. However, when an institution opens an overseas campus, filling it with staff and students from many countries, the nature of what is then on offer is inevitably very different from its original, although not necessarily the worse for it. Thus the use of a traditional university brand has a prestige benefit – and associated dangers, as discussed later – and should perhaps lead to a questioning of whether a national branding is honest or sustainable.

Although governments and state agencies are changing the space in which higher education takes place internationally, Marginson argues that higher education institutions are themselves the most active and influential and that 'Globalisation rests on, and has advanced, the "entrepreneurial" or "enterprise" University' (2010, 151). In the longer term, one can expect governments to have a decreasing amount of control over major, externally facing institutions. As the influence of the nation state decreases, there are stronger possibilities for institutions to work autonomously and globally. Institutional and individual academic prestige can be gained through unfettered global competition and collaboration. Research-intensive institutions across the world may come to have the same kinds of independence from government that has always been the position of major US universities, operating largely independently of federal influence. Certainly nation states retain an ability to control or influence 'their' institutions, through assertion of rights of governance, funding and the award or withholding of recognition of quality, but the fluidity of globalisation is eroding this position, and the conundrum of government is how to retain influence over institutions whilst encouraging them to be more outward-facing and entrepreneurial, developments which bring with them a tendency to have a global rather than a national outlook. As higher education becomes more global, a similar pattern may emerge as in other areas of economic activity, when companies often use their ability to relocate activities from one country to another to make best use of market, labour, raw materials and government-subsidy opportunities. There is no obvious curb to this, given that there are no international bodies with jurisdiction over higher education practices and no immediate likelihood of them developing. The global environment for universities is in some ways like the internet itself, dynamic and hard for any single state to govern. This open collaboration, trading and competition zone is thus likely to foster the best aspects of unregulated space, encouraging enterprise, innovation and diversity of institutional mission. On the other hand, there may be space opened up for less admirable practice if the quality of provision is not monitored effectively.

Wider issues

A major literature focuses on a number of interlinked phenomena that tend to be grouped under the broad heading of globalisation. Economic forces, including trade liberalisation, together with improving communication technologies, are making higher education a truly global and not solely a national concern. This suggests that much of what happens in higher education can only be explained now by reference to global forces. The process of globalisation may be seen as producing something that is much the same as happened before, but in a way that is bounded at a global level rather than at the level of the nation state. I will argue here, as have others, that a significant set of issues affect profoundly the nature of all higher education, to varying extents. There are many accounts and analyses of the effects of the intersection of globalisation, massification and privatisation and it is not intended here to produce a parallel account. Instead the intention is to explore what might be the prestige implications of such changes.

Globalisation is relevant in a number of ways to the manner in which prestige works in higher education. The first and most fundamental is that globalisation may be changing the nature of the role of universities, in teaching, research and outreach, fundamentally. This may happen because the ways in which knowledge is generated, shared and owned in the world may change. Indeed, the kinds of knowledge that are valued may shift. Since universities have historically had an important role in the generation, sharing and validation of knowledge and its possession, this is bound to affect the role of universities. These changes are so far-reaching that many current assumptions about the nature of academic life and work are brought into question. From a prestige perspective, the interesting question is to consider what alters and what endures, as a consequence of such radical and continuing change.

Tensions in the process make the present picture very hard to analyse, let alone imagine the future. Principally, the speed, ease and cheapness of communication, across national boundaries, means that whilst most government remains at the level of the nation state, we are in an era of greater openness than, perhaps, has ever been experienced. It is increasingly difficult for nation states or institutions to achieve the enclosure of any knowledge or social domain. Lying behind this process is what some (Rifkin, 2014; Marginson, 2010) have described as a crisis for capitalism, held to be bringing about its own downfall by the extent of its success. Rifkin speaks of the strong tension between the neo-liberalism that appears to be inherent in globalisation and the creative commons that universal web access enables, because knowledge can be so quickly shared in a far less hierarchical environment. Each of these is in play and each has potential for the nature and patterns of prestige at individual, institutional, disciplinary and national levels in universities. Openness and closure are central conceptions in this view of possible futures for universities.

Possible futures: openness and closure

Universities in the Western world in the twentieth century generally enjoyed a relatively stable position, although it might not have felt so at the time. They have been long-lasting institutions, usually strongly supported financially by governments, serving students who were mainly from the country's middle classes. The right to award degrees was not easily won by others wishing to do so, conferring a huge market advantage on those universities that had that right. Even as an overseas teaching market grew, mainly of postgraduate students, Western universities benefited from an inflow of overseas students, but there was little incentive for home students to go abroad. The English language helped to secure hegemony for Anglo-Saxon institutions. Governments also favoured universities in the distribution of research funding. Much of it could be bid for only by universities. With no explicit link made with the needs of the national economy, universities were left, relatively speaking, to their own devices. In this smaller number of universities, a higher proportion of staff could expect to spend a career, full time and secure, within higher education. Universities, in many ways, had benefits of closure, existing in relatively stable contexts with limited and slow competition, protected by statute, custom and culture. Institutional prestige in such a culture would be based on longevity and on the institution's role in providing a higher education to a relatively elite section of society. The prestige of an institution would lie in shared implicit understandings, which the institution would do little overtly to bring about, other than to go about its business in ways that were in keeping with expectations. For academic staff, prestige would rest mainly on the esteem of fellow academics, more than the approval of client groups such as students, or others beyond the university.

That slightly rose-tinted vision of higher education is already outdated, supplanted by a trend towards new public management and the deliberate marketisation of higher education by government. In this inevitably more open environment, with increasing flows of people and ideas, universities seek to make safe space, through forms of closure. Internally, the active management of teaching quality and the control of research focus and productivity, through the use of metrics and other means, are ways of ensuring that all of the efforts of the academy are directed towards the achievement of institutional goals. A concern for international league table positions, for creating and exploiting patents, for membership of peer institutional groups and interinstitutional agreements offering some form of favoured status are all forms of closure, understandable corporate responses in the face of a more uncertain and challenging environment.

Prestige becomes a very live and more complex issue, because every league table can increase or damage institutional standing, in an environment that is now global rather than national. There are more stakeholders, making more demands, with more access to data that depict quality than ever before. The development and maintenance of prestige becomes a central institutional activity, through the management of press and publicity and through marketing. Academic staff find that their personal prestige requires regular close attention, because the measurement of academic work and associated performance management makes it necessary to be able to demonstrate continuous excellence across a wide range of activities.

It would be easy to characterise globalisation as a natural evolution of the concept of the market economy, with faster flows of people and ideas, aided by communications technologies, and characterised by intense competition in global markets, with increasing transparency provided by international rankings and league tables. The discipline and demands of the free market, that were already operating in other parts of the economy, are now in play in these formerly privileged areas. Universities are seen to be producing quantifiable private goods, whether educational or research outputs, in an economic market. However, that is to assume that the future will look much like the present, but faster, and also that globalisation necessarily means a further turn towards unmoderated capitalism. Rather than driving neo-liberalism, some commentators have claimed that globalisation may be inhibiting it (Marginson, 2010, 143). Globalisation is a process that makes closure of any kind very hard to achieve. The inherent openness of a more free-flowing world may be leading to much more fundamental change. When many goods and services, and the means of exchange, can be available for free or almost free, the development and maintenance of markets becomes much more difficult. A more complex analysis of the process of globalisation may be needed, with openness and closure at its heart.

Jeremy Rifkin (2014) has imagined a world in which knowledge and the ability to make use of it is more widely distributed than ever, at little or no cost. Data about every imaginable human activity have been collected, collated and made available as 'big data'. Products can be designed and manufactured using 3-D printers that are cheap and universally available. Such developments take place using freely shared software, tapping into the willingness of thousands of people to contribute their time and ideas. Some parts of this vision are more convincing than others perhaps, but clearly some aspects of this imagined future have already come into being, and with extraordinary speed. In a way that would have been inconceivable twenty years ago, the internet not only enables free or almost free communication among billions of people worldwide, regardless of national boundaries, but it also supplies vast amounts of information, at no cost to the user, across most of the world. The market in some fields, such as that of recorded music, has been transformed and, in some aspects, destroyed. Spotify and other streaming websites offer most of the recorded music that is available, free, so there is no longer any need to buy music in a physical form. YouTube makes available vast amounts of film, supplied free and accessed at no cost. Newspapers struggle to find a pricing model that enables them to deliver their services electronically whilst making money. Universities are tempted into supplying web-based materials such as massive open online courses (MOOCs), again with no financial model but, rather, a hope that the prestige benefit will make the investment worthwhile through recruitment into conventionally taught courses. In all of these cases, providers can no longer achieve closure of a market in order to exploit it financially.

Rifkin's analysis is that capitalism is the victim of its own success, outmoded because of its ability to stimulate high levels of production whilst driving down costs virtually to zero. He points out that much productive human activity is not even being recorded by government: gross domestic product is an archaic way of understanding what a society produces, because much is in the form of social capital, mediated through the web, the production and exchange of which is not being monitored. He argues that automation and the use of sensors and 'big data' will make all productive processes very much cheaper. Any attempt to establish a protected area is likely to be outflanked as another provider, for reasons of philanthropy or the hope of financial gain, offers a product or service at low or no cost, to anyone with internet access.

Openness makes a profound difference to individuals and groups of faculty. Paradoxically, as previous safe spaces disappear, the opportunities for individuals to make their own academic lives are increasing, particularly in liberal democracies, as other restrictions necessarily fall away. The opportunities of network communication mean that work can take place among individuals who are less often tied by formal organisational relationships. This allows greater autonomy, a broader range of views and a less hierarchical way of working. The advantages of working together globally are that it is free and it is attractive because it means dealing with places different from our own. It provides a space that is sympathetic to creativity, enabling results and reputations to be spread quickly across the world. Any attempts to frustrate those connections or to contain creativity will quickly be overturned because of the ease of the medium and its freedom. It is interesting to consider how this plays out in terms of prestige. Theoretically an open communication medium places all participants on an equal level, provided they have the basic requirements to participate, which increasingly includes mastery of English. Marginson suggests that looser networks are likely to foster intellectual rather than positional status (2010, 134). Whether such potential sweeps away existing differentiation by institution or country is an open question, for although the potential for open collaboration exists, there remain political and cultural reasons why it might not happen. However, the promise of autonomy, and connection with anyone who has something useful to say and is also willing to listen, are likely to be strong motivators. A global stage is a hugely attractive one for an academic mind, offering not only connection and stimulus but also prestige on a global scale. National and institutional concerns are apt to seem parochial in comparison.

Noting the scale and speed and apparent inevitability of globalisation, Marginson is optimistic about opportunities for individuals. He suggests that one of the dangers of thinking of globalisation in this way is that we may lose a sense of agency and be unaware that it is a process that is amenable to influence. Citing the central role of communications, he also argues that the impact of networks, with a free availability of knowledge and contacts, have weakened 'economic determinism' and shown that people do things for reasons other than financial (2010, 122). He notes that many of a university's activities are not designed to make money and that creativity is not necessarily an aspect of neo-liberalism, but can be seen as an alternative to it. Like Rifkin, he suggests that rapid change in technologies makes new human activities possible so that the development of innovations 'races ahead of profit-making and all deliberative intentions'. The emergent outcomes of technological change are happening so quickly that they cannot be controlled. However, Marginson points out, it is human beings who can exploit the technologies and the opportunities that they open up. Many of the economic constraints to academic enterprise have been hugely reduced by the affordances of technologies, so that the remaining difficulties are mainly cultural ones. There is more room for agency than ever before, but it requires a recognition of this by individuals and an ability to grasp opportunities.

Openness, the removal of barriers of many kinds, is clearly both a problem and an opportunity for organisations, fundamentally challenging ways in which higher education is thought about, organised, led and managed. Equally, openness presents problems and opportunities for members of faculty, profoundly altering the nature and likely course of an academic career. In all this, the relationship between the individual academic and the institution is of course different too. These are forces that may be beyond the power of the individual, or even the single institution, to influence. It is possible, however, to take a position in relation to openness and closure. Marginson suggests a need to be watchful:

> We can evaluate global projects in terms of who gains from the moves to widen openness, who gains from the tactics of closure, and how deeply those closures become entrenched.
>
> (2010, 132)

He suggests that the pressure for closure to protect individual interests should be resisted in that it reduces the potential for new and larger-scale solutions to problems. This offers, perhaps, a way of evaluating the working of prestige too – whether its existence in any social or economic setting enables or inhibits the solution of significant problems.

Where does the university sit in relation to this? It is probably naïve to think that all of the functions that are currently carried out by universities will be subverted by collaborative, web-based activity. Governments will remain important and will seek ways of implementing economic and social policy.

Marginson notes that all countries offer either free or relatively cheap tuition and governments continue to finance basic research across the world. Although universities have been encouraged by policymakers to move from basic into commercial research for many years, industry generally provides a relatively small proportion of research funding (2010, 142).

However, some aspects will change. It could be argued that the university has for many years been in a privileged position in society, receiving preferential access to funding for both teaching and research. As has been outlined, this protected position has been eroded.

Rifkin's vision of the future assumes that goods can be produced on a zero marginal cost basis. Whether educational goods can be produced in this way is open to debate. Whilst one can imagine that relatively low-level and routine courses may well be deliverable largely by distance learning on a massive scale with very little human intervention, the very term 'delivery' points to the weakness of the proposal, in its indication of a one-way process. MOOCs offer an interesting example. A huge amount has been written recently about MOOCs, and their capacity to offer the very best teaching to anyone at no cost. However, as is equally well-known, there is not yet a financial model that supports this and ensures that the tutoring and assessments that are such important parts of educational provision can be made available. These aspects are unlikely to become cheaper as they are labour-intensive, particularly at higher levels of learning. When knowledge is freely available, including through MOOCs, other aspects of the university experience, that cannot easily be replicated without attendance, become relatively more important, including the embodiment of expertise in the person of the supervisor. MOOCs and similar developments may well help to distribute educational opportunity more widely, which is praiseworthy. Prestige will continue to exist, despite the democratising effect of such developments.

In summary, the sociological and psychological reasons for the existence of prestige will endure, as will prestige, despite the democratising effects of some of the developments that have been discussed. However, the speed and ubiquity or communication and the pace of technological and cultural innovation will make the maintenance of a prestige position more difficult to sustain, the possibility of losing it more likely and potentially more speedy. Thus there may be a greater incentive than ever for institutions to seek and safeguard their prestige, in a world where historically-based prestige can be less relied upon. There will be continuing battles over the right to recognise and accredit, which means in part having the right to confer prestige through official validation within disciplines and professions. As more and more teaching and research activity becomes subject to measurement, there is a danger to prestige universities in a national system if it can be shown that on a number of key indicators they are performing no better than less prestigious or expensive institutions. It may then be even more attractive to emphasise an institution's strength in aspects that cannot readily be measured. One can also expect more ostentatious display, more costly signalling, as many more intellectual products and resources come into being and are distributed freely and at no cost.

References

Aghion, P., Dewatripont, C., Hoxby, A., Mas-Colell, A. and Sapir, A. (2007) Why reform Europe's universities? *Policy Brief 2007/04*. Bruegel: Brussels.

Altbach, P. and Salmi, J. (2011) *The road to academic excellence: The making of world-class research universities*. Washington, DC: World Bank.

Blackmore, P. (2013) *Academic work and motivation in universities: An international perspective*. London: Leadership Foundation for Higher Education.

Blackmore, P. and Kandiko, C. (2012) *Strategic curriculum change in universities: Global trends*. London: Routledge/Society for Research into Higher Education.

Clark, B. (1983) *The higher education system: Academic organization in cross-national perspective*. Berkeley, CA: University of California Press.

Emons, W. (1997) Credence goods and fraudulent experts, in *Rand Journal of Economics* 28, 1: 107–19.

Jenkins, A. (1996) Discipline-based educational development, in *International Journal for Academic Development* 1, 1: 50–62.

KLI (2012) The King's-Warwick project: Creating a 21st century curriculum, http://www.kcl.ac.uk/study/learningteaching/kings/kwp-summary2010.pdf, accessed 5 May 2015.

Marginson, S. (2010) Higher education as a global field, in S. Marginson, P. Murphy and M. Peters (eds), *Global creation: Space, mobility and synchrony in the age of the knowledge economy* (pp. 201–228). New York: Peter Lang.

McNay, I. (1995) From the collegial academy to corporate enterprise: The changing cultures of universities, in T. Schuller (ed.), *The changing university?*: 105–15. Buckingham: Society for Research into Higher Education/Open University Press.

Rifkin, J. (2014) *The zero marginal cost society*. New York: Palgrave MacMillan.

Salmi, J. (2009) *The challenge of establishing world-class universities*. Washington, DC: World Bank.

Treiman, D. (1977) *Occupational prestige in comparative perspective*. New York: Academic Press.

Tsui, A. (2012) Transforming student learning: Undergraduate curriculum reform at the University of Hong Kong, in P. Blackmore and C. Kandiko, *Strategic curriculum change: Global trends in universities* (pp. 62–72). Abingdon: Routledge/Society for Research into Higher Education.

UNESCO (2014) *Global flow of tertiary-level students*, http://www.uis.unesco.org/Education/Pages/international-student-flow-viz.aspx, accessed 11 August.

Whitchurch, C. (2007) *Professional managers in higher education: Preparing for complex futures*. London: Leadership Foundation for Higher Education.

Chapter 5

National prestige
Global hubs

More students than ever before are choosing to study abroad and the trend is sharply upward: over 4 million students went abroad to study in 2012, increased from 2 million in 2000 (UNESCO, 2014). Expansion of provision for overseas students is being made in areas that have not traditionally attracted large numbers of students and that have traditionally been student exporters. The same source cites major growth areas as: China, Malaysia, the Republic of Korea, Singapore and New Zealand in East Asia and the Pacific; with Egypt, Saudi Arabia and the United Arab Emirates in the Arab states. This chapter is about more than mapping the increase in provision for overseas students that has either taken place or is planned in many countries. It is concerned with the ways in which the nation state has to be projected as a suitable environment for higher education to be located, so that it can attract both faculty and students. In part this means the state improving the quality and attractiveness of its higher education, both to retain its home students and to bring in students from overseas. However, there is also a broader prestige issue that extends to the ways a country chooses or tries to present itself to outsiders.

Underlying these developments are differences in the reasons for developing an overseas student capacity. Changing purposes are signalled in terminology. Several eras have been proposed. 'International education' was a favoured term until the start of the 1980s, succeeded by 'internationalisation' and more recently 'globalisation'. Underlying the terms are three distinct approaches: 'a development co-operation framework, … a partnership and exchange approach, and now … a commercial and competitiveness model' (Knight, 2014, 3). The model took largely as a given the predominance of Western universities, in a world where countries tended to be either exporters or importers of students. At one end is a relatively liberal conception of purpose, not principally aimed at income generation, indeed often not with that intent at all. It can be seen even today, for example when Germany does not charge fees to overseas students. There are of course 'soft power' advantages that have long been acknowledged, where graduates returning to their own countries remain influenced by their university experience.

Much has changed since these open-handed and perhaps paternalistic times. For some nation states the focus has shifted from the movement of individual students and staff, perhaps the traditional way in which higher education was international, through the provision of programmes and the opening of branch campuses overseas, to major national-level ambitions. Many nation states are now seeing higher education not only as a way of increasing national wealth, but also as wealth-creating in its own right. There are obvious potential advantages. Not only is it possible to earn fees from overseas students, but the outflow of funds that support home students going abroad to study can also be reduced. A second purpose may be to provide a more skilled workforce for a country, by attracting talented students who may then be encouraged to remain. Such an approach requires that a link be made between the extent and focus of higher education provision and the nature and mix of the skills that it is estimated are required for economic prosperity. A third purpose has to do with the idea of a knowledge economy, and the intention of using higher education as an integral part of it. Knight refers to these models as student, talent and knowledge/innovation hubs, respectively (2014, 30–4).

The last of these purposes may help explain the great enthusiasm for education hubs in some countries. In a country that wishes to develop rapidly, higher education may be seen as an area where a substantial investment may be expected to yield a return, if proven models and ways of working are adopted and skilled staff and able students can be attracted. There may also be a rhetorical benefit: achieving education hub status is itself a way of gaining a prestigious position in a relatively short time period (Dessoff, 2012). Knight refers to the 'exuberant' use of the term and notes the possibility of its being used for branding (Knight, 2010). Nations that have set out to be education hubs have done so in different ways and, although the picture changes rapidly, have varied considerably in what they have attempted to do and in the extent to which they have been successful to date. More established education providers have in their turn been prompted to review their provision in the light of this new competition for students by, for example, increasing their emphasis on postgraduate provision (James and McPhee, 2012, 147).

Singapore

An interesting example can be seen in the development of Singapore as an education hub. This may be the most significant in that it is probably the most advanced and coherent case of a nation state making a bid for increased status in higher education. Singapore has few natural resources and, following independence from Britain in 1965, the Singapore government has been active in encouraging the growth of industry and public education. An early decision that English would be the main official language, used in its education system, was part of a pragmatic intention of positioning Singapore as a major manufacturing and trading nation, a base for foreign firms seeking to expand in Asia and a magnet for other investment. Thus for many years the Singapore government has actively projected the image of the country as vibrant, fast-growing and concerned about the future. The idea of an education hub is consistent with this long-term policy. With major economic growth taking place in China, Singapore has sought to represent itself as a gateway between East and West, a suitable place from which to launch expansion into Asia. Singapore has also traditionally valued overseas expertise to assist in its modernisation, and there have been related concerns that its capacity to be innovative may have been adversely affected (Sidhu et al., 2014, 126). In recent years a government focus has been on the development of industry at higher technological levels as much of the growth had been in people-intensive industry. These are the classic components of a drive to create a knowledge and innovation hub.

The first proposal for an education hub appeared in a government document on the economy in 1986 (Sidhu et al., 2014, 126). Perceptions of a need for wholesale change in education policy can be traced back to a Thinking Schools Learning Nation initiative in 1997 that focused on the need for educational institutions to emphasise the development of critical and creative thinking in Singapore's citizens (Mok, 2008, 531). However, the start in earnest was famously signalled by the Minister of Education's intention that Singapore should become 'the Boston of the East' (Teo, 2000), and prompted by a perceived need to expand provision with limited state resources. Singapore's reforms began with a 'Global Schoolhouse' initiative in 2002, subsequently branded as 'Singapore Education'. Other examples of the branding of Singapore include 'Renaissance City' and 'Intelligent Island' (Sidhu et al., 2014, 122). Governance and management arrangements for public institutions were changed to 'corporatise' the institutions, with the intention of stimulating enterprise whilst retaining strong government influence. The Singapore Management University was established on a private footing. Invitations were issued to selected high-prestige overseas institutions to establish a presence in Singapore (Mok, 2008). This has meant borrowing the successful brand of the partner universities, which have also had to make their own decisions as to whether location in Singapore is a prestige benefit to them, since it may put their brand at risk. Asian campuses have been established by INSEAD, the University of New South Wales, the University of Chicago and the Technical University of Munich. In addition to provision on these campuses, joint academic programmes are also offered with a range of US and UK institutions. The Singapore government has from 2000 also sponsored growth in biomedicine by investing heavily in the support of research. From its announcement in 2008 a Campus for Research Excellence and Technological Enterprise (CREATE) has provided a home for research centres linked with prestigious overseas institutions, such as Massachusetts Institute of Technology (MIT), which has had a very significant involvement in Singapore. Profit has not been the strongest motive for Singapore. There has been a concern to encourage talented young people to come to Singapore, often by providing bursaries. Singapore uses its education system to extend its 'soft power' in the region by offering university placements and professional development to colleagues from other Asian countries (Sidhu et al., 2014, 126).

The decision to invite an overseas institution is politically sensitive, as is its acceptance or otherwise. Little information is publicly available about some of the negotiations. However, a particularly well-publicised attempt to attract a UK institution demonstrates some of the stakeholders and concerns. A plan by the University of Warwick in the UK to set up a campus was described as part of its institutional vision 'to take its place among the elite group of leading universities from across the world' (Baty, 2005). However, the proposal was abandoned following extensive controversy and a vote in the university's senate, owing to concerns about academic freedom. Issues were said to include gay rights and execution rates for prisoners. Requests by Warwick for guarantees of a number of freedoms on campus were not confirmed (Burton, 2005), whilst a number of earlier cases were cited of writers who had experienced severe difficulty in publishing. There was also significant concern over the cost of the project, almost £300m, and whether it would prove possible to attract able students and staff to a Singapore campus. Following extensive debate, the university senate voted against the development, unwilling to accept the Singapore government's requirement that an international educational institution must not interfere in its affairs. In Singapore, Warwick's strength in social sciences was noted as a possible basis for opposition and the refusal was interpreted as a snub for Singapore and a setback to its plans to be an education hub (Prakash, 2005). The same writer offered a more nuanced interpretation, suggesting that there may have been a failure to understand the ways in which some stories become particularly politically charged in a different political environment, and that conceptions of freedom cannot simply be transferred from one culture to another.

An interesting aspect of the case is that this was a major initiative that had the strong support of the executive, but that failed to carry the academic body with it. Warwick students were also quite vocal. A poll captured the range of views, with 43 per cent declaring it a bad idea, 14 per cent believing it a good idea but one that could be damaging to Warwick's reputation and a similar number saying that it was a good idea but with too great a financial risk (Baty, 2005). It is interesting to note that institutional prestige was a concern for students as well as for staff. Warwick's plans were not entirely lost. In 2006 the Warwick Manufacturing Group (WMG) signed an agreement with the Singapore Institute of Management and Singapore Institute of Manufacturing Technology to launch a WMG Master of Science in Engineering Business Management in Singapore (SIM, 2006). Other universities took different decisions. A number of UK institutions, including Cambridge, were approached but declined, but the University of New South Wales' academic board unanimously agreed to do so, its vice-chancellor declaring that it was a safer location than most in the region and a move that an Australian institution was better placed to make. In the meantime the University of Nottingham had opened a campus in Malaysia and the University of Liverpool was planning to do so near Shanghai (Thompson, 2006). This demonstrates the sense of competitiveness among institutions to achieve prestige through such developments, the motivation to seize opportunities that are presented and the magnitude of the strategic decision that then has to be taken.

United Arab Emirates

The United Arab Emirates offers another important example, with a very distinctive history. The federation of six emirates, including Abu Dhabi and Dubai, took place in 1971. The region has immense mineral wealth, with Abu Dhabi estimated to have 7 per cent of the world's oil reserves. The UAE's population doubled to over 8 million in the five years to 2010, 7 million of whom are expatriates. The three public higher education institutions are mainly restricted to Emiratis, so a large expatriate population requires alternative access to higher education. Fifty other institutions belong to the private sector, half of them outposts of overseas institutions, the largest number of international branch campuses in the world. They are licensed by a Knowledge and Human Development Agency and based in economic free zones that make them largely exempt from government quality assurance arrangements. Programmes have a predominantly professional focus and there is significant duplication (Lane, 2010). An early decision was taken that English would be the language of instruction and that English-speaking faculty would be recruited to the public universities (Fox and Shamisi, 2014). This policy, taken up in the private universities, has helped Dubai to make its offer more attractive to overseas students and to its expatriate population.

There are clear advantages to government in allowing a varied system to develop, and to work at arms-length from it by insisting only that overseas campuses provide an education that is the equivalent of the home campus, overseen by the University Quality Assurance International Board. However, there is inevitably confusion as a result of the variety, as there is no common standard, and the Dubai government does not recognise degrees from those institutions. In addition, such provision is not linked with Dubai's workforce requirements – but then many of the students will not remain in Dubai after graduating. This presents an interesting prestige problem, of building the prestige that is borrowed from host institutions into a Dubai brand, and assuring quality, whilst allowing the diversity that is necessary for the external provision to be attractive to potential students.

Such a major growth in higher education provision has clearly been sanctioned for a purpose. Lane (2010) suggests a number of mainly prestige reasons, to do with international perceptions of Dubai. He suggests that it is a symbol of modernity, and one that gains attention for the state. In addition, bringing prestigious overseas institutions into the country implies that the quality of Dubai's education is comparable and that Dubai is sufficiently important to be taken seriously by those institutions. Finally, the diverse range of nations is evidence that the UAE is global in its outlook.

Malaysia

In countries where the government decides that higher education can be beneficial for the economy, there is a potential advantage for the higher education sector that more funding may flow into it, but along with this may come approaches to the strategic management of the sector that are less than welcome. Malaysia also has ambitions to be an education hub. Malaysia has developed an alternative version of the Asian education hub model, with higher education identified as a national key economic area aiming to achieve 200,000 international students by 2020. The initial incentive came from the large number of Malaysian students who were studying abroad, which was costly for a developing nation, but ambitions have grown over the twenty years (Richards, 2012) beyond this initial objective. A largely private model has been adopted. Richards compares Malaysia's 'emergent' model, slower and linked with the local labour market, with Singapore's 'ambitious model of top-down policy engineering', commenting that the former, more sustainable, approach is to an extent giving way to the latter in Malaysia (Richards, 2011). Like Singapore, Malaysia could claim to be a place where East meets West, although it is a developing and not yet developed nation. There are several prestige issues suggested by Malaysia's situation. Firstly, the assurance of quality continues to be a central concern, without which it is hard to project an attractive image of Malaysian higher education. As a developing nation, Malaysia has particular challenges in developing high-quality capacity with limited funds. Richards points out the potential pitfalls in an understandable wish to gain higher international rankings quickly. Taking an increasingly top-down approach to development and quality, specifying educational standards and recruitment targets, will not of themselves foster a high-quality culture of teaching and learning. Richards argues that a partnership model is needed rather than a policing model (2011, 6). He also points out that the simultaneous setting of high expectations for research productivity may detract from the improvement of teaching. An Asian top-down model is seen as a potential danger, and a 'middle way' is urged, tempering capitalism with a more responsible and sharing approach. Secondly, Malaysia benefited from the political and social consequences of the 9/11 destruction of the World Trade Centre in New York, following which many Middle East Muslim students found it harder and less attractive to enter a Western university (Dessoff, 2012). The same writer claimed that twenty-five overseas institutions had applied to establish campuses in Malaysia. If accurate, this indicates the increasing competitiveness in establishing overseas provision, with many institutions manoeuvring for a global position.

Hong Kong

The historical and cultural context for Hong Kong has helped to shape its higher education system and the nature of its bid to be an education hub. A British colony until 1997, its education system has been strongly modelled on

UK practice. The University Grants Committee oversees the eight publicly funded institutions serving a population of 7 million. Four of the universities – the University of Hong Kong, Hong Kong University of Science and Technology, the Chinese University of Hong Kong and the City University of Hong Kong – appear in the Times Higher Education top 200 world university rankings, a significant concentration for a small region. In addition, there are six private universities. For overseas companies Hong Kong has the benefit of being part of China, with its huge markets, although there are attendant political risks.

Hong Kong's education developments were initially aimed at improving the skills of the Hong Kong population. A review undertaken by the Hong Kong Special Administrative Region (HKSAR) after 1997 concluded that education was an important part of its economic future (Education Commission, 2000). Reforms in recent years have been far-reaching, and distinctive in that they have involved the entire education system. Until recently the region's education system has been highly selective and academic. The final two years of secondary education were principally a preparation for university study, but only 18 per cent were then admitted to university (Tsui, 2012, 62). The reforms reduced the secondary stage by a year while universities moved to a four-year university undergraduate programme, in order to make space for a broader curriculum with attention paid to the development of general skills and experiential learning, and with a liberal arts component. This met with concerns from some members of faculty, particularly in sciences, technological disciplines and professional groups that depth would be sacrificed – an issue returned to later in the chapter on curriculum. In recent years, as part of the region's re-orientation as a city within China, the HKSAR has set out to attract non-local students, from China or elsewhere, to study and then stay in the region. The HKSAR now considers the development of an education hub to be a major contributor to the region's economic success, building on significant existing strengths, although it has been claimed that policy is not entirely coherent between exporting education and attracting workers for the region, and there have been calls for clearer leadership. It has been suggested that Hong Kong has a student hub, and possibly elements of a skilled workforce hub, but has yet to develop a research and innovation hub (Mok and Bodycott, 2014). A comparative study, drawing examples from the UK, Australia and Singapore, concluded that whilst Hong Kong has made progress, the lack of a central authority is hindering efforts, and recommended an increased spending on research, more government-level agreements on issues such as degree recognition and credit transfer, the greater use of overseas offices, recruitment agents and marketing information (Cheung et al., 2011).

Hong Kong's education hub ambitions may to some extent have been cooled by its equivocal relationship with the country of which it is now a part. Recent concerns in 2014 over the manner of selection of candidates for HKSAR elections are a strong outward sign of the inevitable tensions when a former colony, with its own history, traditions and social and cultural norms, is joined again with a much larger and very powerful nation. However, Hong Kong's location in China offers the prospect of future major expansion beyond its home population base of 7 million people. The Chinese government's 2008 plan to unite the nearby nine cities of the Pearl River Delta, the most economically productive region of China, with infrastructure that will bring over 50 million people within an hour's travelling time of one another, has major implications for Hong Kong. Transport routes from Hong Kong to the mainland are also being improved and, despite local sensitivities about mainlanders, and the maintenance of some border restrictions, Hong Kong is increasingly being drawn into the larger region. Even if it can remain relatively separate, it runs the risk that its current strengths will be replicated elsewhere if it does not engage. Hong Kong's future status as an education hub is therefore more likely to come from servicing the human resource needs of the Pearl River Delta (Cheng et al., 2011). The same authors cite two tensions: between a global/regional and a local orientation and between a market-driven and public-funding approach. Each of the options offers a rather different future, and a different form of prestige. A global and publicly funded route leads to world-class universities, with international exchange and collaboration. An outward orientation and market approach will lead to a marketised export model. More locally, public funding will be accompanied by greater engagement in manpower planning and in nation-building, while a private model will lead to more locally provided higher education, privately provided. All of these directions can be seen to some extent, but Hong Kong has yet to contemplate the scale of increase that will be needed if it is to serve its wider region.

This significant point in Hong Kong's development is an excellent illustration of the importance that higher education has now achieved in national planning, both for its potential for supporting and enabling economic growth and for the projection of political and social influence. In confronting its integration into a much larger country, Hong Kong has an opportunity, through its education hub ambitions, to develop 'soft power' in the wider region, and there is a relationship between the extent of educational growth on an industrial scale and capacity for soft power building, as an increasing number of students and professionals pass through its higher education system. However, Hong Kong's education system is small in relation to the scale of higher education needed in the wider region, and it is also desirable to retain an international presence. The writers' recommendation therefore is for Hong Kong to focus on higher-level study and research, which are most helpful for the development of soft power and are least likely to be replicated elsewhere. The reputation of Hong Kong's universities, evidenced by their strong showing in international league tables, coupled with a sound reputation for quality assurance, are strongly supporting factors. However, it may be that a stronger policy framework and clearer political leadership will be needed (Mok and Bodycott, 2014) in a very complex political context, to take advantage of opportunities.

Conclusions

The successful establishment of an education hub can bring economic and social benefits to a host country, and can draw attention to the country in a positive way, helping to portray it as modern and global in outlook. Some of the benefits are projected long-term ones, such as in the Arab states, where there is a wish to diversify the economy to make it less dependent on oil. Others are benefits in kind, social and political, for there is unlikely to be huge profit to be made, and indeed the developments may be heavily dependent on government subsidy (Marginson, 2010, 171). Factors that may help or hinder such a development include policy and organisational environment on the one hand and cultural issues on the other. A British Council report (2013) named Hong Kong, Malaysia, Singapore and the United Arab Emirates as having above-average opportunities. The report identified three specific areas. The policy environment refers to the host government's efforts to assist and manage transnational education, including the provision of incentives and the implementation of quality assurance arrangements. The market environment is favourable where a country has a high per capita income and a growing economy with a demand for graduates. The mobility environment refers to the ability to attract providers and programmes.

Marginson offers a more sociologically driven analysis. He points out that the policy of separate development in some countries may be done for good reasons but may hinder progress. To be separate from the local setting, often quite deliberately in order not to offend tradition, is a weakness – 'Location, identity and capacity matter' (2010, 170). The location is more attractive if it is at the heart of a vibrant and well-connected society, attracting people who are creative. National, regional and city prestige are extremely important. Marginson proposes three conditions that must be met if a region is to be organised successfully: 'geographical proximity, cultural commonality, and political will' (2010, 173). He cites Japan as an example of a country that is for political and cultural reasons unable to look much beyond its borders.

Status benefits accruing to a country as a result of improved perceptions internationally are particularly difficult to quantify. One might expect that improved international league table results would be a proxy measure. However, as the British Council reports, interviews with staff involved in higher education in Malaysia suggest a perception that their transnational activities have given the country global status even though there is no visible league table improvement. The same source suggests that Abu Dhabi and the United Arab Emirates have gained in status.

There are risks to parent institution in setting up campuses overseas, some of which were rehearsed in the Warwick in Singapore debate reported earlier. There have been well-publicised problems that have not reflected well on the parent institution. The University of Waterloo closed its Dubai campus owing to a lack of students (Carrington, 2013) and Michigan State University closed its undergraduate provision in Dubai before any students graduated (Lane, 2010). Marginson summarises a number of concerns, noting that franchised campuses are prone to a lack of control from their home base, may have weak levels of equivalence with the home degree, and from time to time the local partner collapses, producing a reputational risk (2010, 179).

Trends in relative national prestige now make major news stories. For example, recent trends in Times Higher Education rankings have led to a claim that the US is in decline and that Asian universities are increasing in status (Baty, 2014). The sheer number of Chinese institutions – over 2,000 – the level of investment in higher education and the continuing high rate of economic growth seem highly likely to make China a more attractive destination for overseas students. It has been claimed that China might be Asia's next higher education hub (Iqbal, 2011). The same source suggests that China's growing influence in the world is a significant factor – one where the country's prestige leads to prestige for its education system. The education hub developments discussed here are only part of a much larger picture. Knight (2010) also chooses Botswana and Qatar as leading global hubs, with emerging hubs in South Korea, Sri Lanka, Mauritius and Bahrain.

Institutions will find themselves increasingly subject to international competition from both state and private providers. Indeed, a number of the traditional functions of universities may no longer need an institutional home, especially if governments decline to continue giving preferential status to universities to be in receipt of public funds. However, the most prestigious institutions award not just degrees but social capital – connections and networks. They can also offer an experience that is qualitatively different and that is not easily reproducible by 'lesser' institutions and not captured readily through learning outcomes. There will continue to be a market for this, because these are the sources of the kinds of prestige that count the most. The story of global hubs so far is that it takes considerable effort and investment over a very long period to generate a hub with a sound reputation, let alone a prestigious one. The advantage lies very heavily with those who are already established, in the race for the most mobile and advantaged students.

References

Baty, P. (2005) Freedom row fails to sink Warwick's Singapore plan, in *Times Higher Education*, 21 October, at http://www.timeshighereducation.co.uk/news/freedom-row-fails-to-sink-warwicks-singapore-plan/199217.article, accessed 15 October 2014.

Baty, P. (2014) Tectonic shifts point to Asia taking on the mantle, in *Times Higher Education*, 2 October.

British Council (2013) *The shape of things to come: The evolution of transnational education: Data, definitions, opportunities and impacts analysis*. London: British Council.

Burton, J. (2005) Warwick votes against Singapore campus, in *Financial Times*, 14 October, http://www.ft.com/cms/s/0/39f13dfc-3c9b-11da-83c8-00000e2511c8.html#axzz3GQPBQszH, accessed 15 October 2014.

Carrington, D. (2013) Oxford, Yale or Abu Dhabi? Middle East aims to become hub for universities, in *CNN International Edition*, http://edition.cnn.com/2013/11/27/business/harvard-oxford-or-abu-dhabi-universities/, accessed 16 October 2014.

Cheng, Y., Cheung, A. and Yeun, W. (2011) Development of a regional education hub: The case of Hong Kong, in *International Journal of Educational Management* 25, 5: 474–93.

Cheung, A., Yuen, T., Yuen, C. and Cheng, Y. (2011) Strategies and policies for Hong Kong's higher education in Asian markets: Lessons from the United Kingdom, Australia, and Singapore, in *International Journal of Educational Management* 25, 2: 144–63.

Dessoff, A. (2012) Asia's burgeoning higher education hubs, in *International Educator*, July–August, http://www.nafsa.org/_/file/_/ie_julaug12_asia.pdf, accessed 15 October 2014.

Education Commission (2000) *Review of education system reform proposal: Excel and grow*. Hong Kong: Government Printer.

Fox, W. and Shamisi, A. (2014) United Arab Emirates' education hub: A decade of development, in J. Knight (ed.), *International education hubs: Student, talent, knowledge-innovation models* (pp. 63–80). London: Springer.

Iqbal, I. (2011) *China: Asia's next higher education hub?*, http://www.topuniversities.com/where-to-study/asia/china/china-asias-next-higher-education-hub, accessed 16 October 2014.

James, R. and McPhee, P. (2012) The whole-of-institution curriculum renewal undertaken by the University of Melbourne, 2005–2011, in P. Blackmore and C. Kandiko (eds), *Strategic curriculum change: Global trends in universities*: 145–59. London: Routledge.

Knight, J. (2010) Regional education hubs: Rhetoric or reality?, in *International Higher Education* 59: 20–1.

Knight, J. (2014) *International education hubs: Student, talent, knowledge-innovation models*. London: Springer.

Lane, J. (2010) *International branch campuses, free zones, and quality assurance: Policy issues for Dubai and the UAE*. Dubai: Dubai School of Government.

Marginson, S. (2010) Making space in higher education, in S. Marginson, P. Murphy and M. Peters (eds), *Global creation: Space, mobility and synchrony in the age of the knowledge economy* (pp. 150–200). New York: Peter Lang.

Mok, K.H. (2008) Singapore's global education hub ambitions, in *International Journal of Educational Management* 22, 6: 527–46.

Mok, K.H. and Bodycott, T. (2014) Hong Kong: The quest for regional education hub status, in J. Knight (ed.), *International education hubs: Student, talent, knowledge-innovation models* (pp. 81–99). London: Springer.

Prakash, J. (2005) Singapore learns hard lesson, in *Asia Times*, 16 November, http://atimes.com/atimes/Southeast_Asia/GK16Ae01.html, accessed 15 October 2014.

Richards, R. (2011) Higher education marketisation, privatisation and internationalisation: Singaporean vs. Malaysian models of the Asian Education Hub policy. Proceedings of INCUE Conference, Kuala Lumpur, 7–8 December.

Richards, R. (2012) The emergence of the Malaysian education hub policy: Higher education internationalisation from the perspective of a non-Western developing country, in T. Stiasny and T. Gore (eds), *Going global: The landscape for policy makers and practitioners in tertiary education*: 157–68, Bingley: Emerald.

Sidhu, R., Ho, K.-C. and Yeoh, B. (2014) Singapore: Building a knowledge and innovation hub, in J. Knight (ed.), *International education hubs: Student, talent, knowledge-innovation models* (pp. 121–143). London: Springer.

SIM (2006) Singapore Institute of Management to offer the University of Warwick's masters programmes, http://www.simtech.a-star.edu.sg/press-releases/singapore-institute-of-management-to-offer-the-university-of-warwicks-masters-programmes.aspx, accessed 16 October 2014.

Teo, C.H. (2000) *Education towards the 21st century: Singapore's universities of tomorrow*, paper presented at the Alumni International Singapore (AIS) lecture. Singapore: Ministry of Education, 7 January.

Thompson, M. (2006) Why Singapore can't attract any UK universities, in *Independent*, 16 March, http://www.independent.co.uk/news/education/higher/why-singapore-cant-attract-any-uk-universities-470023.html, accessed 16 October 2014.

Tsui, A. (2012) Transforming student learning: Undergraduate curriculum reform at the University of Hong Kong, in P. Blackmore and C. Kandiko, *Strategic curriculum change: Global trends in universities* (pp. 62–72). Abingdon: Routledge/Society for Research into Higher Education.

UNESCO (2014) Global flow of tertiary-level students, http://www.uis.unesco.org/Education/Pages/international-student-flow-viz.aspx, accessed 11 August 2015.

Chapter 6

League tables and international clubs

Introduction

The ranking of universities through the publication of league tables has become a major feature of the landscape of higher education, and a cause of much controversy. Despite a widespread distaste for them in universities, rankings have quickly become highly significant influencers of individual and collective behaviour. More recently, global league tables have been a significant development not just for individual institutions but at the level of national systems. An European University Association report listed thirteen (Rauhvargers, 2011, 12) international league tables and the number increases annually. Rankings are thus one of the most obvious contemporary sites for the negotiation of prestige in academic life.

The earliest rankings of institutions occurred in the US in the 1920s, in relation to graduate schools. Thereafter rankings have developed strongly in the US and in Japan, which also has a strongly stratified higher education system. The US World and News Report published the first global survey, commencing in 1983, which continues to be influential. Rankings arrived in Europe relatively recently, either because national systems were not very strongly differentiated, which meant there was no purpose in distinguishing among institutions, or else because enough was known informally for decisions to be taken. Now a broader higher education sector in most countries and the need to target research funding have led to greater interest, compounded by the development of global rankings (Teichler, 2011, 56). Toutkoushain and Webber point to the growth in science research funding as having diverted universities away from teaching as their main mission and having stimulated state interest in evaluating its impact (2011, 123).

Most commentators see the current high level of interest in rankings as a facet of globalisation, with growth in mass higher education increasing investment in it, both by nations and individuals, and consequent concern about value for money. When knowledge is 'the foundation of economic, social and political power' (Hazelkorn, 2012), higher education may be seen as a major source of new knowledge, and therefore key to gaining advantage over other nations. International organisations such as OPEC and the World Bank now routinely review higher education in nation states, seeing it as an indicator of economic progress. Thus, as Hazelkorn points out: 'The performance and quality of higher education has become a vital sign of a country's capacity to participate in world science and the global economy' (2012, 2). Rankings are now being used as the basis for international comparisons of economic health, at the level of nation states and beyond. They have thus become indicators of national worth. Hazelkorn places global rankings against a broad backdrop of relative economic stagnation in Western advanced countries since 2008, whilst economies such as Brazil, China and India have grown strongly. This has led to shifts in relative strength among nations and sharpened competition (Hazelkorn, 2013, 13). Growth in research and development spending in developing countries, coupled with a huge increase in demand for higher education arising from a rapidly increasing world population both point to a major increase in the number of universities and the extent of competition among them and at system level. The European Commission has expressed fears that the EU is falling behind in relation to emerging economies, by investing relatively less (Europa, 2011). The Times Higher Education's judgement on their 2014 rankings was that the US is showing signs of losing its dominance and Asian countries are gaining ground (THE, 2014, 8). In this way league tables help to set broad perceptions of relative strength and decline. They are thus a spur to international competitiveness in a highly sensitive area politically; that of economic strength. League tables generate web traffic and rankings make news. Stories about the actual and possible changing fortunes of nations and institutions make good copy, and so most of the more influential rankings are of commercial value to their publishers.

The main argument advanced in support of rankings is of transparency. There have always been informal views about the 'best' institutions in a national system. Rankings promise a more objective measure, partly because they are not produced by the universities themselves, so there is supposedly no vested interest in their production, and partly because they use a limited number of numerical indicators. A range of stakeholders – governments, potential and current students, research funders and others – thus have information available that enables them to make informed choices. By exposing institutions to continual comparative scrutiny, league tables may be felt to encourage a constant concern for the improvement of quality, for the benefit of stakeholders. It can be argued that the production of global rankings has in some ways been beneficial, questioning the easy assumptions of superiority that have been felt for many years by universities in the US and the UK. They may challenge 'self-perceptions of greatness' by requiring evidence of performance (Hazelkorn, 2013, 23), prompting debate at a national level to identify the key factors that enable success, leading to policy change (Rauhvargers, 2011, 16). The publicity attached to league tables raises questions about how a system can increase its number of high-ranking institutions, and this in turn draws attention to governance and to financial issues, particularly the overall spending on higher education as a proportion of GDP and the size of research and development budgets. As will be explored later, the behaviours of national systems, institutions and individuals do appear to be influenced quite profoundly, far beyond the initial expectations of those who generate the rankings. The significance for the ways in which prestige is enacted is obvious. League tables generate prestige, by adding a quantitative aspect to judgements that would in some cases previously have been made informally anyway, thus making the implicit explicit. By providing apparently solid measures of quality they offer a currency which enables a prestige economy to flourish, prompting a desire for the possession of those highly visible expressions of prestige and stimulating interinstitutional competition.

However, although league tables may be devised to drive up standards, they may also have a perverse effect, which has to do with prestige scarcity. In any league table there can be only a few winners, so in either generating new or confirming existing prestige, league tables make a scarce good available. Thus league tables label some universities and what they produce as prestigious and others as less so. This would not be so problematic if it were desirable for all institutions to be alike. However, there may be good reasons for institutional missions and priorities to differ. An important difficulty with university rankings, as explored later, is the favouring of a particular kind of institution at the expense of other, also valuable, possibilities. Current interest in 'world-class' universities usually takes into account 500 universities at most. Generally, tables tend to be limited to 100–200 institutions. Since there are over 17,000 universities in the world, this is a discussion that concerns three per cent of universities at most, yet it affects very many more. It can of course be argued that league tables can be constructed around any indicators that the compilers wish to encourage, or an audience wants to consider. The idea of choice is built into the EU multiranking development, referred to later. There is no reason why a university cannot be found to be excellent for its attainment in social inclusion, for example. However, quality indicators and rankings are themselves subject to judgements about prestige. There is little kudos in being top of a table that is not cared about by the most prestigious institutions, that are meanwhile demonstrating their excellence through success against more prestigious measures.

There is now a large literature on university rankings, dealing with their social and political significance and with the technical aspects of data production, interpretation and presentation. Much of it explores the consequences, intentional and incidental, beneficial and malign, but on balance the literature is strongly negative about the accuracy and impact of rankings. The full range of arguments will not be attempted here. Teichler has produced a summary of nine major weaknesses (2011, 62–6). Issues of greatest interest here include the dangers of using data for purposes for which it was never intended, including aggregating them to make very general judgements about institutions; privileging particular kinds of institution; and inviting game-playing and exercises in performativity that distract attention from more important activities. The European University Association advises against taking rankings too seriously, pointing to numerous inherent problems of method and to a large number of ways in which institutions can alter their score, without necessarily improving quality (Rauhvargers, 2011, 66–7). The chosen indicators should correspond to the purpose of the survey. Surveys can work only with the data that can readily be obtained and there may be a mismatch when available indicators are used on the assumption that there is a correlation. This occurs particularly when research performance is taken to be a proxy for teaching quality or for general performance (Vught and Westerheijden, 2010). Some surveys rely on self-reporting by institutions, which opens up the possibility of misreporting for institutional advantage and of interpretations differing among countries.

I will now draw on some of the rapidly growing literature on rankings to explore some of the prestige-related effects at national, institutional and individual levels, making connections with the social psychology of prestige, before turning to the prestige pressures that bear on the producers of rankings.

International dimension

International league tables of institutions highlight major differences in the extent to which nations are represented. US universities are in a commanding position, with substantial UK and Australian representation. Many other countries with developed or strongly developing higher education systems, such as mainland European countries and China, make relatively little showing. Such tables draw attention to national differences and prompt exploration of the possible reasons for them, which may be socio-culturally based or may relate to national policy, particularly on funding and governance. They lead to a higher profile for comparisons among higher education systems worldwide, to explain differing levels of performance and to improve them. They also support popularisation of the idea of the 'world-class university', and the assumption that a principal purpose of a higher education system is to produce such universities, and that all institutions should aspire to be 'world class'.

Global league tables have become a means by which a particular kind of institution – the research-intensive, internationally focused university – becomes the standard against which all others are judged. Within that elite Harvard, at the top of the table, is the key institution to emulate. This effect is particularly apparent in those international tables that pay the greatest attention to research-related measures, such as the QS and the Shanghai Jiao Tung rankings. Teichler refers to the 'imperialism' of rankings that promote a particular view of quality. He comments that Chinese rankings tend to assume that research excellence is a proxy for teaching excellence, that British rankings reward inward mobility whilst neglecting the value of outward, and that there is a tendency for countries to develop more strongly stratified higher education systems, like those that are already well represented in international league tables, so that they can 'produce' a group of elite institutions that can compete internationally (2011, 64). The third traditional academic role, of service, whether within or beyond the institution, is very difficult to define or to measure, and does not generally appear in league tables (Webber, 2011, 115). Larger institutions also benefit, since league tables usually report total productivity per institution. Research-dominated international league tables also signal the importance of working in English, since research publications in any other language are unlikely to achieve the same level of readership and impact.

International league tables are particularly challenging to construct because of the difficulty of obtaining comparable data in widely differing systems. So, whilst some league table measures record productivity by directly quantitative means, such as by counting the numbers of research publications or spending on learning resources, others are reputation-based, asking members of faculty to suggest those institutions that have the highest standing in a particular field. This latter approach is not based on verifiable metrics but on impressions, and thus may tend to privilege the most established and best-known institutions, reflecting past glories. However, it can be argued that such a long-term rounded view may be a more valid indicator of fundamental excellence than a judgement based on snapshots of a number of institutional statistics. It will smooth out some of the temporary and therefore less significant peaks and troughs and reflect, through the capturing of a general impression, some of the less easily measured aspects of excellence. It is certainly an example of an area in which institutional prestige is in play, as an indirect gauge of excellence.

National dimension

Just as international league tables produce a pressure to generate 'world-class' institutions, so too do league tables have a normative effect at national level, where there is a tendency for all universities to be pressed to imitate those institutions that are at the head of the table, ignoring important differences in institutional circumstances. This is reflected even in tables that have a greater teaching emphasis, such as the Sunday Times Good University tables in the UK. In its comment on its 2014 tables, the newspaper labels five institutions as 'the worst', pointing out lower scores in degree completions and professional employment, with no acknowledgement of the very different characteristics of those institutions' student intakes on entry, in comparison with those of 'the best' (*Sunday Times*, 21 September 2014, 5). League tables are often set at the level of institutions and therefore stimulate interinstitutional rivalry. It can be argued that this is an incentive for the overall standard to improve. This is, however, to assume that the model of institution being rewarded is appropriate to all the institutions in the table, that all institutions should develop profiles that are like the most successful in those league tables' terms, and that the spur of competition will encourage institutions to work to become the best, as exemplified by those at the head of the table. However, a developed system of higher education caters for a number of desired ends, academic, professional and social, and these varying ends may most effectively be met through the fostering of a diversity of institutions, each excellent in the achievement of its particular mission. Crude league tables based on a single model of excellence do nothing to help achieve this. Such tables introduce strong incentives for institutions to do whatever scores well and not to do anything that does not have a league table benefit. There are many examples, some of them having to do with social inclusion. When 'value added' is not evaluated, institutions have an incentive to place their greatest efforts to recruit in the direction of the most able students. Where the extent to which an institution is selective is a league table measure, there is an incentive for prestigious institutions to seek to maximise the number of applicants whilst keeping the number of places small (Hazelkorn, 2008, 205).

Quality is now a focus of attention in all developed and developing education systems. As nation states increasingly see advantage in having a strong presence globally in the provision of higher education, so concern about quality assurance grows. National quality assurance arrangements are intended to ensure that institutions are accountable, shifting the community for whom it is important to be prestigious from the institution itself to a wider range of stakeholders (Harman, 2011). League tables have also become a form of quality assurance and it could be claimed that rankings are supplementing other forms of quality assurance and in a desirable way, in the eyes of those who are strongly in favour of marketisation. By placing clear and simple measures of quality in number form in the hands of those who make use of an institution's services, it can be argued that this locates quality assurance where it should be – with those who are well placed to come to a judgement and who can express their perception of quality through the operation of the market. Indeed, rankings are most widely influential in the countries that have a relatively marketised system. Thus they have great influence in the US, UK and Japan and relatively less in mainland Europe.

Institutional-level league tables have the effect of reinforcing hierarchy in a system, by making overall judgements that produce winning and losing universities. Those that make such general judgements about universities produce a 'halo' effect in that all parts of a successful institution receive a prestige benefit. Meanwhile, pockets of excellence in less highly placed institutions are disadvantaged. This produces an incentive for successful research teams in less well-ranked institutions to migrate to a better-placed institution. Rankings tend to favour the hard sciences, partly because of the size of grants that are awarded. The practice of publishing large numbers of multi-authored papers creates a large number of citations, as compared with disciplines that have traditionally favoured single-authored books. Since bibliometric databases generally pay little attention to books, the social sciences and humanities are systematically disadvantaged by league tables (Rauhvargers, 2011, 15). This tends to decrease the standing of those areas in universities where, particularly in the humanities, they have long had less opportunity to win high-value grants. The publication of league tables that clearly favour the sciences can do little for the prestige of the humanities and social sciences. In this and in many other ways, prestige is being driven increasingly from beyond the academy, institutions are indeed tending to become what is measured, and rankings are a mechanism that is increasingly steering the allocation of both private and public resources.

There have been calls for ranking itself to be more tightly managed and quality assured. In 2006 an International Ranking Expert Group (IREG) founded by UNESCO agreed a number of principles for good ranking practice. Purposes should be clear and design appropriate; rankings should be only one way of assessing higher education, complementing other approaches; rankings should recognise diversity of institution; be clear about sources and messages drawn from them; and specify the education system's context. Indicators should have transparent methodology; be relevant and valid; measure outcomes rather than inputs; and specify weighting. Data should be collected and processed ethically; they should use checked and verifiable data collected properly; be quality assured; and be managed well. Presentation should make clear the factors that are used, offer choice in display of rankings and avoid errors (UNESCO, 2006). The list neatly summarises the problems of rankings.

Prestige clubs

Highly placed institutions make use of rankings to argue for support in becoming or remaining world-class institutions. A group of universities may make a case for the concentration of resources within them, as has happened in the UK where Russell Group universities have over a number of years lobbied to ensure that the national research assessment process concentrates research resources rather than distributing them broadly.

Institutions also benchmark themselves against peers, and in some cases their statistics influence their ability to join international groupings of universities (Hazelkorn, 2007, 14). There are a number of international consortia of research-intensive institutions. Universitas 21, formed in 1997, is the longest established, a network of twenty-seven research-intensive institutions, almost half of which are from the UK, US, Australia and Canada. Member institutions describe themselves as 'research-led, comprehensive universities providing a strong quality assurance framework to the network's activities'. Claiming to be 'the leading global network of research universities for the 21st century' (Universitas 21, 2014), much of the group's emphasis is on the internationalisation of curricula. However, since 2012 it has taken a particularly strategic lead by publishing an analysis of national higher education systems, detailed elsewhere in this chapter. The international character of the group is itself a prestige feature.

The League of European Research Universities (LERU), formed in 2002, is a consortium of twenty-one research-intensive institutions from ten countries, five from the UK and three each from France and the Netherlands (http://www.leru.org/index.php/public/home/). The group pursues its common interest, aiming to influence research policy in Europe, describing itself as 'advocating the promotion of basic research at European universities', and believing that 'basic research plays an essential role in the innovation process and significantly contributes to the progress of society'. LERU aims to further 'the understanding and knowledge of politicians, policy makers and opinion leaders about the role and activities of research-intensive universities' (LERU, 2014). Membership is by invitation, against a set of criteria related to the scale of research activity and taking account of the extent to which the institution can add strength to the group and its lobbying power.

The International Alliance of Research Universities (IARU) is a particularly exclusive group of research-intensive institutions, including Yale University and the University of California Berkeley in the US, the Universities of Oxford and Cambridge in the UK, the European Universities of Copenhagen and ETH Zurich, the Australian National University, the University of Singapore and the Universities of Peking and Tokyo. The group describes itself as 'leading research universities that share a global vision, similar values and a commitment to educating future world leaders' (IARU, 2014) and engages in a range of shared activities. Each institution is represented by its president or equivalent and the chairing of the group rotates among members. In addition to promoting shared research activities on global themes, the group argues for the idea of the research-intensive institution, using the concept of a 'knowledge ecosystem' to describe the co-existence of teaching, research and technology transfer and claiming that the metrics that are normally used do not describe the particular value of such institutions.

Describing itself as 'the most active global higher education and research network' (WUN, 2014), the Worldwide Universities Network (WUN) has eighteen mainly mid-ranking institutions, from the UK and two each from the US and Australia. Its Board consists of the presidents or equivalent of each of the member institutions. WUN sponsors a large number of collaborative research projects on four themes, in partnership with a range of international agencies, and also has researcher development and mobility provision.

These international groups have a number of prestige aspects. Firstly, some of them claim explicitly to wish to influence government policy (and, in the case of LERU, that of the EU). This requires credibility and connections, a point enshrined in LERU's membership criteria. Secondly, they are a way in which institutions can publicly indicate those whom they consider their peers. Each tends to contain institutions of broadly comparable stature, providing the prestige reciprocity that makes the group attractive to all of its members. Each group aims to increase collaboration among the members of that group, presumably in preference to any institutions that are not in the group. Thirdly, some groups argue the case for institutions of their kind, as exemplified best by IARU, which makes a very particular case for a research-intensive institution benefiting from a cluster of related activities. The formation of such groups offers ways in which member institutions can show that they are different from others. The overall effect is to distance a number of largely Anglo-Saxon research-intensive institutions from the rest.

The internal effects of ranking

Use of league tables occurs despite widespread reported dissatisfaction with the ways in which they work and what they measure (Hazelkorn, 2007, 8). Many university staff dislike the existence of such measures. Yet institutional priorities and actions are clearly shifted by such means. The close attention that institutions pay to rankings reflects an evident belief that many of those who are stakeholders are themselves influenced by them, and shows that institutions are willing to compete against one another (Locke, 2011, 204). All league table rankings are of interest to institutions, in that any of them can contribute to institutional prestige, and any of them can produce 'negative prestige' (Vught and Westerheijden, 2010, 10–11). Institutions use league tables and rankings to review their activities and identify weaknesses. Thus rankings tend to prompt change within institutions, becoming prestige weapons, for use within as well as beyond the institution. On the basis of extensive international surveys of institutional behaviour, Hazelkorn noted that 63 per cent of institutions were taking management decisions as a result of rankings (2007, 45). Hazelkorn lists some of the activities that universities are diverted into as a response to rankings: planning for mergers, spending on recruitment and restoration of morale internally and reputation externally (Hazelkorn, 2008, 201). Institutions also improve their management information systems so that they can better measure the data involved (Hazelkorn, 2007, 13). Rankings are also extremely important for marketing and publicity (Hazelkorn, 2007, 11), making the most of those league table placings that show them in the most favourable light. Institutions are quite likely to align their own quality assurance processes so that they measure the same factors as those used by external quality assurance processes. Thus in the UK, the National Student Survey, offered to all final year students each year, is likely to be the template for internal student satisfaction questionnaires in other years, even though an extensive critique of the survey has pointed out its deficiencies against alternatives used elsewhere in the world, an issue returned to later.

One of the institutional effects of rankings may be to stimulate spending on symbols of prestige, which may be iconic buildings, sports facilities or highly rated researchers. This use of rapidly increasing student fees has long been noted in the US, where the increasing cost of degrees, out of proportion with popular perceptions of teaching quality, has been a matter of debate for some years (Archibald and Feldman, 2011). Rankings can also be used by faculty and other staff within an institution as a way of lobbying for positioning and resourcing, if a potential investment or organisational rearrangement can credibly be claimed to have a probable effect on league table placing.

Two processes of internalisation and institutionalisation have been claimed to underlie altered behaviour and lead to undesirable consequences for institutions (Locke, 2011, 202). Espeland and Sauders (2007) Foucauldian analysis of US law schools, points out the increasing quantification of activity in public organisations and note, as did Foucault, the thin line between describing a situation and changing it through statistics. The concept of reactivity supposes that people's behaviour changes when they are observed, including for evaluation, because they are reflexive. A reactive measure is therefore one which changes as a result of the measurement taking place. They name two mechanisms which act to produce change: self-fulfilling prophecy and commensuration. The former occurs when people change their behaviours to act in conformity with the measure. An example they offer is that more students may apply to an institution that has scored well for the quality of its teaching, even if the differences rated are in fact very small. Reputation scores given by members of faculty will start to reflect league table positioning because those are the only available data once respondents' personal knowledge has been exhausted. Resources within an institution may be distributed to schools that already score well, to maximise their league table benefit. Finally, rankings encourage the imitation of what is valued, thus discouraging distinctiveness. Commensuration is the process by which we change what we attend to, because what is measured becomes the focus of attention. Much information is thus ignored and what remains is turned into a simple and authoritative metric that is decontextualised. Simplification by reducing to numbers makes it easier to attend and respond to the measure. A measure also becomes the way in which entities are compared. Thus the relationship between institutions is defined as rankings shift from year to year, as is change in a single institution over time. As a result of these processes, they claim, resources are redistributed, work is redefined and the use of gaming proliferates.

Sauder and Espeland (2009) also deploy Foucault's concept of discipline as a means of understanding the ways in which rankings influence institutions, and the apparent inability of institutions to keep their distance. They explore some of the ways in which surveillance and normalisation contribute to a discipline that comes from outsiders and is also self-imposed. Surveillance is continuous, since new league tables are produced and thoroughly publicised each year. The rankings are known almost immediately by current and potential students and by other faculty worldwide. Almost any decision in an institution seems to have a ranking aspect. Thus surveillance is also highly detailed, and often entails the careful gathering of statistics, perhaps at the expense of doing the job itself. Surveillance can also take place at a distance from the institution, since data make the institution so transparent and are so publicly available and apparently easy to interpret. Normalisation is a second mechanism, through which a norm is established, so that institutions can be measured by the extent to which they conform to it. Rankings facilitate comparison, by assuming that all those included are of a kind. Differentiation and hierarchy are made possible through the use of metrics. They also encourage homogeneity, make it more difficult to be distinctive and help to exclude those that do not conform. Rankings are internalised by a number of means. Firstly, they tend to cause anxiety, particularly about status, in part because rankings cannot be controlled by a single institution. Hence staff may have responsibility without control. Secondly, they may prompt resistance, but this is itself a relationship with rankings.

Student and employer behaviours

A number of studies seem to show that potential students pay attention to league tables when making their choices. What is less clear is whether they are the principal means of deciding or whether they confirm a general judgement that has already been made, and whether students' behaviour is uniform across various student categories. A complicating factor concerns the relationship between quality and prestige. This can be illustrated with the UK's National Student Survey, which invites final year students to rate their institution in relation to a number of measures to do with organisation and management, quality of teaching, assessment practices, the availability of resources and a range of other items. These measures have a credible research base in the literature on student learning and taken together are assumed to indicate the quality of the student experience in that institution. Some teaching-led institutions outperform research-intensive ones on measures of teaching quality. It is possible, but not very likely, that this outcome will produce a major loss of students from the research-intensive university in favour of the clearly more teaching-focused institution. What is more likely is that the research-intensive institution will retain its popularity with students despite the league table figures. This suggests that one or more other factors are in play. It is of course a complex question, but it seems highly likely that many students will make their university choice on the basis of an overall perception of an institution's prestige rather than on the quality of its performance in organising for teaching. This is not to argue that the quality of teaching does not matter. It may be that in the long term sustained poor performance in the support of students' learning may well have a detrimental effect on the institution's reputation and thence its prestige, but it appears that any relationship is not direct or immediate.

Hazelkorn cites several studies that suggest that above-average and financially independent students are more likely to take a decision based on general reputation than are those who are less fortunate (2008: 203). It has also been suggested that international students are likely to be more influenced by league tables, and this may perhaps reflect the lack of other sources of information and opinion that might be available to a 'home' student. Some international postgraduate markets appear to be particularly sensitive, especially where the student's home country awards scholarships only to institutions that are highly ranked.

Students are of course able to see that the value of their degree may be influenced by perceptions of the quality of the institution. It has been suggested that some students act strategically to make positive returns on their experience (Clarke, 2007). There have also been reports that this point has been made directly to students by faculty in some institutions in the UK. Student issues are explored in greater depth later.

Hazelkorn suggests that the limited research on employers' choices tends to suggest that choices are made on the basis of a general sense of reputation coupled with a tendency to recruit from the same limited number of institutions that have served them in the past, together with the use of league table data (2008, 205). Stakeholders tend to use rankings to confirm their existing opinion, and to reassure themselves (2008, 16). This appears to support the view that overarching impressions of reputation and prestige weigh most heavily. Detailed statistics help to confirm a picture that has already been formed.

The prestige of rankings

For audiences beyond universities, the increasing credibility of rankings derives from their simplicity and perceived independence from the higher education sector or individual higher education institutions (Hazelkorn, 2008, 21). Faculty in universities may dislike them for much the same reasons, being pressured by externally devised rankings that appear to oversimplify complex issues and thus be misleading. There have at times been attempts to boycott particular rankings or else to sponsor alternatives, but such moves are rarely successful. However, despite the powerful position that rankings appear to occupy, they too have to fight for their space. The number of league tables and the fact that they are in many cases sponsored by for-profit organisations, such as newspapers and periodicals, means that there is competition among the league tables and their originators. In effect, there is a prestige economy of league tables. The main groups whose approval is sought are outlined by Hazelkorn (2008) as: those who use the system, including government, employers, parents and students; higher education institutions that want to maximise their benefit from the system, either by the way they present data or by influencing the metrics; those who are trying to improve the system, including the ranking organisations and government; and those who are critical of the ranking system. A successful league table provider needs to convince its users that it captures accurate and useful information, manages the frequently conflicting requests of those who wish to benefit from or improve the system and maintains sufficient public confidence so that critics of such systems are not able to gain ground.

Three major global rankings compete, in effect, in their representations of higher education globally. The Shanghai Jiao Tung index grew from a local wish to calibrate that institution's research quality against a small number of other institutions, mainly in the US. The Times Higher Education ranking is very clearly associated with a commercial publisher. A change in its supplier of data led to its former partner developing the World University Rankings (Vught and Westerheijden, 2010, 11). There have been attempts to shift the emphasis of global tables. Universitas 21's ranking of education systems is a means of moving attention away from the inspection of the quality of single institutions and towards the national context, which is otherwise invisible in global rankings that tend to operate as if the policy context were the same in all countries. A recent EU development shows the political significance of such rankings, through an attempt to establish an alternative form of ranking that would deliver rather different results for its sponsors.

U-Multirank

The information needs of stakeholders are complex and extremely varied. Even among students, the needs of school leavers, professionals who are updating and members of traditionally excluded groups are very different (Vught and Westerheijden, 2010, 10). A major initiative to reform the operation of rankings has been sponsored by the EU. U-Multirank is an interesting development, both for its approach to ranking and for the discussions that have surrounded its introduction. U-Multirank was first proposed during the French presidency of the EU in 2008, as a means of acknowledging the wide range of higher education institutions, the variety in stakeholders' needs and thus the many ways in which institutions can be excellent. The initiative was described as addressing 'some of the shortcomings of existing rankings' which meant that US and UK institutions were strongly represented and European universities less so (EPRS, 2014). A similar sentiment appeared in European Parliament questions in 2012 asking what measures it would take 'to ensure that the EU's higher education institutions rise to the highest positions in the ranking system' (European Parliament, 2012a). The EU's politically prudent response was that responsibility for quality lay with the institutions and the member states and the Commission's role was a supporting one (European Parliament, 2012b).

A 2010 paper made the argument for transparency. Describing education as in part a 'credence good', meaning one of which the value is not known even after consumption (Vught and Westerheijden, 2010, 3) the writers argued that conceptions of quality vary, as do stakeholders' needs for information. They criticised the methodology informing the most current use of indicators and argued for a better form of transparency based on multi-dimensional tools. A feasibility study reported positively in 2011 and the first ranking was produced in 2014. Described as 'a new multi-dimensional, user-driven approach to international ranking of higher education institutions', U-Multirank offers data on five dimensions: teaching and learning, research, knowledge transfer, international orientation and regional engagement. Thus it is much broader in its focus than other international league tables. Its purpose is to enable the user to find institutions that are similar in profile and to analyse performance against the user's chosen performance indicators. The first survey included 850 institutions from seventy-four countries, with EU institutions heavily represented: 62 per cent are from Europe, 17 per cent from North America, 14 per cent from Asia and 7 per cent come from Africa, Latin America and Oceania (Europa, 2014). The survey offers rankings of whole institutions and also rankings of fields of activity: business studies, physics and electrical and mechanical engineering. Psychology, computer science and medicine will be included next and other fields are scheduled to be added in subsequent years. The data in U-Multirank come from a number of sources, including institutions, bibliometrics, databases and surveys of over 60,000 students at the universities included. The survey does not use composite scores, on the grounds that transparency is lost when scores of different kinds are combined. Initial analyses have shown that no institution achieves 'A' scores across all the measures (A equating to 'very good' and E to 'weak'). Around 100 universities have more than ten 'A' scores and all have at least one. Three hundred universities appear that have never before featured in global rankings, thirty of them achieving 'A' scores of more than ten (Tyson and Gravas, 2014). It could thus be claimed that such a survey displays excellence that would otherwise go unrecognised in other rankings. For example, the survey shows that interdisciplinary research accounts for 7–11 per cent of most institutions' outputs. The five institutions that score best on this measure do not appear in other international rankings. Thus a key function of U-Multirank is to demonstrate that the choice of indicator determines which institutions appear at the top of any ranking. Despite the intention of putting the choice of performance indicator in the hands of the user, a number of 'ready-made' rankings have been published. The use of a number of knowledge-transfer measures highlighted strengths of particular institutions in France, Austria, Sweden, Germany, Japan, the Czech Republic and Iceland, while some approaches to the measurement of research have produced some different orders among the top-rated institutions (MacGregor, 2014).

From an EU perspective, such a development is entirely in keeping with policy objectives, in that it is likely to encourage diversity in higher education systems. Such a tool aims to encourage excellence, but acknowledges that it may come in many forms. It also has the potential to assist the EU in directing research funding and other investment towards excellence, wherever it is to be found. At national level, the aim starts to conflict with another intention, which is to develop or protect 'world-class' institutions. Certainly at institutional level one might anticipate a range of responses to this EU-sponsored attempt to liberalise conceptions of prestige, related to perceived gain or loss. U-Multirank has been funded initially by the EU and developed in academic research centres in the Netherlands and Germany. As a publicly funded initiative, U-Multirank and expenditure on it have been subject to public scrutiny. The response of the Secretary-General of the League of European Research Universities, reported in the Times Higher Education, itself a publisher of league tables and therefore with a commercial interest (Curell, 2013), summarises some of the issues. Describing it as 'at best an unjustifiable use of taxpayers' money and at worst a serious threat to a healthy higher education system', he reported LERU's 'serious concerns about the lack of reliable, solid and valid data for the chosen indicators in U-Multirank, about the comparability between countries, about the burden put upon universities to collect data and about the lack of "reality-checks" in the process thus far' (Gove, 2013). A UK House of Lords report (House of Lords, 2012) was critical of a number of aspects. The majority of those bodies that expressed a view felt that there were already too many league tables, that data collection would be burdensome and that the task was full of methodological difficulties. Indeed, a number of the objections were to aspects of rankings that the initiative aimed to deal with. The other intention, referred to earlier, of wishing to redress the stronger representation of US and UK institutions in comparison with European ones means this is inevitably a politically charged innovation. This is reflected in a UK government ministerial comment to the House of Lords that U-Multirank might appear to be 'an attempt by the EU Commission to fix a set of rankings in which [European universities] do better than [they] appear to do in the conventional rankings' (House of Lords, 2012, 26). The House of Lords' conclusion was that until the new method could adequately deal with the deficiencies in approaches to ranking, the EU should prioritise other activities (2012, 27).

A key distinction underlying league tables, and one that U-Multirank seeks to deal with, is that differences among institutions can be defined both horizontally, by classification, or vertically, by ranking. Classifications are intended to denote difference in kind, rather than differing levels of quality (Vught and Westerheijden, 2010). For example, some institutions have higher degree-awarding powers and others do not. However, in practice difference is often construed to mean differing quality, and the operation of prestige tends to convert expressions of difference into indicators of relative quality, reflecting whatever is most highly valued. The best-known classifications are the US Carnegie classification and the EU's U-Map. Each has attempted to deal with this problem. The Carnegie Foundation's classification has been widely used since its introduction in 1973. Although not intended for the purpose, it became a form of ranking, in that it was deemed more prestigious to be in one category than another. This led to a change to a multi-dimensional approach in 2005 (Vught and Westerheijden, 2010, 7). The U-Map, introduced alongside U-ranking, is designed to provide profiles of institutions against six dimensions: research, innovation, education profile, student profile, internationalisation and regional outreach. It is intended to reflect what an institution is trying to do, rather than its level of achievement. Whilst efforts can be made to prevent the generation of league tables, by producing data that cannot readily be aggregated, underlying perceptions of the prestige associated with a particular focus are likely to remain. A further difficulty for U-Map is that whereas Carnegie can make use of national databases to inform its work, working in the EU means dealing with data that may be collected and stored differently across a range of countries, so that data from different nations may not be comparable (Vught and Westerheijden, 2010, 15).

Conclusions

The continuing growth and popularity of rankings are the despair of many higher education commentators. As noted already, a substantial literature points out methodological deficiencies that are often claimed to be impossible to remedy. Teichler suggests that there may be an inverse relationship between quality and popularity – the poorer quality and more biased the survey, the more popular it is likely to be (2011, 67). However, league tables will not go away. There appears to be a considerable appetite for them from a number of quarters. From the prestige perspective, the power of the movement towards ranking is entirely understandable. Complicated judgements are made easy; a currency of prestige is produced that can be traded. News is generated, especially if there is sufficient churn to provide a regular supply of winners and losers. If we are addicted, individually, institutionally and nationally, to prestige, then rankings feed that addiction by providing a constant input of desirable prestige items, the possibility of reward and the prospect for some of confirming their desired identity and status.

An unlikely benefit may be that some of the consequences of the unthoughtful use of league tables are so obvious that they may work to stimulate more nuanced developments. These may be driven by economic good sense as well as by ideas of social justice. It is reasonably obvious that a developed economy requires more than a few flagship internationally prestigious institutions and that a more far-sighted aim of national policy is to promote breadth in higher education, with a range of institutions pursuing varied and equally valued missions. This is easier said than done given the power of simple prestige stories. However, continued development of rankings themselves can be a way forward, as U-Multirank shows.

As ever, judgement about the desirability of the prestige aspects of league tables and rankings depends on the extent to which their influence is beneficial or malign. It is clear that a drive to attain prestige is very powerful and can stimulate considerable efforts at national and institutional levels to improve comparative performance. However, a narrowly conceived treatment of prestige will produce unintended consequences if all that is required of universities is not included in the survey. Rankings may then prompt institutions to take actions that are not beneficial overall. The experience of being judged yearly against the profile of a 'globally excellent' institution will encourage convergence in institutional mission, when government may wish to foster a broad and differentiated range of institutions. To take a specific concern, universities will not be encouraged to be inclusive and admit 'non-standard' students unless a value-added approach can be found that takes account of students' starting points, an issue returned to later. Prestige of itself is neither good nor bad – it has to be judged on its effects in the world on how people, organisations and systems act. Rankings are a highly obvious example of a feature of higher education practice that continues to need review.

References

Archibald, R. and Feldman, D. (2011) *Why does college cost so much?* Oxford: Oxford University Press.

Clarke, M. (2007) The impact of higher education rankings on student access, choice, and opportunity, in *Higher Education in Europe* 32, 1: 52–70.

Curell, J. (2013) U-Multirank aims to improve HE, not sell newspapers, in *University World News*, 16 February, 259, http://www.universityworldnews.com/article.php?story=20130214134418891, accessed 30 September 2014.

EPRS (2014) *What is U-Multirank*, http://epthinktank.eu/2014/05/23/university-ranking-and-u-multirank-2/, accessed 30 September 2014.

Espeland, W.N. and Sauder, M. (2007) Rankings and reactivity: How public measures recreate social worlds, in *American Journal of Sociology* 113, 1: 1–40.

Europa (2011) *Supporting growth and jobs: An agenda for the modernisation of Europe's higher education systems*. Brussels: Communication from the Commission to the European Parliament, the Council, the European Economic and Social Committee and the Committee of the Regions, http://eur-lex.europa.eu/legal-content/EN/ALL/;ELX_SESSIONID=VHNJJx2MLYvWpDpG7TwMTzS7whJFTrDjZ670PDP8ndvnKSHj13Zq!-1945910639?uri=CELEX:52011DC0567, accessed 4 October, 2014.

Europa (2014) *New international university ranking: Commission welcomes launch of U-Multirank*, http://europa.eu/rapid/press-release_IP-14-548_en.htm, accessed 30 September 2014.

European Parliament (2012a) *Parliamentary questions: U-Multirank*, http://www.europarl.europa.eu/sides/getDoc.do?pubRef=-//EP//TEXT+WQ+E-2012-003668+0+DOC+XML+V0//EN&language=EN, accessed 12 October 2014.

European Parliament (2012b) *Parliamentary questions: Answer given by Mrs Vassiliou on behalf of the Commission*, http://www.europarl.europa.eu/sides/getAllAnswers.do?reference=E-2012-003668&language=EN, accessed 1 October 2014.

Gove, J. (2013) Universities pull out of EU's 'unjustifiable' U-Multirank, in *Times Higher Education world university rankings*, http://www.timeshighereducation.co.uk/world-university-rankings/news/universities-pull-out-of-eus-unjustifiable-u-multirank, accessed 30 September 2014.

Harman, G. (2011) Competitors of rankings: New directions in quality assurance and accountability, in J. Shin, R. Toutkoushain and U. Teichler (eds), *University Rankings: Theoretical basis, methodology and impacts on global higher education* (pp. 35–53). London: Springer.

Hazelkorn, E. (2007) The impact of league tables and ranking systems on higher education decision-making, in *Higher Education Management and Policy* 19, 2: 81–105.

Hazelkorn, E. (2008) Learning to live with league tables and ranking: The experience of institutional leaders, in *Higher Education Policy* 21, 2: 192–216.

Hazelkorn, E. (2012) Understanding rankings and the alternatives: Implications for higher education, in S. Bergan, E. Egron-Polak, J. Kohler, L. Purser and M. Vukasović (eds), *Handbook of Internationalisation of European Higher Education* (pp. A2.1–5). Stuttgart: Raabe Verlag.

Hazelkorn, E. (2013) World-class universities or world-class systems: Rankings and higher education policy choices, in E. Hazelkorn, P. Wells and M. Marope (eds), *Rankings and accountability in higher education: Uses and misuses* (pp. 71–94). Paris: UNESCO.

House of Lords (2012) *The modernisation of higher education in Europe*. London: Stationery Office.

IARU (2014) *International Alliance of Research Universities*, http://www.iaruni.org/, accessed 28 September 2014.

LERU (2014) *The League of European Research Universities*, http://www.leru.org/index.php/public/home/, accessed 28 September 2014.

Locke, W. (2011) The institutionalization of rankings: Managing status anxiety in an increasingly marketized environment, in J. Shin, R. Toutkoushian and U. Teichler (eds), *Ranking, reputation and the quality of higher education* (pp. 201–228). Dordrecht: Springer.

MacGregor, K. (2014) New global university ranking launched, in *University World News*, http://www.universityworldnews.com/article.php?story=20140514061139715, accessed 30 September 2014.
Rauhvargers, A. (2011) *Global university rankings and their impact*. Brussels: European University Association.
Sauder, M. and Espeland, W.N. (2009) The discipline of rankings: Tight coupling and organizational change, in *American Sociological Review* 74, 1: 63–82.
Teichler, U. (2011) Social contexts and systemic consequence of university rankings: A meta-analysis of the ranking literature, in J. Shin, R. Toutkoushain and U. Teichler (eds), *University Rankings: Theoretical basis, methodology and impacts on global higher education* (pp. 55–71). London: Springer.
THE (2014) *World university rankings 2014–15*. London: Times Higher Education.
Toutkoushain, R. and Webber, K. (2011) Measuring the research performance of postsecondary institutions, in J. Shin, R. Toutkoushain and U. Teichler (eds), *University rankings: Theoretical basis, methodology and impacts on global higher education* (pp. 123–143). London: Springer.
Tyson, A. and Gravas, M. (2014) *EAC lunchtime conference: Launch of the world's first global, multi-dimensional user-driven university ranking*, PowerPoint presentation, unpublished.
UNESCO (2006) *Berlin principles on ranking of higher education institutions*, http://www.che.de/downloads/Berlin_Principles_IREG_534.pdf, accessed 1 October 2014.
Universitas 21 (2014) *Universitas 21*, http://www.universitas21.com/, accessed 28 September 2014.
Vught, F. and Westerheijden, D. (2010) Multidimensional ranking: A new transparency tool for higher education and research, in *Higher Education Management and Policy* 22, 3: 1–26.
Webber, K. (2011) Measuring faculty productivity, in J. Shin, R. Toutkoushain and U. Teichler (eds), *University Rankings: Theoretical basis, methodology and impacts on global higher education* (pp. 105–121). London: Springer.
WUN (2014) *Worldwide Universities Network*, https://www.wun.ac.uk/, accessed 28 September 2014.

Chapter 7

Necessary myths
Universities and knowledge

To retain and enhance their position, universities individually and collectively must be seen to be efficient and effective (Diamond, 2011, 2015), using the resources at their disposal in the pursuit of desired ends. The nature of those ends changes over time and is influenced by a number of stakeholder interests and wishes, both within and beyond the institution. The dominant contemporary expectation is that universities should prove their economic usefulness in the knowledge economy, developing and maintaining a place in a 'triple helix' of government, industry and universities (Wilson, 2012). This is to be achieved through research, much of it highly applied, that can be shown to lead to new and improved products and services, and through teaching that produces skilled graduates and a continuously updated workforce.

However, whilst many outputs and outcomes of a measurable kind can be delivered against externally generated and specific requirements, not everything that a university 'produces' can be so readily measured and there are many more interests in play, including those of individuals and groups within the institution. As Cohen et al. (1972) pointed out, universities have purposes that can never be fully defined or agreed and use technologies that cannot be described exactly, in that we do not know how to guarantee excellent student learning or research outcomes. Universities are also driven in part by standards that are generated by academic bodies.

The possession of prestige – and the ability to generate it – carries with it social permissions and opportunities. This applies to higher education as a whole, to groups of institutions, individual universities, groups and individuals. If a recognised and highly valued role is being fulfilled, prestige will be retained, permissions will continue and resources will be available. There has, therefore, to be some accommodation between what is valued in society as a whole and what is valued in a university, the latter of which is signalled by what it spends its time and resources on and the nature of its outputs and outcomes, in both teaching and research. To safeguard that prestige position at an institutional level, it is necessary that certain beliefs and values are held, or perceived to be held. For example, it would be unwise for a university to declare that it was not concerned to make an economic contribution. The beliefs and values serve at least two functions: signalling outwardly that an institution or group of them is delivering that which is valued; and providing a cohering narrative within the institution as a guide to behaviour. This is an immense simplification of course in that what is valued externally is a complex and highly political question, with many actors attempting to influence debate and dominant emphases changing over time. Similarly, within institutions, individual and group interests may vary considerably, with differing values and intentions in play and with competition for status and resourcing.

As demands on universities, and opportunities for them, increase, so does the complexity of generating and sustaining a coherent narrative, with institutions tending to proclaim themselves to be excellent at all things, often attempting to reconcile competing pressures as they seek prestige in areas that have differing values. Among these many tensions, both within and without the institution, a set of central tenets exists, with a powerful cultural, political and economic function. They are developed and defended enthusiastically, precisely because their acceptance or otherwise either confirms or weakens the position of the university and of particular dominant groups within them. They are termed myths here, not because they are necessarily untrue, but because they are ultimately not capable of being proved and yet they have considerable power to influence attitudes and decisions. Neither is an evaluative judgement being made about the myth or the motives of those who support it. There may be self-interested aspects, but it may also be that these are sincerely held beliefs with an internal consistency that sits comfortably within a particular 'moral tribe' (Greene, 2013).

This chapter deals with the significance of myths of this kind in organisations and the ways in which leaders, managers and other staff in a university can generate and make use of myth. Attention then turns to a first central area of myth, surrounding the kinds of knowledge with which the university deals. A second area of myth, to do with the purposes and processes of academic activity, is dealt with in Chapter 8.

The management of myth

I will shortly explore a number of central myths but before doing so will consider the ways in which myths are developed and maintained. Bourdieu (1984) uses the term 'symbolic capital' to describe those kinds of capital that come about through socially learned classification. Thus prestige is a form of symbolic capital. For an item of capital to be held to be prestigious by a group, it has to be accepted at a valuation that has been placed on it – a process that has been termed 'symbolic violence', in that it is a way in which the behaviours of others can be managed, by persuading them to be in alignment with a particular way of viewing a valued item. The stronger the pressure to compete on the basis of the conspicuous holding of various forms of capital, the stronger too is the incentive to seek to manage impressions in order to gain advantage. Attachment to and active support of particular viewpoints can be seen as a form of game, which can happen at the level of the nation state, institution, faculty, department, research group or individual. In an institution, pressure to succeed may increase the tendency to be strongly engaged in a game, in a process that Bourdieu referred to as 'illusio' (Bourdieu, 1993). By this he meant that those who work in a field and become concerned to achieve success in it will increasingly come to believe strongly in the value of what they are striving for and will try ever harder, whether that belief is recognised consciously or held unconsciously. Illusio is that which enables individuals to take a game seriously and give everything that they can to it.

Burton Clark described very strong institutional cultures as 'organisational saga'. Participants would relate strongly to their institution by seeing their practices 'as the expression of a unified and unique approach that has been devised by hard work and struggle' (1983, 9). The story might not be accurate, and would probably be exaggerated, but it would contain some truth. Clark described organisational sagas as being weak, moderate or strong. In very competitive situations, universities may be forced to promote an institutional legend. Within the institution a saga produces loyalty, commitment and a sense of community. It is a form of moral capital, like a bank deposit that can be drawn on in times of difficulty (1983, 11). This is not unlike the concept of the 'reputational reservoir' (Watson and Maddison, 2005), which can sustain an institution through times of difficulty and that is contained in the institution's story of itself. Watson recites a long list of governance and management difficulties that the University of Cambridge weathered, any of which could have been a major shock for a less prestigious institution. Elsewhere Watson comments (2009: 113) that if the reservoir is full, criticism is directed downwards in the organisation. If it is not full, then the criticism may travel upwards. It also enables the institution to attract funding. Clark proposes that a specialist prestigious institution is safer in times of downturn than a generalist institution that is not distinctive. If nothing unique is lost when cuts are imposed then the institution is at particular risk. Strong pride and self-belief brings disadvantages, too. An institution that perceives itself to have a particular strength may be unwilling to adapt in changing times. Individual staff may have such a great investment in the way they do things that change can come about only through appointing new staff. This illustrates the difficult balance to be struck between the continuity that enables the steady build-up of prestige over time and the risk of institutional sclerosis that comes with it.

Not every entity can be prestigious: by definition, prestige is relatively scarce. One of the psychological values of prestige attribution may therefore be to simplify a very complex environment. A clear leader with a plausible story makes the task of valuing and following very straightforward. In an exploration of academic leadership, Bailey suggests that we should look beyond the rational in seeking to understand some leaders' actions. He describes a world where people compete to make their version of what is happening into an accepted reality. He calls these versions myths and points out that they have a 'sacred and derisory' aspect to them. That is to say a leader must prove that their version of the truth is important to follow and that those of others are foolish delusions. An aim of leadership is to make one's story stick. It has to be a simple story and it does not really matter if it is not true. It simply has to be believable. In a messy world, leadership 'is the art of cutting into this chaos and imposing a simplified definition on the situation, that is, making people act as if the simplified picture were the reality'. It is 'a form of cultivating, of stopping doubts and stifling questions' (Bailey, 1988, 2).

Leadership can be gained and retained on a number of bases. It may stem from: an ability to inspire; having shared values; an 'instrumental' approach which involves 'rewards and penalties'; and the position of expert, awarded to somebody who has skills that others simply do not have. Each of these is the basis of trust in the leader, meaning that the person trusted is free of detailed scrutiny and will not be held accountable for every single action. Prestige has a component of trust: having prestige validates what the person has or does and provides room for maneouvre. Prestige makes explanation unnecessary. Indeed, a feature of a person in a prestigious position is that he or she may not feel obliged to explain their actions. To do so would lessen their prestige.

Knowledge myths

There are of course many beliefs in organisational life that have nothing directly to do with prestige. Those chosen here fit the general requirement for myths – that they are widely believed or known about but not easy to prove. However, they are chosen as prestige myths here because they have to do with bestowing a particularly high status on a phenomenon or an activity within universities. The first area of myth is around the nature of the knowledge that universities are believed to be generating and sharing. Some of the claims are that:

- universities have a central role in the production and sharing of knowledge;
- the knowledge they produce is in some ways distinctive and cannot readily be produced elsewhere;
- there is stability in knowledge, represented by stable disciplines;
- universities understand and can facilitate professional practice, including in the visual and performing arts.

There are fairly obvious tensions in this set of myths, not least the respective statuses of the various kinds of knowledge with which a university may deal, which are explored below and which help to illuminate some aspects of prestige in universities.

Knowledge and the university

Universities play an important role in the generation, validation and sharing of knowledge, although they are not unique in society in doing so and their role is increasingly challenged in some aspects. The kinds of knowledge that are associated with the university influence its position in society and thus have a prestige dimension. The relationship between universities and society is reciprocal: universities tend to reflect a set of values in society, and by their work serve to support those values, although aspects of their work may at times generate social change. When those external values shift, particularly when this is reflected in legislative, procedural and funding changes that affect the university, tensions within the institution that may be latent are likely to become more apparent.

The range of disciplines and professional groups present in a university is very wide. Struggles for the intellectual high ground, and more pragmatically for funding, are highly likely to have a prestige dimension. The primacy of science and scientific method has been an enduring feature of universities for many years, a source perhaps of envy and increasingly a focus of critique. Modern debate is often said to have begun with C.P. Snow, who declared that Britain had since Victorian times suffered from an under-valuing of sciences as against the humanities in comparison with the US and Germany (Snow, 1961) and who, significantly for a study of prestige, pointed out the lack of respect for and understanding of the culture of the other. The snobbery of the humanities was made all the more intense by the successes of science, which made it easier for the humanities to retreat to a moral high ground and be dismissive than to engage with those of another tribe. A sociologically based critique has questioned the status of 'hard' scientific knowledge, attempting to show that much of what has been held to be objective scientific knowledge is socially constructed (Latour and Woolgar, 1986).

A related distinction is that between 'hard' and 'soft' knowledge, terms often used to characterise and locate the kinds of knowledge that tend to be valued in universities. Many analyses use Biglan's (1973) three dimensions of knowledge: hard-soft, pure-applied and life-non-life. In hard fields, that tend to be in the sciences, there is an agreed paradigm or theoretical base, whereas in soft areas there are often competing theoretical positions and a lower level of agreement about what is to be known and how. Pure areas of study are not concerned with practical application, whilst life fields are concerned with living systems. Disciplines have commonly been characterised in relation to this framework. Hard-pure disciplines can be represented by mathematics, physics and chemistry. Hard-applied might include engineering and medicine. Sociology, English and music are pure-applied and business, education, social work and nursing soft-applied. Biglan also proposes social dimensions. A convergent discipline has agreed core standards and an enduring elite. A divergent discipline may have a number of schools of thought. Urban disciplines see researchers working closely together in highly defined areas, as would a research team in the sciences. A rural discipline has fewer researchers, often working individually over a wide area, such as history. A number of studies have attempted to show the possible relationship between these largely epistemological distinctions and a range of personal and organisational aspects, such as personal goals, activities and job satisfaction (Creswell and Bean, 1981) and attitudes to leadership and management have also been explored

(Blackmore, 2007), as have attitudes to risk (Deem and Johnson, 2003) and to teaching and assessment (Neumann et al., 2002). Others, such as Trowler (2012), have argued that such differences are over-stated and disciplinary affiliation and influence are in reality much more nuanced. Knowledge tensions in universities are played out in a number of places where different forms of knowledge meet and prestige is in play. These include the development of interdisciplinary and interprofessional research and teaching, engagement with mode 2 knowledge, of which professional learning is an example, and dealing with the visual and performing arts.

Interdisciplinarity

A discipline has been described as: 'any comparatively self-contained and isolated domain of human experience which possesses its own community of experts' (Nissani, 1995, 122). Disciplines have a body of knowledge and a methodology and also require a community that generates, evaluates and passes on the disciplinary knowledge. Therefore, a discipline is also a socio-cultural entity, in which decisions have to be taken about what and who counts within the discipline. Learning within a discipline entails a socialisation process that encourages and sometimes requires a particular worldview (Hall and Weaver, 2001). There are also complex relationships with external bodies, including other disciplines, to be negotiated. For all these reasons, disciplines necessarily include a relationship between knowledge and power (Moran, 2002).

The idea that a university consists of a set of solid, clearly bounded and enduring disciplines is itself a myth. The history of the university is of new bodies of knowledge and areas of professional expertise being incorporated over time, with a steady expansion of what constitutes academic knowledge (Clark, 1983, 3). Once there, disciplines are not usually static. A process of fragmentation and reformation has taken place, in fields such as biological sciences, psychology and economics (Trowler, 2012, 6). Some disciplines reach a point of crisis, while others seem to be constantly in dispute, such as English literature, which has been described from within as having no shared aims or methodology (Eaglestone and Kovesi, 2013). Geography has as a discipline not only changed in its emphases over time, but has developed differently, owing to historical events, so that European geography has a different tradition from that of the US (Bonnett, 2003).

The discipline map of the university is immensely complex and the extent to which interdisciplinarity is practised varies considerably. Some disciplines, such as physics, are relatively strongly boundaried and mono-cultural in discipline terms, whilst others, such as business studies or education, are better described as fields of study, drawing on a number of disciplines, so that they are either multi- or interdisciplinary. Even in many fields of study though, the initial socialisation of academic staff tends to be in a single discipline, reflecting perhaps the relative strength of disciplinarity in the kinds of institution that tend to supply the majority of academic staff.

Interdisciplinarity, which tends to come about as a means of more effectively solving problems, requires the bringing together of two or more disciplines in a way that is more than the sum of the parts. It has been described as 'a process for achieving an integrative synthesis, a process that usually begins with a problem, question, topic, or issue' (Klein, 1990, 188). Concepts, methodologies and tools are combined, forming new relationships. There is a debate as to whether effective interdisciplinarity requires a base of disciplinarity (Foster, 1998). Many of the fastest growing areas of university research are inherently interdisciplinary, and can be carried out only with the creative fusion of disciplines. It is not always easy to develop interdisciplinary approaches, for a number of reasons that have to do with identity and power. For example, the field of biocomputation requires molecular biology, physiology, nutrition, genetics, informatics and statistics. However, working in those fields entails career risk, as exemplified by a PhD student's report (Guardian, 2014) that the interest and excitement of working in an interdisciplinary way, indeed having to do so because of the focus of a grant, is tempered by a sense of unease because 'academia at the higher levels looks worryingly resistant to interdisciplinary research'.

A study of academic staff from a range of disciplines in the UK and Australia (Blackmore and Kandiko, 2011) found a number of barriers to interdisciplinarity, some of which are prestige-related. Faculty in both countries reported that at national level there were disincentives, particularly in the assessment of research. For example, in the UK, the Research Excellence Framework is assessed by discipline-based panels. Although arrangements are in place to signal interdisciplinarity and take it into account, participants nevertheless felt that this was a risk compared with being mono-disciplinary. The most highly regarded journals tend also to be mono-disciplinary. Once again, it may be a risk to submit articles that are beyond the competence of peer reviewers. In a highly competitive field, when there is doubt it is easier and quicker to reject than to seek alternative opinions. Claims by individual members of faculty of being systematically disadvantaged in such a way are not uncommon (Shaw, 2013). At an institutional level, promotion is most straightforward when a member of faculty is working in a single discipline. Becoming interdisciplinary requires time, to develop expertise, establish networks and secure publication, and can reduce or delay opportunities for promotion. At a local level, respondents reported that they often felt isolated for many practical reasons, such as the difficulty in communicating with people outside their own department, and therefore found it hard to be interdisciplinary. For that reason, as reported elsewhere too (Klein, 1990), senior faculty are more likely than junior to choose to undertake interdisciplinary work, because they are established in a field and so their risk is lower. Prestige plays a part in at least two ways. Firstly, an individual risks his or her own personal prestige in stepping beyond conventional boundaries, as a result of being subject to the academic judgement of peers who are strongly professionally socialised into a discipline. Secondly, the extent to which colleagues are prepared to work across boundaries may be influenced by the relative prestige of the other disciplines involved and the esteem in which the activity of interdisciplinarity is or is not held. Thus, tensions play out in a number of ways. In teaching, for example, tensions can be found in the staffing of course components, in terms perhaps of whether the mathematics component of an engineering degree is best taught by engineers or by mathematicians. The dispute is between those who consider themselves to be most expert in mathematics per se, and those who believe that their understanding of the practice of engineering brings greater relevance (Blackmore and Kandiko, 2012).

The development of interprofessional approaches, usually in professional training and development, are differently rooted, in that the discussion is not as much an epistemological one as of finding ways in which a fully rounded professional service can be provided (Kandiko and Blackmore, 2012, 78). However, many of the challenges are rather similar, in that effective interprofessionalism requires co-operation across professional boundaries in a seamless way, bringing together groups and individuals who may have rather different and competing statuses. Thus a school of nursing may have more to gain in prestige terms by co-operating with a school of medicine than vice versa. There may be boundary disputes carried over from the professional world. The question of prescribing rights is an obvious example where current pressures to widen such rights to nurses, psychologists and others in the broader health field have been hotly debated (Horton, 2002; Lavoie and Barone, 2006). These rivalries in professional life can be transferred into the academy.

Mode 2 knowledge

Discussion of interdisciplinarity has focused on those who are already within the university. However, areas of human expertise are continually becoming academicised and being added to the university, including fields that generate what has been termed 'mode 2 knowledge'. The idea that two forms of knowledge production could be identified was popularised in the early 1990s (Gibbons et al., 1994). A distinction was proposed between mode 1 knowledge production, which is framed in disciplines, favours propositional knowledge and is curiosity-driven, and mode 2 knowledge production, emerging in the middle of the twentieth century and a feature of contemporary society, with knowledge generated in a real world context in order to solve a problem. Despite its wide adoption as a way of understanding knowledge however, the implication that mode 2 knowledge production has arisen subsequently to mode 1 may itself be an example of the privileging of a particular form of knowledge. It is self-evident that problems have always existed in the world, such as how to navigate with accuracy and how to transport goods cheaply, and people have done their best to solve them, often methodically, using the best available resources including knowledge to do so. The institution of the university is a later phenomenon, and the idea of science, with a body of empirically derived truth as the dominant paradigm within universities, still later. Fuller suggests that the two modes came into being in Germany towards the end of the nineteenth century (Fuller, 2000). Etzkowitz and Leydesdorff claim that the two modes can be found within science itself, so that mode 2 is 'the material base of science, how it actually operates' and mode 1 is 'a construct ... to justify autonomy for science' (2000, 116). Thus the way in which the story of science is told can contain a bid for prestige, based on preferences for particular forms of knowledge.

The degree to which universities engage with mode 2 knowledge production affects the extent of influence that they have and the funding to which they are likely to be able to gain access, especially when, as is discussed later, a strong emphasis is placed by government on the contribution that universities make to economic growth. Central to this are the ways in which the state, academy and industry are related. In exploring the conditions in which innovation is likely to occur, Etzkowitz and Leydesdorff propose a triple helix view of these relationships. The efficient and effective generation of innovations will happen to the extent that these three components are brought together productively. A state-led model seeks to control industry and academia, and tends to be ineffective. Another model loosely couples the three in a laissez-faire approach that maximises autonomy but does little to promote collaboration. In the third model, the three components are brought together in trilateral networks and hybrid organisations (2000, 111). The kinds of knowledge with which the university is prepared to deal makes a major difference to the kinds of work that can be undertaken and to the nature and extent of co-operation with others beyond the institution. An institution that concentrates on academic-defined knowledge and is not concerned with the usefulness of its research in the world is likely to be sidelined and to lose influence and funding. One that leaves its relationships with outside bodies to chance and personal motivation may have more impact and thus a little more influence, but opportunities will be lost. One that tries to work seamlessly with other bodies will broaden its access to funding, but is bound to experience greater tensions, which many institutions have dealt with by setting up arm's-length quasi-academic departments, science parks and other hybrid organisational arrangements. These issues are discussed in the next chapter.

Professional knowledge

Some critiques of universities have suggested that there is a tension between propositional knowledge that is standardised and relatively easy to describe and the knowledge that professionals and others actually use. In his work on professional thinking, Donald Schon (1983) argued that universities prefer an epistemology that pays little attention to how professionals think and act in practice. Schon noted a crisis of confidence in the professions, an increasing unwillingness to trust professional judgement or claims to particular knowledge, leading to a questioning of what is appropriate preparation for professionals. Growing complexity faced by professionals leads to a need for ever more flexible and adaptable practice that is hard to achieve and difficult to describe in order to teach it. Professionals do in fact frame and solve problems, but with a kind of artistry that is hard to encapsulate. Schon notes that the art of professional practice exists: it can be learnt even if it cannot be taught. This is a challenge both to the professional area in practice and to the university. There is a clear pressure to find a description of professional practice and what enables it that is solid and dependable, describable and reproducible. Reviewing many years of discussion on the nature of professions, Schon chooses Glazer's (1974) distinction between major and minor professions as having particular explanatory power, based on the idea of technical rationality. The major professions can lay claim to a body of solid, propositional knowledge, universal in its validity and application. Medicine, law, business and engineering are cited as examples. Other minor professions are less clear about their purposes and cannot develop a systematic knowledge base. Central to this distinction is the relationship between performance and what enables it. The most common conception is in effect one of a building with foundations, with practice underpinned by propositional knowledge, so that practice is advanced by the absorption of further propositional knowledge and its application to practical situations. Schein identified three levels, underlying or basic science, applied science and skills and attitudes. Discussion about 'bench to bedside' research reflects this view of knowledge (1973, 43). If basic science has the highest cultural value in a society, then it is in a profession's interest to lay claim to a body of propositional knowledge that it can call its own, and to turn its back on the less quantifiable practical knowledge that is involved in the performance of many professional tasks. However, an emphasis on propositional knowledge may distract attention from the question of how proficient practice is actually enabled, an important issue because the ways in which knowledge informs practice cannot simply be assumed. Another factor is the extent to which the professional has autonomy in the carrying out of duties, which may involve dealing with infinite varieties of unpredictable situations. Two wholly different responses may be made: either one emphasises the propositional knowledge base and allows considerable latitude for professional judgement, or one attempts to specify the competences that an individual must have in order to deal with all likely situations.

This hierarchy and the autonomy aspects can also be seen in the ways in which professional development curricula are thought about. Elliott (1993) listed three forms. A rationalist model has a long tradition, with a belief that professions work for the common good and an emphasis on a large body of systematic knowledge that has to be learnt over a long period, deployed in the solution of professional problems that, because of their requirement for judgement, mean that the professional should be autonomous, guided by a set of professional values. The second view, born out of a distrust of the autonomy enjoyed by the professional, is a social market one, in which professional learning can be expressed as 'quantifiable products which can be clearly pre-specified in tangible and concrete form' (16–17). The competence movement in training is informed by this conception, in which knowledge is not the starting point for designing professional curriculum or a professional. Instead, it is what the competent professional can actually do. The approach has been critiqued extensively (Ashworth and Saxton, 1990; Hyland, 1994; Eraut, 1994), in part for its reduction in the space for autonomy and of the importance of personal values. Finally, Elliott notes a practical science view, invoking Stenhouse (1975) as a major figure. In this, the individual practitioner develops by examining his or her own professional practice. Knowledge may be personal and practice-created, and not readily generalisable from one situation to another. Whilst this may reflect the actuality of the ways in which professionals learn and the basis on which their decisions are made, it clearly has a low status in a system that prefers generalisable propositional knowledge.

One way in which professions can develop and buttress their claims to status is through their relationship with universities. Entrance to the university requires that the profession's way of viewing its own expertise should be congruent with the ways in which knowledge is viewed in the university. Schon describes the growing influence of positivism in Western thought, to the point that it became dominant and little questioned by the end of the nineteenth century. With it came the assumption that the development of theory was separate from and superior to practice. Being able to lay claim to being a profession is itself an act that provides prestige. Membership of the university is part of that prestige claim. Most professions have entered the university; to do so they have had to borrow the clothes of those who are already there.

Knowledge and the arts

The visual and performing arts also have a complex relationship with the academy, because some strong beliefs and values that tend to be held in the arts do not sit comfortably with dominant academic structures and processes. Arts educators have been spoken of as preferring 'mystery over certainty, process over outcome, and individuality over uniformity' (Eisner, 1996, 3). Fields that emphasise creativity, which is inherently unpredictable and very hard to define (Kleiman, 2008) are a problem for the implementation of outcomes-based curricula, with their requirement that what is to be learnt should be pre-specified. The issue of artistic process is also complex, with a long debate on the nature of creativity, whether the creative process is intuitive or rational, whether it can be quantified and at what point it is best assessed (Cowdroy and deGraff, 2005). Assessment can be particularly problematic. Words in the form that are generally asked for in universities are relatively easy to assess. Well-understood expectations about form, structure and argument make it reasonably straightforward to make judgements but also, because words are permanent and portable, to verify that those judgements are sound. Contrasting this convenience with the leap of a dancer illustrates the difficulties of moderating and standardising assessment. What can more easily be accommodated in the academy is word-based discussion of the arts, which may mean art history, or the philosophy of art or the critiquing of art

– indeed everything about art except, one could argue, for the practice of art. Thus is set up a distinction between art as it exists in the world as a practice and art as it is talked about in universities. A further prestige dimension is that evaluative judgement in the arts is inevitably highly contextual, since many aesthetic judgements cannot readily be reduced to rules. This means that much evaluation, and a great deal of the standing of artists, is prestige- rather than reputation-based. This is reflected in assessment processes that bring to bear a number of individuals' views. The requirements of validity and reliability may drive some of the reality of professional judgement underground, with requirements for objectivity making the admission of subjectivity difficult. This opposition may not reflect the reality of artistic judgement. Bourdieu rejected the dualism of objectivity and subjectivity, claiming that all judgements were both, a claim supported by Shay who, in her analysis of a complex task, in this case the assessment of a final year engineering project, found an iterative judgement process, making use of both perspectives (Shay, 2005).

Orr notes some of the challenges in art and design assessment, suggesting that it is an 'artful social practice', inevitably subjective and best done by bringing to bear the shared understanding of groups of experts, a community of practice (Wenger, 2004), as it is a form of 'connoisseurship' (Orr, 2007). Beyond this, of course, is the question explored by Bourdieu (1984) of the extent to which aesthetic taste is a means of confirming a social position.

The definition of creativity itself is politically infused. In reviewing higher music education, Odena (2014) notes that creativity is increasingly associated with being a means of advancing the knowledge economy, related to a move in the twentieth century from thinking in a romantic sense of creativity, to a universal definition, analogous to solving problems. An emancipatory tradition in the arts has seen them as having the function of freeing people, particularly children in schools, from convention, and enabling authenticity. In current higher education terms, this may be described as personal fulfilment (Kleiman, 2008, 215–16). This can be linked with a strong tradition that places arts of many kinds beyond society, with artists deliberately positioning themselves as outsiders (Becker, 1963).

To some extent, also, conservatism within the academy may reflect conservatism within the arts, for example in tensions between the preservation of musical traditions as against music that is created from and about contemporary society (Jorgensen, 2014, xxii). Changes in the ways in which the arts are practised present new challenges to what has previously been held to be prestigious. The availability of cheap recording technology for music and the ways in which music can instantly be shared, sampled, incorporated and reproduced blur the distinction between artist and audience, question the 'high art' conception of creativity as an individual phenomenon and take place in a communication medium that means that ideas, individuals and groups can rise to prominence quickly, often completely circumventing traditional ways of attributing cultural worth, including the university, a development explored by Burnard (2014, 4). The conventional 'hierarchy of value' that ascribes greater worth to creativity than to performance is questioned. Such changes call into question the kind of professional preparation that is appropriate for musicians and the warrant for institutions of higher education to be making academic awards.

Comment

The history of universities over several hundred years shows that different forms of knowledge acquire differing statuses, and an individual's or group's relationship with particular kinds of knowledge can confer prestige. Whilst universities have over very many years extended the kinds of knowledge with which they deal, current circumstances, already signalled in this chapter but dealt with also in Chapter 8, make a complex socio-cultural situation all the more complicated. Universities now inescapably have to face in a number of directions, paying attention to the needs and wishes of a variety of stakeholders. There will be differences in emphasis: the priorities and practices of an institution that emphasises basic research are rather different from one that spends much of its energy on community engagement. The kind of knowledge in which the pure mathematician engages is different in kind and in purpose from that of the practising professional. Working in the presence of social and cultural influences that transcend institutions, universities have to find ways of valuing many different kinds of knowledge, which come with greater and lesser opportunities for the gaining of prestige, depending on the socio-cultural context in which they are being used. Notably, where interdisciplinary developments are desired, it is essential that the institution does not frustrate its own intentions, by neglecting to foster a climate in which this might take place or even by visibly valuing some kinds of knowledge over others. For individuals, it means that very careful judgements have to be made about where to put the balance of effort in allocating time, and in the planned trajectory of an academic career. The prestige that can be gained by remaining closely within a discipline has to be weighed against the potential opportunities that working in a more applied and therefore probably more multidisciplinary or interdisciplinary way might bring. As Chapter 8 will explore, the call for universities to be ever more involved with the knowledge economy presents major prestige challenges.

References

Ashworth, P. and Saxton, J. (1990) On 'competence', in *Journal of Further and Higher Education* 14, 2: 3–25.
Bailey, F. (1988) *Humbuggery and manipulation: The art of leadership*. Ithaca, NY: Cornell University Press.
Becker, S. (1963) *Outsiders: Studies in the sociology of deviance*. New York: Free Press.
Biglan, A. (1973) The characteristics of subject matter in different scientific areas, in *Journal of Applied Psychology* 57, 3: 204–13.

Blackmore, P. (2007) Disciplinary difference in academic leadership and management and its development: A significant factor?, in *Research in Post-Compulsory Education* 12, 2: 225–39.

Blackmore, P. and Kandiko, C.B. (2011) Interdisciplinarity within an academic career, in *Research in Post-Compulsory Education* 16, 1: 123–34.

Blackmore, P. and Kandiko, C.B. (2012) *Strategic curriculum change in universities: Global trends.* London: Routledge/SRHE.

Bonnett, A. (2003) Geography as the world discipline: Connecting popular and academic geographical imaginations, in *Area* 35, 1: 55–63.

Bourdieu, P. (1984) *Distinction: A social critique of the judgment of taste*, trans. Richard Nice. Cambridge, MA: Harvard University Press.

Bourdieu, P. (1993) *The field of cultural production: Essays on art and literature*, trans. Randal Johnson. New York: Columbia University Press.

Burnard, P. (2014) *Developing creativity in higher music education: International perspectives and practices.* Abingdon: Routledge.

Clark, B. (1983) The higher education system: Academic organizations in cross-national perspective. Berkeley, CA: University of California Press.

Cohen, M., March, J. and Olsen, J. (1972) A garbage can model of organizational choice, in *Administrative Science Quarterly* 17: 1–25.

Cowdroy, R. and deGraff, E. (2005) Assessing highly-creative ability, in *Assessment and Evaluation in Higher Education* 30, 5: 507–18.

Creswell, J. and Bean, J. (1981) Research output, socialization and the Biglan model, in *Research in Higher Education* 15, 1: 69–91.

Deem, R. and Johnson, R. (2003) Risking the university? Learning to be a manager–academic in UK universities, in *Sociological Research Online* 8: 3, http://www.socresonline.org.uk/8/3/deem.html, accessed 3 January 2006.

Diamond, I. (2011) *Efficiency and effectiveness in higher education: A report by the Universities UK efficiency and modernisation task group.* London: Universities UK, http://www.universitiesuk.ac.uk/highereducation/Documents/2011/Efficiencyin HigherEducation.pdf, accessed 24 March 2015.

Diamond, I. (2015) *Efficiency, effectiveness and value for money.* London: Universities UK, http://www.universitiesuk.ac.uk/highereducation/Documents/2015/Efficiency EffectivenessValueForMoney.pdf, accessed 24 March 2015.

Eaglestone, R. and Kovesi, S. (2013) English: Why the discipline may not be 'too big to fail', in *Times Higher Education*, http://www.timeshighereducation.co.uk/features/english-why-the-discipline-may-not-be-too-big-to-fail/1/2008473.article, accessed 9 March 2015.

Eisner, E. (1996) Overview of evaluation and assessment: Conceptions in search of practice, in D. Boughton, E. Eisner and J. Ligtvoet, J. (eds), *Evaluating and assessing the visual arts in education* (pp. 1–16). New York: Teachers College Press.

Elliott, J. (1993) *Reconstructing Teacher Education.* Basingstoke: Falmer Press.

Eraut, M. (1994) *Developing professional knowledge and competence.* Basingstoke: Falmer Press.

Etzkowitz, H. and Leydesdorff, L. (2000) The dynamics of innovation: From National Systems and 'Mode 2' to a triple helix of university–industry–government relations, in *Research Policy* 29, 109–23.

Foster, H. (1998) Trauma studies and the interdisciplinary: An overview, in A. Coles and A. Defert (eds), *The anxiety of interdisciplinarity:* 157–68. London: BACKless Books.

Fuller, S. (2000) *The Governance of Science*. Buckingham: Open University Press.
Gibbons, M., Limoges, C., Nowotny, H., Schwartzman, S., Scott, P. and Trow, T. (1994) *The new production of knowledge: The dynamics of science and research in contemporary societies*. London: Sage.
Glazer, N. (1974) Schools of the minor professions, in *Minerva* 12: 346–64.
Greene, J. (2013) *Moral tribes: Emotion, reason, and the gap between us and them*. London: Atlantic Books.
Guardian (2014) *Interdisciplinary research: Why it's seen as a risky route*, http://www.theguardian.com/higher-education-network/blog/2014/feb/19/interdisciplinary-research-universities-academic-careers, accessed 1 March 2015.
Hall, P. and Weaver, L. (2001) Interdisciplinary education and teamwork: A long and winding road, in *Medical Education* 35: 867–75.
Horton, R. (2002) Nurse-prescribing in the UK: Right but also wrong, in *Lancet* 359: 1875.
Hyland, T. (1994) *Competence, education and NVQs*. London: Cassell.
Jorgensen, H. (2014) Foreword, in P. Burnard, *Developing creativity in higher music education: International perspectives and practices* (pp. xxii–xxiv). Abingdon: Routledge.
Kandiko, C. and Blackmore, P. (2012) Shaping the curriculum: A characteristics approach, in P. Blackmore and C. Kandiko (eds), *Strategic curriculum change in universities: Global trends* (pp. 73–91). London: Routledge.
Kleiman, P. (2008) Towards transformation: Conceptions of creativity in higher education, in *Innovations in Education and Teaching International* 45, 3: 209–17.
Klein, J.T. (1990) *Interdisciplinarity: History, theory, and practice*. Detroit, MI: Wayne State University Press.
Latour, B. and Woolgar, S. (1986) *Laboratory life: The construction of scientific facts*. Chichester: Princeton University Press.
Lavoie, K. and Barone, S. (2006) Prescription privileges for psychologists: A comprehensive review and critical analysis of current issues and controversies, in *CNS Drugs* 20, 1: 51–66.
Moran, J. (2002) *Interdisciplinarity: The new critical idiom*. London: Routledge.
Neumann, R., Parry, S. and Becher, T. (2002) Teaching and learning in their disciplinary contexts, in *Studies in Higher Education* 27, 4: 405–17.
Nissani, M. (1995) Fruits, salads and smoothies: A working definition of interdisciplinarity, in *Journal of Educational Thought* 29, 2: 119–26.
Odena, O. (2014) Facilitating the development of innovative projects with undergraduate conservatory students, in P. Burnard (ed.), *Developing creativity in higher music education: International perspectives and practices*. Abingdon: Routledge.
Orr, S. (2007) Making marks: Assessment practices in Art and Design, http://www.adm.heacademy.ac.uk/resources/features/making-marks-assessment-practices-in-art-and-design/, accessed 24 March 2015.
Schein, E. (1973) *Professional education*. New York: McGraw Hill.
Schon, D. (1983) *The reflective practitioner: How professionals think in action*. New York: Basic Books.
Shaw, C. (2013) Research that doesn't belong to single subject area is deemed 'too risky', in *Guardian*, http://www.theguardian.com/higher-education-, accessed 2 March 2015.
Shay, S. (2005) The assessment of complex tasks: A double reading, in *Studies in Higher Education* 30, 6: 663–79.

Snow, C. (1961) *The two cultures and the scientific revolution.* Cambridge: Cambridge University Press.
Stenhouse, L. (1975) *An introduction to curriculum research and development.* London: Heinemann.
Trowler, P. (2012) Disciplines and interdisciplinarity: Conceptual groundwork, in P. Trowler, M. Saunders and V. Bamber (eds), *Tribes and territories in the 21st century: Rethinking the significance of disciplines in higher education* (pp. 5–29). Abingdon: Routledge.
Watson, D. (2009) *The question of morale: Managing happiness and unhappiness in university life.* Maidenhead: Open University Press/McGraw Hill.
Watson, D. and Maddison, E. (2005) *Managing institutional self-study.* Maidenhead: Open University Press/McGraw Hill.
Wenger, E. (2004) *Communities of practice: Learning, meaning and identity.* Cambridge: Cambridge University Press.
Wilson, T. (2012) *A review of business-university collaboration,* https://www.gov.uk/government/publications/business-university-collaboration-the-wilson-review, accessed 17 February 2015.

Chapter 8

Necessary myths
The university as economic powerhouse

Introduction

The last quarter of a century has seen a decisive shift in expectations of universities from the pursuit of knowledge for its own sake to that of knowledge for what it can do in practical terms, from valuing 'knowing that' to 'knowing how to' (Barnett, 1994). As suggested earlier, in the discussion of globalisation and the emergence of nations as global hubs, there is now a much stronger expectation that investment in higher education in a national system will yield an economic and a social return. National governments aiming to produce economic growth look to their universities to help to provide it, through the generation of ideas that can be exploited commercially and the provision of highly skilled and immediately employable graduates. Within government, those who manage university funding have to be able to demonstrate that the investment has been a sound one. Universities that wish to receive public funding for both research and teaching need to show that they do indeed provide benefits that are worth paying for. It is in all sides' interest to ensure that investment in universities pays and is perceived to pay an economic dividend. Prestige plays a major part in commuting and frustrating these efforts.

Chapter 7 explored the kinds of knowledge with which universities deal, noting an increase in these over time, and some of the tensions that come with the differing statuses of knowledge. This chapter is closely connected with the previous one, in that the increased expectation that universities will directly and obviously generate economic benefit compounds the tensions that already exist in what is held to be prestigious, by institutions and by groups and the individuals within them. The second set of myths has to do with the purposes and processes of activity. These include claims that

- the work of universities has economic benefits;
- there is value in curiosity-driven research that has no immediate practical usefulness because basic research eventually feeds into improvements in the real world;

- higher-level teaching is distinctive, through the presence of research;
- higher-level teaching leads to more skilled 'job-ready' graduates.

External perceptions of need

The UK provides an excellent example of government concern that universities should contribute to economic growth and of the prestige issues that are raised. A series of reports over the past ten years has developed a series of themes that has been consistent across administrations: the certainty that universities had an important role to play in ensuring economic success, and the need to achieve greater efficiency and effectiveness, all against a background of rapidly strengthening overseas competition. The areas of greatest concern have been: the teaching of economically valuable skills, matched with the requirements of the economy; working with business and industry; and ensuring that research is focused on economic needs and has practical impact. The Leitch review of skills needs is a typical example, claiming that the UK's skill base had at that time improved but was behind those of many countries that were increasingly competitive. The report argued for a strong focus on 'economically valuable skills' (Leitch, 2006, 3) so that a decisive shift would be achieved by 2020.

Commissioned as part of the 2007 comprehensive spending review, the Sainsbury report suggested that the UK had improved in some critical economic areas, including knowledge transfer from UK universities. However, it saw blockages in innovation in industry and argued for improvements in knowledge transfer and a move into 'high-value goods, services and industries' (Sainsbury, 2007, 3). With many developing countries able to produce with low labour costs, a more educated and trained workforce would thus become essential to achieve the kinds of growth for which the UK was well placed. The report pointed directly at a number of prestige issues, in calling for:

> a diversity of excellence ... with research universities focusing on curiosity driven research, teaching and knowledge transfer, and business facing universities focusing on the equally important economic mission of professional teaching, user driven research and problem solving with local and regional companies. Research, teaching and knowledge transfer are fundamental roles for any HEI. But the way these are done will be very different and some students will be attracted by one type of educational experience and some by the other.
>
> (Sainsbury, 2007, 5)

There are major political and cultural challenges in achieving such apparently rational aims. The report presumes that universities and the knowledge with which they deal will neatly classify themselves into two kinds. However, there is no clear distinction in reality between 'curiosity driven' and 'user driven', and it is not obvious that knowledge transfer relates to the first and not the second. It is also unlikely that an institution will voluntarily move out of a field in which there is profitable work to be won and possibly prestige to be gained: many universities would claim to be both research-intensive and business-facing, or would aspire to be so. A two-tier system raises the problem of parity of esteem, which is extraordinarily difficult to achieve for the social and cultural reasons cited earlier. In teaching, this major issue is apparently to be solved by students making choices. However, unless the institutions on offer have parity of esteem and unless access is managed on an equitable basis, student choice, where students have it, is not simply a matter of preferring one kind of university to another, as is explored in Chapter 10.

In less confident times, following the banking crash and recession of 2008, a further government report pointed to the need for 'high levels of skills and creativity' (DIUS, 2009, 10) and technological change. Investment in science and research was to be ring-fenced as an essential requirement for the support of economic growth. Applicants for Research Council grants would have to show that their proposed research would have economic impact and this principle was also to be included in the new Research Excellence Framework. The report signalled a move into a highly contentious and important area for academic prestige, the relative importance of basic and applied research. With it came the implication that continued levels of funding were dependent on directly economically useful outputs and a shift from academic dominance in determining what is researched and how it is evaluated to the representation of the wishes and needs of external stakeholders. Renewed attention would be given to the development of skills for the UK workforce and universities would have an incentive to respond to need and would also be inclusive of a wider range of students.

A report in the same year by the employers' organisation the Confederation of British Industry took as its starting point that 'universities are a vital public good, making a crucial contribution to the intellectual, cultural, social and economic well-being of the UK' (CBI, 2009, 5). It offered a broader view than comparable central government documents, in acknowledging that universities have a number of stakeholders. However, it considered universities to be vital to business and also stressed that business needed to support students and graduates and to be more closely engaged in research and innovation with universities. At a time of financial constraint, employers would have to do more to invest in higher education. Recommendations included the abandonment of the 50 per cent participation target and careful organisation of tuition fee loans to ensure that university education was affordable for those who need it. Again, there were calls for 'employability skills ... developed alongside the academic qualifications, and ... seen as an integral part of higher education' (CBI, 2009, 8), raising prestige issues both of parity of esteem and of the place of employability skills within a formal curriculum.

The white paper 'Students at the heart of the system' (BIS, 2011) followed on from the previous administration's Independent Review of Higher Education

Funding and Student Finance, known as the Browne Review (2010), and set out the Coalition Government's ambitions for universities. The most controversial aspects were to do with student finance reform. However, the foreword to the white paper asked also for 'a renewed focus on high-quality teaching in universities so that it has the same prestige as research'. Thus the white paper points to one of the most enduring prestige issues in higher education. This was to be achieved by the empowerment of students through better-quality information, backed with a regulatory framework which would see the Higher Education Funding Council for England becoming a 'consumer champion'. The assumption that the parity issue would be solved by consumer pressure is optimistic. That of itself, as explored in Chapter 10, is not likely to change attitudes to what is held to be prestigious. Further prestige issues are signalled with the recommendation of increased diversity of provision to meet student demand and the expectation of new providers entering the market and teaching in innovative ways. Underlying this is a rationalist assumption that consumer choice will match students with programmes.

The more recent Adonis report notes economic strengths but also areas of weakness – low productivity, low investment in research and development, uneven development focused on London, high youth unemployment and low pay. Two of the UK's major strengths are held to be: 'world leading universities' and 'an outstanding science research base' (Adonis, 2014, 4). Solutions lie in government sponsorship of innovation, empowerment of regions, a better matching of available and needed skills and support for growing companies. The recipe of strong enabling central government and strong local government, in partnership with businesses, says very little about universities, other than that they should be included. Local enterprise partnerships (LEPs) (Pickles, 2012) should be improved, supported by increasingly devolved funding, and 'all universities within that area should be represented' (2012, 8), a proposal repeated later in the report. Proposals for skills improvement mainly concern the development of youth apprenticeships, and the establishment of a hundred university technical colleges by 2020, focusing on economic growth areas and offering technical education for fourteen- to nineteen-year-olds. Further education would have a more focused role in technician-level skills. The Times Higher Education global rankings are cited, to demonstrate that the UK has a large number of highly rated institutions. The relatively high productivity of UK academic researchers is recognised and their contribution to GDP and employment. In a substantial analysis of business needs, a brief ending comment notes that almost a fifth of businesses collaborate with universities extensively and 60 per cent do so to an extent, but 40 per cent not at all. A Small Business Research Initiative that provides funding for businesses to meet government innovation needs would be scaled up. Universities are not mentioned as part of this process. Overall, the report does not achieve a focus on universities or on how they can be enabled to make the desired contribution.

The Heseltine report, prepared with civil service support, is another attempt to tackle the problem of wealth creation. Written from the other side of the political divide, it shares with the Adonis report a lack of a sense of what might be a role for universities in economic and social development, deferring to the Wilson report (2012) for a view of collaboration between universities and business. It argues for stronger local government, with clear leadership, particularly in cities, that can form effective alliances with business in a stable climate for planning. A similar attitude to universities can be seen here with praise for 'four of the six best universities in the world' coupled with a complaint about skills gaps (Heseltine, 2012, 21). Heseltine's analysis is that for over a hundred years power has become centralised in the UK, so that local business people have taken less interest in community governance. Local government has emphasised social provision rather than economic development. The solution is for revitalised and extended LEPs, led by business, to assemble strategic local plans and bid for central funding. A National Growth Council would take a cross-government view on growth and wealth creation, linking together disparate departments. Universities do not feature strongly in this report. They are occasionally mentioned incidentally as potentially making a contribution to innovation, and there is reference to some universities having expertise in knowledge transfer, but the major players are national and local government and business leaders. Heseltine's section on higher education concentrates on the development of student employability and the publication of data that enable choice. This report and the others show that universites do not necessarily have a place at the table; it has to be earned.

Higher education response

There is plentiful evidence that universities are trying to show that they are delivering what has been called for. Universities UK, the organisation for heads of higher education institutions, published a fourth report (UUK, 2009) in a series starting in 1997 detailing the extent of the impact that they believed universities have on the UK economy. Benefits in direct and indirect employment, contribution to gross domestic product and overseas income were noted and the need for continuing public investment to sustain this was emphasised.

The Wilson report, the commissioning of which was signalled in the 2011 white paper, and led by the then vice-chancellor of the University of Hertfordshire, is not surprisingly more positive and detailed in its advocacy of the importance of university and business links, commencing with Lord Dearing's comment that universities are 'the source of strength in the knowledge-based economy of the 21st century' (Wilson, 2012, preface). The complexity of the field is shown in his list of contents: 'applied research in advanced technologies, in company upscaling of employees, ... bespoke collaborative programmes, science park developments, enterprise education, entrepreneurial support for staff and students, higher level apprenticeships, skills development of postdoctoral staff' (2012, 1). The relationship between business and universities is held to be a complex one, not simply a chain. He suggests that there is no single source of authoritative knowledge in the field and that one should be established, led by business and university leaders sitting as equals, thus signalling a prestige aspect. It is proposed that universities should collaborate to clarify their areas of strength and to be able to refer enquiries to the place where they can be dealt with best. This would improve the reputation of the sector as a whole. Collaboration between employers and universities over curriculum design is recommended, although employability, enterprise and entrepreneurial skills should be taught in ways that universities will decide. Here again is a site of tension. Further government investment is advocated in innovation and knowledge centres such as Catapult Centres and also in encouraging the sustaining of research collaboration through strategic partnerships. Universities can play a major role in LEPs and make business connections by so doing. As the LEPs become more established, there will be opportunity for universities to become more involved. Closer links are recommended with enterprise zones near institutions. Universities could offer their strength and reputation in promoting them, thus attracting business interest. The report considers the best way of producing change, turning away from greater regulation or, in the main, from increased government investment. Instead, improvements will be gained through cultural change 'promoting behaviours that may be supported or inhibited by reward, structures, regulations and procedures' (Wilson, 2012, 14). This can be supported through leadership and commitment in universities, in businesses and at government level. Overall, the Wilson report supplies important detail about the role that universities can play, and in doing so raises prestige questions about how business and universities can be mutually respectful and work with one another, which of the universities will take up this work and how it will be related to other areas of work. Importantly, in its concern for the shaping of behaviours, and the signalling of the importance both of structures and of incentives, the report starts to get to the heart of what has to be done if the vision is to come fully to fruition. All of the economic aspiration rests in the end on individual and group behaviours, influenced by beliefs, values and interests, in both senses.

Mission groups are also keen to show that they make a positive difference economically. In a commissioned report (Russell Group, 2014), the Russell Group attempts to quantify the economic impact of the capital investment of its members. The report emphasises the group's value to the UK as an economic asset and claims a major impact on the gross value added of the UK economy and on jobs. It is claimed that each pound invested generates almost £5 in gross value added. The benefits are in construction and the purchase of equipment in the short term. Longer-term operational impacts come from the direct effects of using the facilities. More conjecturally, longer-term catalytic impacts are claimed to include: graduate productivity; returns on medical research; commercialisation and innovation, such as through licensing and company start-ups and spin-outs; an enhanced ability to attract research funding; a tourism benefit when students and staff are visited; and an improved learning environment making the university more attractive to students. Numerous examples are given of university developments that are leading to greater efficiency and effectiveness. The report also notes that some benefits are very hard to quantify in monetary terms, including the reputation of UK education internationally, the contribution to scholarship and improvements in quality of life, including health and the environment. The report also draws attention to but does not attempt to quantify the cost of not investing in such facilities in terms of lost opportunities and market share. Although the report includes a lengthy explanation of methodology, inevitably calculations contain a large number of conjectures and assumptions, given the nature of what is being measured.

The Higher Education Funding Council for England (HEFCE), which remains a major distributor of government funding to higher education for research and teaching, although less of the latter than formerly, also has to demonstrate that it makes the right kind of difference so that government funding will continue to be allocated to HEFCE and through them to the universities. A report (HEFCE, 2014) explored the impact of the Higher Education Innovation Fund (HEIF) on knowledge exchange performance. In so doing it focused on the central concern of government that investment in universities should make a difference to the economy. The report points to structural limitations on what can be done. These include the complex and difficult relationship between businesses and universities that might potentially be partners for innovation. The abolition of the regional development agencies and the less than perfect establishment of LEPs are cited as areas of difficulty. The report suggests that investment in knowledge exchange yields a substantial return and is thus an argument both for the continuation of this form of funding and for the role of the Funding Council in managing it.

At an institutional level, too, more attention is being paid to demonstrating the value of a university to the economy and the community. For example, the University of Hertfordshire has developed a strong reputation for being business-facing, and like a number of other institutions now takes care to show the benefits that it generates in its contributions to employment and the local economy, and its attraction of business investment as well as its value in social and cultural life. Making use of expertise in its business school, published information includes estimates of gross value added per employee in comparison with the sector as a whole, return on investment in terms of higher economic activity, international income and success in widening access (University of Hertfordshire, 2014).

The themes of these reports taken together are clear and relatively consistent. What can also be seen for the most part is an under-consideration of the social and cultural issues that underlie apparently straightforward intentions. Universities should work more closely with business; there should be different types of institution with parity of esteem; research and teaching should be valued equally. In these and a number of other issues, beliefs, values and social practices are strongly entrenched. Against this background several myths can be seen to provide rallying points in the academy, embodying deeply held beliefs that help to sustain a particular view of the academy and of the role of the academic that do not always fit comfortably with the agenda that has been set out to this point. The first of these has to do with the purposes of research.

The purposes of research

A university's research is increasingly expected to make a direct contribution to the knowledge economy. However, research is an uncertain business. It is not possible to ensure that good ideas will come into being. The usefulness of basic research outcomes cannot be guaranteed, whether or how they will flow through into changes in practice. Thus the likely return on investment in basic research and its timescale are not usually known. Much research requires specialist knowledge to interpret and evaluate it, so the wider world is inevitably dependent to an extent on the research community itself to come to judgements of worth, which may mean that the community serves the discipline at the expense of other stakeholders. Cohen et al. (1972) famously summarised these issues in claiming that universities can be thought of as organised anarchies, with problematic goals, unclear technology and fluid participation. This produces an area of tension with government, usually the largest research funder in a national system, about what is being paid for, and at what cost. Institutions have to show that they can conjure certainty out of an uncertain world, guaranteeing research outcomes that will have an impact, when in fact basic research is unlikely to have a short-term impact and is often conducted by people who are not addressing such practicalities.

Curiosity-driven research is attractive to many in academic life. Much of it is basic research, undertaken without direct concern for its practical usefulness, and tending to have higher status than applied research in universities. Basic research is more likely to take place in universities, where public and charitable funding is more available to support it, than in industrial and commercial settings. Thus, apart from its possible intrinsic value, basic research is attractive to universities because it is what universities do, using funding that is often in effect ring-fenced for them. Basic research is often justified on the grounds that it may in due course result in improvements at a practical level. In biomedicine, for example, this continuum has been termed 'bench to bedside' (Woolf, 2008), and translational research has grown as a recognised field that bridges the two traditional categories of basic and applied research. However, the nature of that supposed link has been hotly debated, arguments that without basic research there can be no new breakthroughs countered by those who believe that too many basic research outcomes do not in the end have a practical use, so that money would be better invested in translational and applied research and in practical implementation. Universities' and researchers' attachment to basic research reflects another necessary myth, with a tension between advocacy for funding and dispassionate analysis (Glover et al., 2014).

Recent debate is often traced back to an article in the 1960s that claimed that twenty important military weapons developments over the previous ten to twenty years had taken place with little support from universities, only 0.3 per cent having come from undirected research (Sherwin and Isenson, 1967). The study suggested that the transition might require a fifty-year timescale. The relevance of this to other fields has been contested, including a study in various medically related fields that concluded that 41 per cent of clinical advances were based on research that was not clinically oriented (Comroe and Dripps, 1976). The following year Comroe published a supporting article on the many valuable but unpredictable consequences of basic research (Comroe, 1977). A range of other studies have made the case for basic research and its value – for example Garfield's spirited defence of US research spending in the face of proposed federal spending cuts (Garfield, 1981), repeating comments that stories of lives saved were no longer enough – there needed to be proven financial benefits (Fudenberg, 1978). More recently, the US National Institutes of Health's focus on translational research has been criticised as taking attention away from the basic research that is claimed to be responsible for the majority of breakthroughs in science (Collins, 2012).

The value of basic research has been challenged, particularly in biomedicine, which is an interesting field in this regard since one might suppose that it would be relatively straightforward to track ways in which basic research has fed into patient outcomes by, for example, examining the evidence base cited in clinical guidelines (Grant et al., 2000). A *British Medical Journal* article questioned Comroe and Dripps' methodology, including their definitions of research and their unclear methods of selecting important advances and significant papers, cast doubt on their conclusions and pointed out that they had not dealt with the key question of how to assess which basic research areas are likely to lead to clinical advances (Smith, 1987). A number of research projects in recent years have sought to use improved methodologies to provide estimates of the nature and extent of the relationship between basic research and application. An investigation into the economic returns of cancer-related research (Grant et al., 2003) used the concept of the quality-adjusted life year to place a monetary value on quality of life and concluded that after seventeen years, between 2 per cent and 21 per cent of clinical advances were underpinned by basic research. A large scale study of over 25,000 reports published in important basic science journals between 1979 and 1983 produced a remarkable outcome, finding that of the 101 that claimed clinical potential, five had proceeded to licensed clinical use by 2003 and of those only one was widely used (Contopoulos-Ioannidis et al., 2008). A case study review of sixteen grants both basic and clinical in arthritis research (Wooding et al., 2004) concluded that the translation of research into practical improvements could usually be related to the drive, commitment and networks of a specific investigator rather than to the type of funding.

A study funded by the Wellcome Trust, the Academy of Medical Sciences and the Medical Research Council (Buxton et al., 2008) concluded that medical research provided a 39 per cent health and GDP return over the period 1975–92. Whilst not differentiating between basic and clinical research, the report noted the need to understand the time lag between research-spending and health gain, and that the greatest benefit in cardiovascular health gains was through smoking cessation. An investigation into returns from cardiovascular and stroke research (Wooding et al., 2011) differentiated between 'academic' and 'wider' impact and concluded that each grant had many impacts that required careful case study work to discover; that basic biomedical research has a greater academic than wider impact; and that in over fifteen to twenty years, all of the clinical studies had wider impact as against only six of fifteen basic research studies. Most economic impacts came from a small minority of projects. Collaboration and co-location were features of projects that had wider impacts. The study found no connection between the extent of knowledge production and wider impact. A mental health Retrosight project (Wooding et al., 2013) aimed to find out which aspects of research, including researchers and context, led to improvements in care, by tracing links forwards from the original research and backwards from treatment advances, and concluded that clinical research had a greater effect on patient care than more basic research.

Waste of research resources has been explored and the need to increase basic research yield (Chalmers et al., 2014), with problem areas identified in the needs of potential users being ignored, the failure to use what is known already and to know what is concurrently being researched. The writers claim that over half of UK research investment is in basic research, but evidence for its value is not strong. The consequences of misdirected research effort are examined at a global level by Røttingen et al. (2013), who suggest that a global observatory is needed to keep track of health research and development data. They argue that there should be greater investment in clinical and health services research and point to an injustice in world health that illustrates another shortcoming in the current focus of research: very little research investment is used to investigate diseases that afflict low- and middle-income countries the most.

The case of biomedicine illustrates the steady growth of interest in finding ways of demonstrating the economic value of basic research, the considerable methodological challenges of linking basic research with making a difference in the world, and a range of studies that point to the desirability of rebalancing research spending towards clinical research. There are significant interests at stake, for universities as a whole to show that basic research funding has economic value. The necessary myth sits comfortably with a dominant prestige aspect of universities, a deep-seated cultural valuing of basic over-applied research, of curiosity-driven research over the provision of a service.

The politics of pedagogy

Higher education is not a precise science, in that what and how an individual learns cannot be guaranteed. Neither can there be universal agreement about what knowledge should be contained in a syllabus or what learning processes should be in a curriculum. The question of what constitutes an educated person is a socio-cultural one, a matter of belief, varying with context and time. Even in what one might think were simpler areas to pin down, such as in professional and vocational curricula, which are at least anchored in the requirements of competent practice, there will be uncertainties about what a practitioner at a particular level should be able to do, what kinds of knowledge inform that capability, how the knowledge informs practice and is generated and tested by practice and, once again, what are the optimum conditions for that learning to take place. Across all forms of learning, there are associated difficulties in assessment, in knowing what needs to be asked and answered in order to demonstrate competence, proficiency or capability. However, teaching has, in practice, to be organised and resourced and students have to be attracted to a university. Thus universities must show that they know how to teach and that they have taught effectively.

The need for the mastery of skills and a capacity for enterprise are consistent themes in analyses of the needs of the economy and the shortcomings of graduates. The two aims may be in tension with each other, if the former is construed to be about the learning of set processes and procedures and the second requires flexibility and imagination. To achieve the flexible and imaginative and practically skilled employee requires a sophisticated pedagogic approach blending these two rather distinct requirements. Universities are in some ways very well placed to supply learning opportunities that offer such a blend, but in others they are less so, owing to some long-standing beliefs, values and interests that tend to make pedagogic practice resistant to change. Prestige plays a part in the preferring of practices that look educative but may not be, and that are in keeping with a particular construction of how education takes place. Prestige concerns also influence the preferences of academic staff for the roles that they play.

Some teaching traditions have endured for centuries: indeed, it could be argued that teaching methods have changed remarkably little in over 2,000 years. The lecture hall's purpose would be recognised by a visitor from ancient Greece. A lecture theatre is a space that conveys prestige, with the lecturer as the focal point, in whom is vested the right to speak most, if not all of the time. Beneath teaching methods lie assumptions about the ways in which teachers, learners and what is to be learnt are related, and these too have prestige aspects. A long-standing dichotomy in views about teaching centres on whether it is or should be teacher- or student-centred. Broadly, a teacher-centred view sees the principal responsibility for the organisation of learning to lie with the teacher, whose role is to impart knowledge. A student-centred view argues that learning is in the end done by the learner, who should be encouraged to be increasingly autonomous, making many or all of the choices about what and how to study. A student-centred view has a long history, often traced back to Socrates and, in more recent times, to Jean-Jacques Rousseau and John Dewey (1916, 1938). Carl Rogers (1983), writing from a humanistic psychology perspective, was an influential exponent. Famously, he argued that: 'We cannot teach another person directly; we can only facilitate his learning' and that 'A person learns significantly only those things which he perceives as being involved in the maintenance of, or enhancement of, the structure of self' (1983, 389). Malcolm Knowles (1978) popularised the idea of andragogy, in which similar principles were applied to adult learning. Brandes and Ginnis made a case for student-centredness in a set of principles (1986, 12–15) partly paraphrased thus: the learner has full responsibility for her own learning; the subject matter has relevance and meaning for the learner; involvement and participation are necessary for learning; the relationship between learners (including teachers) is one of equality; and the teacher becomes a facilitator and resource person.

Student-centredness changes in its meaning according to context. The use of the term may mask practice that remains heavily teacher-centred (Lea et al., 2003). It is as likely to be used to describe the availability of services for students or the provision of programmed learning materials. It has itself become a prestige term, meaning more or less 'student-sensitive' or 'student-aware'. However, setting these other uses of the term to one side, there remains the pedagogic distinction that has been drawn. It can be seen today in the advocacy of peer learning, in which students are encouraged to take shared responsibility for their learning and to contribute reciprocally to the learning of others. Despite a rhetoric of student-centredness over many years, it could be argued that most higher education remains quite strongly teacher- and subject-centred. There may be many reasons advanced for this, such as the need for a significant body of knowledge to be internalised before an individual can participate in an informed way in discussion, and the requirements of safe and effective professional practice. However, prestige plays a part in this apparent conservatism and resistance to changing practice. Academic prestige is closely associated with the mastery of a knowledge domain. A system that emphasises the member of faculty as the expert maximises prestige for the academic. The alternative approach, which casts the member of faculty in the role of facilitator, is threatening to that status. Epistemologically, the academic claim to expertness then rests on the soft knowledge of pedagogy rather than the probably harder knowledge of the subject domain. There is a related difficulty in 'mode 2' knowledge, generated beyond the academy. Unless the academic has experience beyond the academy and works in an environment that values that experience, there is more kudos in demonstrating mastery of the knowledge generated within the academy.

In tension with ideas about student-centredness, there has for many years been a tendency for higher education programmes to be more fully described, in terms of aims, objectives and intended learning outcomes. This movement, influenced in part by vocational education, has a long history with sources in nineteenth-century attempts in the US to make the school curriculum more narrowly vocational (Hyland, 1994). It has also been traced to mid-1960s economic concerns and a demand that education should be more accountable (Tuxworth, 1989), which led to the US Office of Education offering grants to develop training programmes for teachers, focusing on the specification of the behaviours of teachers and of what was to be learnt. A related tradition on the specification of learning objectives is usually linked to the curriculum evaluation work of Tyler (1949). It constitutes a technology of education, most recently finding expression in the idea of constructive alignment (Biggs, 1996). The key ideas of constructive alignment include instructional design, which has focused on the need for alignment between a course's objectives and what is assessed, and constructivist learning theories, which emphasise that the learner is active in making meaning. Despite the concern for the ways in which learners learn, this is a strongly teacher- and subject-centred approach, with emphasis on the skills of those who design learning experiences for others. It is attractive to those who fund higher education in that it appears to specify what is being paid for, and it makes the job of evaluation much easier, if everything that is to be learnt has been pre-specified. It has become a dominant paradigm in the preparation for teaching in higher education and also forms a basis for the ways in which academic programmes are approved and reviewed. As such its adoption and use, particularly rhetorically, can assist in the assurance of academic reputation.

However, certainty and learning have an inconvenient relationship. It can be argued instead that much high-level learning cannot be pre-specified, either in its outcomes or its processes. Curiosity-driven research, for example, starts from a position of not knowing something. Famously, a number of critically important inventions have arisen from failure or from unintended consequences of planned experiments. A reputable research tradition holds that higher-level learning, both in terms of the process of learning and the state of knowing, is qualitatively distinct from lower-level learning and that taking a model of how a novice or a competent person may work, by memorising and deploying standard knowledge and procedures, is not a good guide to the more flexible operation of expertness (Dreyfus and Dreyfus, 1986). This presents a major problem for universities to deal with in a more regulated era when closer specification can strengthen a claim that a service has been provided to a user or customer. Despite the use of student-centredness at a rhetorical level, it is ironic that some of the most traditional practices in universities have in some sense been a good deal more student-centred, depending on how the term is defined, than are more contemporary practices. Thus, a traditional lightly tutored PhD has placed significant responsibility on the shoulders of the student to manage their own learning, whilst more recent tendencies require students to move through tightly defined stages of thesis preparation and to undertake skills training programmes of various kinds. The latter may perhaps be justified in that it takes the students' needs into account and provides helpful structure, and can thus be claimed to be student-centred. I am not here arguing that teaching that pays little attention to pre-specified learning outcomes is necessarily student-centred. It may be highly teacher- or subject-centred. The question is not simply whether there are detailed intended learning outcomes, but who has influence over what is to be learnt and how, and over how learning is assessed. The highest prestige institutions are probably the least concerned to pre-specify learning outcomes or to demonstrate constructive alignment. Such critiques of a detailed technology of education are not confined to the most prestigious institutions, but it may be that they and those who work in them are most confident to resist the orthodoxy, even if a show of surface compliance has to be made.

A possible outcome of pressures to perform against particular measures is a tendency to avoid risk. One aspect of this, related to the marketing of higher education, is in the commodification of learning (Shumar, 1997). It has been suggested that the growth in demand for higher education is offering an incentive for learning to be seen as a commodity in a market. Learning is thus broken down into conveniently sized pieces that can then be 'delivered', often using learning technologies, to large numbers of students. A related aspect of this is that students become consumers, rather than equal participants in an educational activity or even as authors of themselves. Naidoo has compared this with a more traditional model of education, a higher level of face-to-face interaction and many more individual opportunities to study. She notes that commentators suggest: 'While first order learning may be more open to standardisation, second-order learning is unpredictable and requires exposure to uncertainty and risk taking on behalf of both students and lecturers' (Naidoo, 2005, 255). A feature of second-order learning is that if experiences and outcomes are less predictable it requires a higher level of trust between universities and their stakeholders – and also presumably between teachers and students. There is therefore an incentive for a teacher to take no risk of dissatisfying students.

Thus it can be argued that some of the most pedagogically desirable aspects of universities – that they can be places where students learn to be creative and to work autonomously – have always been compromised by the prestige-driven cult of expertness that makes it hard for an academic to be a facilitator rather than a lecturer. This negative tendency is increasingly reinforced by pressures for greater specificity of learning processes and outcomes that makes it less rather than more likely that graduates will be creative and autonomous, key components of enterprise.

Research-teaching nexus

One of the most hotly contested questions over the last twenty years has been whether and how research informs teaching, the so-called research-teaching nexus. The politically significant nature of the link, and the dangers in overclaiming, became apparent when in the US the Boyer Commission criticised research-intensive institutions for failing to give their undergraduates access to the best researchers or the experience of research (Boyer Commission, 1998). This is only in part a pedagogic question, and on it rests at least two prestige issues. One of them is whether there is anything distinctive about higher-level learning, a question which is related to resourcing. Another has to do with buttressing the place of research in universities.

A very large literature (summarised in Lindsay et al., 2002), explores the possible relationship, perhaps stemming from Humboldt's claim in 1809 that teacher and researcher alike were engaged in learning (Humboldt, 1970). The two have also been held to be incompatible, different functions requiring different skills that together would require too much time and effort (Newman, 1852). A series of myths exists: that research and teaching have a mutually beneficial relationship; that it is generalisable and static; that scholarship is separate from research and teaching; that those who research will lecture better; and that research into the relationship is disinterested (Hughes, 2005). Barnett has described these, taken together, as 'an academic ideology' (2005: 12). A rather different approach was taken by Brew and Boud (1995) who, echoing Humboldt, proposed that the two activities are different, but united by learning. The partisan nature of the claims made for the contribution of research to teaching can be seen in that they were for many years made as if it were universally and equally true. Only relatively recently has significant attention been paid to possible differences attributable to discipline (Healey and Jenkins, 2003) and to academic level (Coate et al., 2001). The most celebrated study to date has been a meta-analysis of fifty-eight attempts to show a connection between the quality of teaching and of research. Hattie and Marsh (1996) concluded that there was in general no correlation, except possibly in the liberal arts, where the correlation was low. This is not to say that there cannot be a connection, and it has been argued that there can be one, but that it might need to be designed (Blackmore and Fraser, 2003).

A number of forms of link have been proposed. Perhaps the most obvious is the subject matter link, the proposition that a member of faculty will use the outcomes of research in teaching. Another draws on the idea that education and research share a common aspect, which is that of learning, and that higher and better levels of learning can be achieved if students learn in a research-like way, becoming junior researchers themselves.

Claims have often been made that research funding for universities should be preserved, on the grounds that there is a teaching benefit. This may be driven by a sincere belief that this is so. Repeatedly, when surveyed, faculty declare that the presence of research activity is a benefit for education. However, it is also a convenient belief in that it protects a highly valued activity, research. The supposed nature of the link is also contentious, in that arguments for a subject matter link sit most comfortably within a research-intensive environment, where most teaching staff are likely to be active researchers, whereas research as a learning process link suggests that most, if not all, institutions can link research and teaching, if they use the right pedagogic approach. With a significant proportion of higher-level learning now taking place in further education institutions, often on a lower unit of resource, with staff who do not have the opportunity or the expectation of undertaking research, it is clearly in the interest of universities to show that their way of teaching is better, and one way of doing so is by claiming that it is research-led. Even among universities there are differences in that as research funding comes to be concentrated in a few institutions, many more universities are teaching on a scholarship rather than on a research base. Even within the most favoured research intensive institutions the increasing separation of research and teaching means that much teaching may be undertaken by faculty on teaching-only contracts and by graduate teaching assistants. Thus research-informed teaching is a highly political area, related to academics' sense of self-identity and, at times, self-interest.

Conclusions

Universities have for some years been faced with a policy and funding environment that emphasises the need for economic competitiveness. The reports that have been reviewed here contain a number of consistent themes that suggest some particular challenges for the UK's universities. A major challenge is to be in the economic game at all. Others have to do with tensions between the often prestige-related practices, underlying beliefs and values of universities and what they are being asked to do.

The main policy discourse on universities focuses on the quality and cost of higher education and on skill requirements. A reading of policy documents indicates that business–industry links are a largely separate discussion in which the role of universities is underplayed and unclear. There have been reports focusing on the relationship between business and universities, the Lambert review (2003) and the Wilson report (2012) being two major examples, but most general reports on economic growth see the main players as central and local government and business representatives. Growth will come when central and local government work together to create the conditions that will allow private businesses to develop and expand. In some there is a clear underplaying of the part that the state plays in all modern developed economies. The role of the university is only part of a larger omission. This under-consideration of universities is reflected in the ways in which regional government in the UK has been structured to deal with economic growth, and in the ways it actually operates. When regional economic growth responsibility is focused on LEPs, universities do not always have membership of such bodies or influence within them, and as noted in the comments of heads of institutions in the national study in Chapter 9, some feel that what they have to offer may easily be overlooked because they lack prestige. This, coupled with a tendency at a national level to regard 'world-class' universities as being the desired model, leaves a gap for the economically engaged university to fill. This is a prestige problem. Some of the institutions that might be well placed to make a contribution do not have the prestige to be included. Those that have may be less interested to do so. One solution is to imagine a high-prestige, research-intensive and economically engaged institution. This is not to argue that such institutions do not exist. Clearly they do – the University of Warwick is perhaps an early example of a university that sought to square this circle. An alternative is for different types of institution to work together, contributing their distinctive strengths. A consequence of current local government arrangements and the culture of higher education is that the case for university involvement has continually to be made, and prestige aspects play quite strongly against optimal involvement.

The higher prestige accorded to basic research continues to be an issue if what is required is a system that is geared to making the greatest possible improvement in the real world. Some rebalancing may be needed, but not in ways that appear to be opposed to the carrying out of basic research. The charge of the basic researcher that we do not know which piece of basic research will be a winner in practical terms is a perfectly sound one. It points to the need to understand more about how many and which basic research projects yield a practical outcome, and the conditions under which this is more likely to be achieved. Discussion of the ways in which basic research can be helped to come to practical fruition may be more productive than blanket criticism of basic research.

A major problem for teaching remains that it is less highly valued than research. Beyond that, there remains the conundrum of how the requirement for employable and enterprising graduates can be met through a largely discipline-based curriculum. There is no simple answer, partly because employability and enterprise are such contestable terms and the human capabilities that they allude to are very complex, situated and gained as much through fairly open educative processes as through the tightly structured acquisition of propositional knowledge. Many members of faculty construe their role as teaching 'their discipline' rather than teaching skills. This may lead to the development of skills programmes that are taught outside a disciplinary context and indeed outside the formal curriculum, where they are hard to resource, may be harder for some students with work and other commitments to attend and may have low status.

One part of the way forward is to acknowledge what underlies apparent resistance to change. Reasons can be found in what yields prestige – the primacy of research, the associated status of the teacher as knowledge expert and the influence of the discipline. Properly articulating the possible relationships between research and teaching and gaining their benefits remains an important need, which again can be tackled only by paying attention to the prestige associated with the varying bases of academic identity. If higher-level teaching is provided increasingly from a base of scholarship rather than original research, then that practice has to be esteemed, the skills required for it developed and recognised.

If universities are to be more extensively involved in the fostering of economic growth, the issue of interinstitutional prestige has to be addressed. It is unlikely that the sector will neatly divide itself into those institutions that undertake world-class research and those that concentrate on applied research and economic development. The two areas of activity are not separable in the real world. It is also unlikely that any institution will willingly cut itself off from a field of activity that is potentially profitable, either in prestige or in financial terms. The Wilson report called for collaboration, and for institutions to know all of their respective strengths and work together to allocate work where it is best done, but the growing competitiveness of universities, spurred on by government action, works against this, as do some of the prestige dynamics referred to already. Regional collaboration is possible, and there are examples that can be learnt from, but incentives are needed to encourage it.

A drive towards specificity of learning outcome – being quite clear about what has been taught and learnt – may be at one level commendable. If one can define what is learnt, then students need not re-learn what they already know, and can gather academic credit in a number of places, cashing it in for an award when they have amassed sufficient learning. This is a model that has been remarkably slow to take root, and prestige lies behind the problem, as well as institutional self-interest. The most prestigious institutions are not likely to wish to agree that what they offer has the same value as the offering from a less highly rated institution. For all of these reasons, both virtuous and otherwise, universities may not always deal very effectively with calls for more flexible, credit-based systems that assist in 'upskilling' the workforce.

The central political theme today is of economic competitiveness, universities being considered as enablers of economic growth, through the education and training of graduates with skills that make them employable, enterprising and productive, and through applied research that makes a difference in the world. However, I would suggest that many of those who work in universities, whilst no doubt aware that this agenda exists, are not drawn to it or driven by it, but rather tend to engage as they must, in order to secure funding and other resources, but with continuing attachments to older and more deeply rooted sources of identity and values. There are many signs of change. We know that academic autonomy has been significantly curtailed in many institutions, that many staff are more corporate in their outlook and that much of the growth in roles in universities is in blended academic and professional roles that may be less culturally tied to strongly discipline-based senses of identity. However, it has sufficient validity to need to be taken into account. Talking more loudly about economic imperatives will not of itself produce more effective communication. However, the adjustment of systems to encourage desired behaviours is likely to have an effect over time. All human systems tend to be adaptive. An example would be the inclusion of a requirement to demonstrate impact in the Research Excellence Framework in the UK. This has introduced a need to think hard about application of research into the working life of every member of faculty who aspires to be recognised for excellence at research. As such it is a major strategic intervention that can over time be expected to shift notions of what is held to be prestigious. It has the further political benefit that judgements continue to be made by academic communities, so it is to an extent owned by them.

References

Adonis, A. (2014) *Mending the fractured economy: Smarter state, better jobs*. London: Policy Network, http://www.yourbritain.org.uk/uploads/editor/files/Adonis_Review.pdf, accessed 17 February 2015.

Barnett, R. (1994) *The limits of competence*. Buckingham: Society for Research into Higher Education/Open University Press.

Barnett, R. (2005) *Reshaping the university: New relationships between research, scholarship and teaching*. Maidenhead: Society for Research into Higher Education/Open University Press.

Biggs, J. (1996) Enhancing teaching through constructive alignment, in *Higher Education* 32: 347–64.

BIS (2011) *Higher Education: Students at the heart of the system*. London: Department for Business, Innovation and Skills, https://www.gov.uk/government/uploads/system/uploads/attachment_data/file/31384/11-944-higher-education-students-at-heart-of-system.pdf, accessed 17 February 2015.

Blackmore, P. and Fraser, M. (2003) Research and teaching: Making the link, in R. Blackwell and P. Blackmore (eds), *Towards Strategic Staff Development* (pp. 131–141). Buckingham: Open University Press.

Boyer Commission (1998) *Reinventing undergraduate education: A blueprint for America's research universities*. Stony Brook, NY: State University of New York at Stony Brook for the Carnegie Foundation for the Advancement of Teaching.

Brandes, D. and Ginnis, P. (1986) *A guide to student-centred learning*. Oxford: Blackwell.

Brew, A. and Boud, D. (1995) Teaching and research: Establishing the vital link with learning, in *Higher Education* 29: 261–73.

Browne, J. (2010) *Securing a sustainable future for higher education: Independent review of higher education funding and student finance*, https://www.gov.uk/government/uploads/system/uploads/attachment_data/file/31999/10-1208-securing-sustainable-higher-education-browne-report.pdf, accessed 20 February 2015.

Buxton, M., Hanney, S., Morris, S., Sundmacher, L., Mestre-Ferrandiz, J., Garau Garau, M., Sussex, J., Grant, J., Ismail, S., Nason, E., Wooding, S. and Kapur, S. (2008) *Medical research: What's it worth?: Estimating the economic benefits from medical research in the UK*. London: Wellcome Trust/AMS/MRC.

CBI (2009) *Stronger together: Businesses and universities in turbulent times*. London: CBI, http://www.cbi.org.uk/media/1121439/cbi_he_taskforce_report_strongertogether.pdf, accessed 17 February 2015.

Chalmers, I., Bracken, M.B., Djulbegovic, B., Garattini, S., Grant, J., Gulmezoglu, A.M., Howells, D., Ioannidis, J.P.A. and Oliver, S. (2014) Increasing value and reducing waste when deciding what biomedical research to do, *Lancet* 383: 156–65.

Coate, K., Barnett, R. and Williams, G. (2001) Relationships between teaching and research in higher education in England, in *Higher Education Quarterly* 55, 2: 158–74.

Cohen, M., March, J. and Olsen, J. (1972) A garbage can model of organizational choice, in *Administrative Science Quarterly* 17, 1: 1–25.

Collins, F. (2012) NIH Basics, *Science*, 337: 503.

Comroe, J. (1977) *Retrospectroscope: Insights into medical discovery*. Menlo Park, CA: Von Gehr Press.

Comroe J. and Dripps R. (1976) Scientific basis for the support of biomedical science, in *Science* 192: 105–11.

Contopoulos-Ioannidis, D., Alexiou, G., Gouvias, T. and Ioannidis, J. (2008) Life cycle of translational research for medical interventions, in *Science* 321: 1298–9.

Dewey, J. (1916) *Democracy and education*. New York: Free Press.

Dewey, J. (1938) *Experience and education*. New York: Simon and Schuster.

DIUS (2009) *Building Britain's future: New industry, new jobs*. London: HMSO, http://webarchive.nationalarchives.gov.uk/20100222165247/http://www.dius.gov.uk/~/media/publications/N/new_industry_new_jobs, accessed 17 February 2015.

Dreyfus, H. and Dreyfus, S. (1986) *Mind over machine: The power of human intuition and expertise in the era of the computer*. Oxford: Blackwell.

Fudenberg, H. (1978) Informing the public: Fiscal returns of biomedical research in H. Fudenberg and V. Melnick (eds), *Biomedical scientists and public policy*: 35–48. New York: Plenum Press.

Garfield, E. (1981) The economic impact of research and development, in *Essays of an information scientist*. Philadelphia, PN: ISI Press.

Glover, M., Buxton, M., Guthrie, S., Hanney, S., Pollitt, A. and Grant, J. (2014) Estimating the returns to UK publicly funded cancer-related research in terms of the net value of improved health outcomes, in *BMC Medicine* 12: 99 (doi: 10.1186/1741-7015-12-99).

Grant, J., Cottrell, R., Cluzeau, F. and Fawcett, G. (2000) Evaluating the 'payback' on biomedical research by characterising papers cited on clinical guidelines: An applied bibliometric study, in *BMJ* 320: 1107–11.

Grant, J., Green, L., Mason, B. (2003) Basic research and health: A reassessment of the scientific basis for the support of biomedical science, in *Research Evaluation* 12: 217–24.

Hattie, J. and Marsh, H. (1996) The relationship between research and teaching: A meta-analysis, in *Review of Educational Research* 66, 4: 507–42.

Healey, M. and Jenkins, A. (2003) Discipline-based educational development, in R. Macdonald and H. Eggins (eds), *The scholarship of academic development* (pp. 47–57). Buckingham: Society for Research into Higher Education/Open University Press.

HEFCE (2014) *Knowledge exchange performance and the impact of HEIF*, http://www.hefce.ac.uk/pubs/rereports/year/2014/keheifimpact/, accessed 17 February 2015.

Heseltine, M. (2012) *No stone unturned in pursuit of growth*, https://www.gov.uk/government/uploads/system/uploads/attachment_data/file/34648/12-1213-no-stone-unturned-in-pursuit-of-growth.pdf, accessed 17 February 2015.

Hughes, M. (2005) The mythology of research and teaching relationships in universities, in R. Barnett (ed.), *Reshaping the university: New relationships between research, scholarship and teaching* (pp. 14–26). Buckingham: Open University Press.

Humboldt, W. (1970) On the spirit and the organizational framework of intellectual institutions in Berlin, in *Minerva* 8: 242–67 (originally published 1809).

Hyland, T. (1994) *Competence, education and NVQs*. London: Cassell.

Knowles, M. (1978) *The adult learner: A neglected species*. Houston, TX: Gulf Publishing.

Lambert, R. (2003) *Lambert review of business–industry collaboration*. London: HMSO, http://www.eua.be/eua/jsp/en/upload/lambert_review_final_450.1151581102387.pdf, accessed 17 February 2015.

Lea, S.J., Stephenson, D. and Troy, J. (2003) Higher education students' attitudes to student-centred learning: Beyond 'educational bulimia', in *Studies in Higher Education* 28, 3: 321–34.

Leitch, S. (2006) *Prosperity for all in the global economy: Final report*. London: HMSO, http://www.delni.gov.uk/the-leitch-review-of-skills, accessed 17 February 2015.

Lindsay, R., Breen, R. and Jenkins, A. (2002) Academic research and teaching quality: The views of undergraduate and postgraduate students, in *Studies in Higher Education* 27, 3: 309–27.

Naidoo, R. (2005) Universities in the marketplace: The distortion of teaching and research, in R. Barnett (ed.), *Reshaping the university: New relationships between research, scholarship and teaching* (pp. 27–36). Maidenhead: Society for Research into Higher Education/Open University Press.

Newman, J. (1852) *The idea of a university*. Notre Dame, IN: University of Notre Dame Press.

Pickles, E. (2012) *Local Enterprise Partnerships (LEPs) and enterprise zones*, https://www.gov.uk/government/policies/supporting-economic-growth-through-local-enterprise-partnerships-and-enterprise-zones/supporting-pages/local-enterprise-partnerships, accessed 1 May 2015.

Rogers, C. (1983) *Freedom to learn for the '80s*. New York: Merrill.

Røttingen, J.-A., Regmi, S., Eide, M. et al. (2013) Mapping of available health research and development data: What's there, what's missing, and what role is there for a global observatory?, in *Lancet* 382: 1286–307.

Russell Group (2014) *Economic impact of the capital investment plans of the Russell Group universities*, http://www.russellgroup.ac.uk/uploads/Economic-impact-of-the-Russell-Group_1.pdf, accessed 17 February 2015.

Sainsbury, D. (2007) *Review of science and innovation: The race to the top*, http://www.rsc.org/images/sainsbury_review051007_tcm18-103118.pdf, accessed 12 August 2015.

Sherwin, C. and Isenson, R. (1967) Project Hindsight, in *Science* 161: 1571–7.

Shumar, W. (1997) *College for sale: A critique of the commodification of higher education (knowledge, identity and school life)*. Abingdon: Routledge Falmer.

Smith, R. (1987) Comroe and Dripps revisited, in *British Medical Journal*, 295: 1404–7.

Tuxworth, E. (1989) Competence-based education and training: Background and origins, in J. Burke (ed.), *Competency-based education and training* (pp. 10–25). London: Falmer Press.

Tyler, R. (1949) *Basic principles of curriculum and instruction*. Chicago, IL: University of Chicago Press.

University of Hertfordshire (2014) *Vision, value and vitality: The economic, social and cultural impact of the University of Hertfordshire*. Hatfield: University of Hertfordshire.

UUK (2009) *The impact of universities on the UK economy (4th report)*, https://globalhighered.files.wordpress.com/2009/11/economicimpact4full.pdf, accessed 17 February 2015.

Wilson, T. (2012) *A review of business–university collaboration*, https://www.gov.uk/government/publications/business-university-collaboration-the-wilson-review, accessed 17 February 2015.

Wooding, S., Hanney, S., Buxton, M. and Grant, J. (2004) The returns from arthritis research, volume 1: Approach, analysis and recommendations, http://www.rand.org/pubs/monographs/MG251.html, accessed 14 November 2013.

Wooding, H., Hanney, S., Pollitt, A., Buxton, M. and Grant, J. (2011) Project Retrosight: Understanding the returns from cardiovascular and stroke research: The policy report, http://www.rand.org/pubs/monographs/MG1079.html, accessed 14 November 2013.

Wooding, S., Pollitt, A., Castle-Clark, S. et al. (2013) Mental health retrosight: Understanding the returns from research (lessons from schizophrenia): Policy report, http://www.rand.org/pubs/research_reports/RR325.html, accessed 14 November 2013.

Woolf, S. (2008) The meaning of translational research and why it matters, in *Journal of the American Medical Association*, 299, 2: 3140–8.

Chapter 9

Heads of institutions and prestige

This book has proposed that prestige is a significant factor that helps to explain values, attitudes and behaviours in higher education. A distinction has been drawn between the seeking of prestige and of reputation. In 2014–15 a research project undertaken by the author and funded by the Leadership Foundation for Higher Education took an opportunity to explore the role of prestige in academic life, through the perceptions of heads of UK higher education institutions. Heads were asked to comment on a number of aspects of prestige – whether and how it played a part in their own professional life and in working both within and beyond their institution. Discussion of careers explored the process of selection and appointment, the nature and degree of fit between the individual and the institution, and the ways in which heads gained and retained personal credibility. Discussion of prestige within the institution focused initially on the management of a disparate range of disciplines and professional groupings. The opening focus of the discussion on external prestige was that of the placing and projection of the institution.

Twenty vice-chancellors or other institutional heads were interviewed, the sample drawn from across the range of pre- and post-1992 institutions in England, Scotland and Wales, thus representing both research-intensive and teaching-led universities. Interviewees had a variety of levels of experience, from the recently appointed, through the more experienced, sometimes in a second head of institution role, to those who had recently completed their time in the role. Six female heads were interviewed, a larger proportion than is suggested by the number in the overall population of institutional heads, but chosen in order to ensure sufficient breadth of perspective. Each head of institution participated in an extensive interview of between one and two hours, responding to semi-structured questions about the above issues. Extensive fieldnotes were taken and permission was sought to use specific quotations on an anonymous basis for both individual and institution. A number of richly interesting analyses of the head of institution role were obtained which are explored here as a way of considering the extent to which ideas of prestige and of a prestige economy might be of explanatory value in university leadership. Whilst the research was entirely UK-based, it may have some value in illuminating likely issues and concerns in other national systems and also suggests that some comparative work would be useful.

Attitudes to prestige

Initial discussion focused on the possible meanings of the term, both in general and to the interviewee. There was wide agreement that prestige stood beyond reputation and that, whilst it can be powerful in its effects, it is difficult to define. Distinctions between the two that emerged in discussion have already been suggested earlier: that prestige is measured relative to others, rather than in absolute terms; it is defined by insiders rather than outsiders; it is developed and lost slowly; and it can be held by only a few, not universally. A number of issues that were felt to have a prestige aspect were frequently cited early in discussion, including the National Student Survey of student satisfaction and its effect on interuniversity comparisons; the Research Excellence Framework and its influence on the nature of academic work and the status of teaching; and the influence of mission groups, particularly the Russell Group, which consists of a number of research-intensive institutions in the UK.

Some responses showed that prestige was itself a contested term in two senses. Firstly, a small number of interviewees did not feel that it described their institution, other than perhaps in small parts of it. For a number, the term 'reputation' better represented what they felt they could and should aspire to achieve. Interviewees either engaged unambiguously with prestige, seeing it as a central part of what they and their institutions did, or believed that reputation was a more realistic aim. A more nuanced picture emerged in institutions that had pockets of prestige within a more reputationally focused institution. Thus the research outcomes broadly support the proposal of Brewer et al. (2002) that institutions can be described as prestige-maximising, reputation-maximising or prestige-seeking, the last named describing an institution that has reputation but seeks to move beyond that to prestige.

Secondly, differences in view could be seen in personal attitudes to the idea of prestige. Some heads were entirely comfortable with the term, seeing it as part of their working life and of the institutions that they led, and aware of its usefulness as a leadership tool:

> I am very comfortable with the term. It is articulated in a number of ways in my institution. It means you don't have to explain yourself.
>
> (Interviewee 4)

A small number expressed a distaste for it, seeing it as an expression of exclusion and privilege, sometimes not properly earned:

> I don't like the elitist connotations of prestige … I am more interested in esteem.
>
> (Interviewee 8)

Heads of pre-1992 universities, in which there tends to be a greater concentration on research, were generally more positive about the idea of prestige and its applicability than some heads of post-1992 institutions tended to be. The latter were more likely to have to manage tensions between prestige and reputation within their own institution, and to face the consequences of prestige-related events that had a negative impact on perceptions of their institution and on the morale of the staff within it, as will be explored later. In the analysis that follows, the terms pre- and post-1992 institution are used where sufficient distinctiveness of view emerged to make such references meaningful, but their use should not be taken to mean that the two parts of the sector are entirely distinguishable in relation to prestige. It is a far more complex picture.

Personal prestige

Interviewees were invited to outline the basis on which they personally had high standing in the academic community, both the qualities that they believed had enabled them to gain the appointment and how they were perceived within their institution. For some, the foundation of this was their standing as a researcher. Particularly in pre-1992 institutions, heads tended to feel that they had at least at some point in their lives to have crossed a threshold to the achievement of high credibility as a researcher, even if it was not now possible personally to engage in research, as was the case for almost all of those interviewed. This made it more possible to have detailed conversations about aspects of research but also meant that faculty knew that one understood what they had to do.

> My personal prestige was derived from success over twenty years. If someone questioned me I could say that this is what I have done over the last four RAEs [research assessment exercises]. I also have mastery of a field, albeit necessarily a small one. You have to have this in a university like X. They challenge credentials.
>
> (Interviewee 4)

Academic prestige could also be gained, and was frequently retained, through membership of senior academic bodies, such as research councils, which allocate funding and evaluate research. Credibility was at least as often seen to be about mastery of some of the main academic processes within institutions and proven success in some of the set-piece management tasks, typically through the management of external inspection, such as a research excellence submission or academic audit of teaching. In post-1992 institutions, proven management experience, particularly knowledge of sector funding and experience in and with national-level bodies, were often held to be particularly important. Overall, appointing panels were often described as having a problem that they wanted solved, whereas heads perceived that across the institution there had been a wish for a person who seemed to fit the culture.

A number of heads spoke of an amalgam of academic understanding and a strategic sense, an ability to bridge two worlds:

> You have to understand the intellectual issues. You need an intellectual or an academic imagination. Decisions cannot be entirely financially led. You need to think of the other side of it too. You need to see whether there is a gap in the knowledge base. I use my skills in critical appraisal a lot.
>
> (Interviewee 18)

There was almost universal agreement that each interviewee's institution was not ready for a 'non-academic' head. This was always held to be the case in pre-1992 institutions and generally thought to be so in post-1992 ones, although several interviewees acknowledged that there are examples of non-academic institutional heads in the UK having been judged to be effective. Two interviewees in post-1992 institutions had been appointed from outside the academy, one with a great deal of leadership and management experience outside academia and another with national policy and funding experience related to higher education. Both felt that this was not a problem within their institution: they believed they were judged on whether they could do the job.

Most interviewees had worked either entirely in pre-1992 institutions or solely in post-1992 institutions. Those who had crossed the former 'binary divide' had moved from pre-1992 to post-1992, not the other way. Heads described their choice of institution to apply to as one of finding a 'fit'. They wanted to work in the kind of institution in which they would feel comfortable. Some believed that they did not have the sort of background and experience that would carry weight in a particular institution, and so chose not to put themselves forward for a process that they felt would be bruising and probably unrewarding. Heads therefore seemed to filter themselves out of particular institutions, in a process that is similar to that which some prospective students have been reported to use in deciding to which institution to apply, as discussed in Chapter 10. Others felt they were particularly advantaged for pre-1992 appointments if they came from a high-prestige institution – Oxford, Cambridge and the University of London were mentioned.

The head of institution role carries prestige that is separable from the role holder. Some, particularly in post-1992 institutions, had not expected it to make such a difference:

> The role of the VC has a surprising element of prestige beyond the person inhabiting it. I am surprised by the extent of deference. I am taken seriously in the city establishment. People defer to me. It gets you through doors. You become aware of how you act – there is a way you should be as a VC. It wasn't the same to be DVC.
>
> (Interviewee 6)

The step up from a deputy or pro-vice-chancellor role was felt to be quite marked. Others who felt they had particular prestige beyond the institution were heads of pre-1992 institutions in Scotland and Wales, who were frequently consulted on higher education and related policy, a tendency they attributed to the smaller scale of government and their relative closeness to senior ministers.

Some felt that prestige had its part to play among heads of institutions. A typical observation from a head of a post-1992 institution was that:

> When you are in a group with other vice chancellors, then the institution you come from makes a difference.
>
> (Interviewee 6)

Heads of pre-1992 institutions who commented did not believe that there was a pecking order.

To maintain the prestige that came with the role, it was necessary to behave appropriately. Several heads described activities that they would not engage in, including charity 'stunts' that would not have been appropriate, and examples were cited of colleagues who had lost credibility through highly public actions that were not in keeping with the position. It was also deemed necessary by several heads not to take a party political position. Indeed, one had withdrawn from a former role as a political commentator for that reason.

The majority of female heads did not believe that they had received unfair treatment that could be attributed to gender in their working lives. This should perhaps be set alongside the relatively small number of female heads of higher education institutions in the UK. It is possible that some of those who have not achieved senior positions might have a different view, but this was beyond the scope of the research. Basic attitudinal differences were attributed to gender by one interviewee:

> A woman VC provides a role model and encourages women to apply. Women usually wait until they have a pocketful of riches, whereas men will apply if they just have a couple of pennies.
>
> (Interviewee 18)

The most common observation by women interviewees was that there are too few role models at all levels to encourage and show how it can be done. One interviewee pointed out that it would be simplistic to characterise all women as having the same leadership approach, and another offered a categorisation of the perceived leadership styles of her female peers.

The first few months following appointment were widely held to be important in establishing credibility. Some felt they brought it with them. In particular, those who had already been a head of institution elsewhere and who were believed to have been a success felt that they had more permissions and were able to act more swiftly, aided in part by their greater knowledge of the ways in which key functions of an institution operate. Others concentrated on what they believed might be quick wins, particularly those that had a means of measurement attached so that success could be demonstrated. Others again found that relatively small changes made a significant symbolic difference:

> It was a quick win to make the university driver redundant ... I was surprised how great an impact that decision made.
>
> (Interviewee 8)

New heads felt that there was an expectation that they would act decisively, perhaps radically. For those in pre-1992 institutions, this tended to be tempered with a perceived need to be respectful of and sympathetic to the culture of the institution. Approaches that were simply imported without change from elsewhere would not only be likely to fail but would also be perceived as showing a lack of understanding of the new institution, a belief which if widely held could lead to a loss of support.

Relationships with staff were most often commented on by heads of pre-1992 institutions. Gaining and retaining the confidence of both academic and professional staff were felt to require consistent attention and behaviour over a long period and could be lost quite quickly. There were balances to be struck, between gravitas and approachability, and between being consultative and being decisive. One head of a pre-1992 institution described the relationship as one of 'quasi trust'. One could not expect whole-hearted support from all staff. Many just wanted to be left alone and would accept decisions provided that they perceived that those that had been taken in the past had tended to be the right ones. Different registers were needed: one head of a pre-1992 institution felt the need to be able to speak as an academic and also as a businessperson. The latter was acceptable to staff provided they knew that you were capable of the former.

Within the institution

There was strong support for the suggestion that universities are tribal, and many caricatures of disciplines and professions were readily cited:

> Becher was exactly right about tribes in universities. There are differences and it is necessary to be respectful of the expertise of people but not to tolerate any ya-boo behaviour.
>
> (Interviewee 4)

Tribalism tended to produce real or perceived differences that had to be managed. One was between 'problem-solving' groups, commonly identified as medicine and engineering, set against 'problem-framing' groups such as within the humanities. This difference was also described as being between professional groups and disciplines, in that there was held to be a tendency for the former to need to be direct in their impact and for this to encourage a focus on the swift achievement of practical outcomes. Another fault line lay between clinical and non-clinical work. Apart from the practical nature of the former, the necessity to remain in good clinical standing meant that many members of faculty remained partly within a medical or health-related culture, which often had different values from the institution as a whole. These differences had a number of effects, including the tendency for interdisciplinary and interprofessional research and teaching to be hard to establish and maintain, unless there was mutual respect for the different kinds of knowledge and the differing cultures that were thus brought together.

It has often been claimed that there is a division between the academy and the administration in universities. There was wide support for this view and an awareness that often lack of understanding of others' contributions led to a lack of respect:

> An academic said I should get the bureaucrats off our backs, with no perception of how she sounded. She had no understanding of others doing different jobs.
>
> (Interviewee 3)

This traditional division between the academy and the administration appeared still to be strong in heads' minds. For most it was a lived experience. Relationships between the academy and the administration might be positive or negative, but for the most part they remained separable bodies of people. It was interesting to note that discussion of prestige focused for most of the time on academic aspects and staff members. The idea of being prestigious appears to sit more comfortably with academic than administrative endeavour, which is entirely in keeping with the suggested distinction that can be drawn between prestige and reputation. It also suggests that patterns of motivation may in some aspects to be different in some parts of the academy than in the administration. Heads generally expressed themselves as sitting between the academy and the administration and therefore able to perform a particularly useful role: a number of heads felt that they were well placed to be aware of the actions of the administration, to understand how these might be interpreted through academic eyes and to be prepared to modulate actions and messages if need be. However, although administration is often dealt with as if it were a homogeneous whole, and although the institution's administration was held to be more cohesive and inclined to be corporate than the academy, a number of heads noted some separateness within the administration too, between student- and research-related administration and between student-facing and 'back-office' staff. A shared view was easier to maintain within a central administration than among those who were dispersed across the institution, and partly for this reason the extent to which the administration should be centralised was a recurring topic within institutions.

The tribal differences noted so far could be further heightened by tensions between the two major academic activities: research and teaching. This was an issue for all heads, although it presented itself very differently given the variety of institutional mission. There was wide agreement that research remains dominant, even in those institutions that have relatively limited amounts of research activity. The head of one such institution commented that research was more important to some of their staff than it was to the institution. It was therefore necessary to pay constant attention to asserting the value of teaching, even in strongly teaching-led universities, as another head of such an institution said:

> You have to work on this all the time. If you take your foot off at all or disengage your mouth, academics will disappear back into the cupboards.
> (Interviewee 19)

One difference that was widely noted was in the availability of metrics that support the demonstration of research quality, and the relative difficulty of 'measuring' the quality of teaching. It was suggested that until this was done, teaching would always remain a poor relation, because claims about quality would be perceived to be only assertions. Another area of challenge was in a perceived tendency for some staff to believe that they would get on faster if they did as little teaching as possible and concentrated on research. This view could be strengthened if research 'stars' were brought into the university.

The regular national assessment of research quality, through the Research Excellence Framework (REF) exercise was believed to be the strongest driver in universities. All interviewees acknowledged a potential cost that teaching would not be valued by staff. For some institutions that are strongly teaching-led and have a major social inclusion role, there was some sense of resentment that both the REF and the National Student Survey regularly showed their institution in a poor light. This was felt to be unfair in that their particular strengths were not being reflected in these prominent national contests. The good work that was done through many forms of community engagement could easily be forgotten amid talk of 'world-class' universities and global rankings. Staff morale could be damaged by repeated apparent failure and part of the role of the head of institution was to reinforce the message about what the institution was actually trying to achieve.

Heads of the most research-intensive pre-1992 institutions were particularly aware of the need to attract the best possible researchers to the institution. This meant that the university had itself to be seen to be prestigious, and thus a good base from which to develop an academic career. Once appointed, there would be the previously mentioned difficulties of apparent lack of parity of esteem between the new researchers and those staff already present. There was a tension between the wish to have academic stars to display and the fact that it takes a very long time for truly 'stellar' quality to emerge, frequently extending past the researcher's working life or indeed life span. Long-term investment was needed, together with an awareness that it is possible to invest in stars that have already given their best and are likely to decline. Thus, attracting and retaining the very best researchers who had been recognised publicly as such was a significant concern, fuelled in part by esteem factors such as Nobel laureateships that are included in global rankings. This concern led to a further activity, that of tracking previous members of academic staff who might have moved on elsewhere but some of whose lustre could be claimed for the institution.

As previously suggested, whilst some heads believed that their institution was mainly engaged in gaining reputation rather than prestige, almost all institutions were held to have aspects of prestige, either in whole or in part. All heads could name one or more areas in which they felt that their institution could claim to be genuinely world-leading. Those who felt they were managing an institution with a prestige area had often inherited the strength through institutional merger. This required a judgement about what constituted legitimate difference and what had to be brought into line, for overall organisational efficiency and effectiveness:

> When the medical school joined the University, they had many different ways of doing things. I'm quite hot on the implementation of standard procedures. Cultural differences are really rather more tricky, and in some cases could not be changed, and perhaps only needed to be changed if they were holding the institution back.
>
> (Interviewee 5)

Very commonly, smaller institutions that had been merged into a larger one had a strong niche market. Not only was there a risk that the market might be lost by an abrupt change of identity, members of staff also might be unwilling to become fully part of what they might see as an alien institution. A further difficulty came with the inheritance of geographically distant physical sites. Some heads believed that often the best way of achieving unity was to move inherited additions physically, where it was possible to do so.

There was considerable variety of view in the desirability of merging institutions. Some felt that it could lead to cohesiveness and an opportunity to establish a new and attractive brand, while others believed that its cost and the inevitable dislocation of many aspects made it an expensive option. The small number of mergers that have taken place was noted by some, who attributed it in part to institutional pride and individual self-interest. One interviewee noted the lack of cohesion of the University of London and commented that if it were able to merge its constituent institutions, that have for some years been increasingly independent or have departed altogether, it would be an institution to rival Harvard.

Beyond the institution

Heads of institutions generally believed that they had an important role in representing the institution to the outside world. Indeed, the role of the head was seen by some as being increasingly external, thus justifying in some cases the establishment of a complementary internally facing 'provost' role. Overall, institutional prestige was therefore a major part of the work of the head, even though the term might not always be used. A strong theme was that prestige acts as a reservoir that can be drawn upon and that enables things to be done. If an institution has prestige, built up through long-term presence, then it does not have to spend time explaining what it is or what it does. This is an argument for conservatism in some of the most prestigious institutions, where some heads felt that continuity was itself a significant asset that should not be thrown away. There was some skill in tempering this with necessary change. Heads frequently referred to their role in managing impressions of the institution, perhaps supporting what one interviewee referred to as the 'ineffable' nature of prestige. Heads turned to metaphor to depict these aspects of their role: it meant finding stories that could be told of an institution's excellence that would stay in the mind, of playing new tunes on the university or of painting a picture of it.

Some institutions had spent much time in reviewing their name. Sometimes this was driven by a perception that emerging overseas markets could not be assumed to have an understanding of the significance of particular terms, and which might translate unfavourably. Thus, terms like Institute or College might be felt to be a disadvantage, compared with the apparently unambiguous University. A similar concern could be seen in a widespread move from vice-chancellorships to the title of chief executive or president, for the head of institution.

Most heads named peer institutions. For those at one end of the institutional spectrum, the comparison was an international one, and often quite aspirational. Heads wanted to compare their universities, and to be allied if possible, with institutions that would add lustre to their own. Those with international links sometimes found them of doubtful practical value but felt that they had a symbolic use, signalling their own quality and outward orientation.

> Being international sends a signal that you are worthwhile to work with.
> (Interviewee 18)

In more regionally focused universities, heads generally named four or five institutions that tended to score at an equivalent level in league tables and that were within easy travelling distance. There were a few exceptions to these patterns. The head of one pre-1992 institution claimed that they sought no peers but simply did what they thought best, declining to copy institutions that might look similar but in fact be rather different. Another, a head of a post-1992 institution with a very varied profile, felt that it was not possible to have a single peer group. Individual parts of the institution had to be set at their own level.

The only UK mission group that was mentioned, and then quite extensively, was the Russell Group. It was widely felt that the Russell Group had been immensely successful in achieving a position of prestige, so that the term was now coming to be synonymous with excellence.

> The Russell Group is a fantastic brand and very valuable to my institution. Who outside it would say no if they were given an opportunity to join it? The only way of damaging it would be if an elite left, perhaps Oxford, Cambridge, Imperial, UCL and LSE.
>
> (Interviewee 5)

Other pre-1992 institution heads fully realised that they were thus disadvantaged, and tended to feel that this was unfair, claiming that at a discipline level the provision of their own institution was frequently better than that of many in the Russell Group. Nevertheless, there was no shared view on the wisdom of reconstituting the 1994 group, the other alliance of pre-1992 institutions that ceased to exist several years ago when some key members joined the Russell Group. Several heads felt that the Russell Group brand was an unhelpful influence, and that there should be room for another, perhaps based around a creative and more applied combination of research and teaching. However, a desire for prestige clearly works against the re-establishment of what might be seen as a second tier body.

> Everyone would want to be in another league so it would be hard to achieve common cause. A pity because I feel the Russell Group represents a conservative view of a university and it should be possible to project an alternative model.
>
> (Interviewee 3)

Others suggested that the future for some might lie in regional groupings. Successful examples were cited, but with a recognition that there are inherent difficulties in bringing together institutions of differing missions and statuses.

Some international groups were named as sources of prestige. The League of European Research Universities was believed to be an effective lobbying voice in Europe for research for research-intensive institutions. Universitas 21 was also named. Both were felt to gain some of their strength from exclusivity of membership.

League tables were discussed extensively, whether international or national. Heads of pre-1992 institutions tended to be clearest about their immense importance:

> League tables are totally important, life and death.
>
> (Interviewee 12)

Others, generally in post-1992 institutions, felt that league tables did not represent their strengths, and so tended to ignore them where possible and to act against what they saw as the unhelpfully distorting influence league tables could have on their institution and staff morale.

> I don't take a great deal of notice of league tables, because they do not really fit the kind of institution that I run.
>
> (Interviewee 18)

One spoke of what he termed 'cultural cringe' that teaching-led institutions could develop when repeatedly scoring badly in contests not designed for them. In institutions that did not have strong self-belief, the head needed to bolster this. The attitude of the board of governors was felt by several heads to be important here. They might be very concerned about performance against such a public measure or relaxed about it, and this belief might be associated with their general sense of confidence in the head of institution.

Regional and local alliances often had prestige dimensions. Underlying these appeared at times to be an intention that any relationship into which an institution enters would produce a net gain in prestige rather than a loss or lending of it to others. There were accounts of interinstitutional rivalries, where heads of prestigious institutions were unwilling to work with less prestigious ones, unless on terms that confirmed the institutional pecking order by allocating the most prestigious tasks to the most highly ranked institution. Research contracts would be valued highly, while skills training delivery would be less prized. One significant area was in relationships with the area's Local Enterprise Partnership, public bodies that are intended to enable local authorities and businesses to work together to direct local public investment (Pickles, 2012). For some this was a central aspect of their work, through which they were deeply involved in local regeneration. For others there appeared to be no engagement in their local bodies, that were at times perceived not to be very effective. There were also claims that local government bodies preferred to work with the most prestigious institutions, even if they were outside the region. In such a competitive situation, where neither membership of the prestige economy nor one's part in it could be assumed, some institution heads reported that they had to work hard to convince others that their institution had something to offer.

Applying and critiquing the idea of a prestige economy

Prestige and economies of prestige are valid conceptions if they successfully illuminate aspects of the social and psychological environment being studied. In this they are likely to have strengths and weaknesses, to fit in some places and not in others. A further brief depiction of the characteristics of prestige and of a prestige economy may help to frame the question of whether and where the concept may usefully be applied in the areas explored by this study.

Prestige, in contrast with reputation, is not readily measured, is often driven from within the academy rather than by stakeholders beyond, is scarce, in that not all can have prestige whereas all may have a good reputation, and is usually slower to gain and to lose. At a basic level, a prestige economy is a bounded area within which some forms of capital are valued highly. Thus a prestige economy is likely to have a number of features:

- an identifiable area or field, or at least one where the connections amongst those who are part of that network are stronger than with those who are outside it, in relation to the focus of the prestige economy;
- a currency of some sort, which may be thought of as forms of capital;
- those within it who have prestige, who seek it and acknowledge it;
- brokers or fixers.

Another dimension of a prestige economy would be that of time – it would require enough continuity for valuations to become established as prestige often takes a significant amount of time to build.

The research suggested that the study of prestige and the contexts in which it operates is potentially fruitful for increasing an understanding of values, attitudes and behaviours in universities, and for differentiating between types of institution and kinds of activity within them. One of the clearest messages emerging from interviews was that some institutions and their heads relate readily to prestige and see it as a central part of what they are and what they do, while some others believe that they are aiming to maximise reputation rather than prestige.

The interviewees named a number of areas which appeared to have all of the aspects of a prestige – and in some cases a reputation – economy. All heads of institutions were highly conscious of their university's standing as compared with other institutions, and readily listed comparator or peer institutions. Some were internationally focused, some national and others regional. Prestige and reputation can be associated with many things, but the most obvious contemporary manifestation is that of league tables, which provide a highly visible stage and also a form of capital. The compilers and publishers of the league tables are brokers, as are those who generate the data that enable the compilation of the league table. Another customary feature of prestige is that it is generally assessed by insiders, in this case academics. This is generally true of international league tables, which rely heavily on broad impressions gained through academic peer review. National league tables tend to use publicly available data about relatively concrete items such as library spending, and in that sense could be said to be reputational rather than prestige instruments, although success in them may help to build prestige. All league tables have the characteristic that a gain for one is a loss to others, in that they identify comparative positions.

Another area widely commented on was of disciplines and professional groups within institutions. Faculties and departments have to convince an institution that they are worth investing in and they therefore compete with one another for scarce resources to appoint staff and provide teaching and research space. The cost of attracting research stars and providing them with the facilities that they need means that an institution will be increasingly careful to focus its resources on those areas that are most likely to generate a return. The publication of an increasing amount of comparative statistical data about such aspects as research grants and publications, student numbers and overall income provide ways of making comparisons. However, the relationship between data and prestige is not always direct. Several examples were given of parts of an institution that were prestigious but that did not cover their costs. Indeed, if decisions were made entirely on the grounds of profitability, a number of disciplines, particularly in the humanities, might quickly become even more scarce in universities. The tendency to cross-subsidy may reflect a sense that a university should have the widest range of disciplines represented in order to be properly a university, but is perhaps also a prestige decision to wish to have those disciplines in the university, even if at a financial loss. Thus, it could be said that the disciplines and professional groupings in a university constitute a prestige economy in their competition for institutional approval and resourcing.

A further area where the idea of the prestige economy appears to have some usefulness is in descriptions of relationships within a region, among local government bodies and higher education institutions. The review of central government publications in Chapter 7 highlights uncertainties about exactly how universities can make a contribution to the desired 'triple helix' of employers, government and universities. This appears to be mirrored in a number of heads of institutions' perceptions of Local Enterprise Partnership relationships, where some are invited to, or learn to, play an engaged role and others do not, in some cases reportedly because of the less prestigious standing of the institution. Similar prestige concerns seem to influence the likelihood of interinstitutional collaboration in a region.

There was evidence too of prestige that arose from membership of groups of institutions that were opportunities for the display of prestige. This could be seen in lobbying organisations such as the League of European Research Universities, and also in Universitas 21 and the Russell Group, where prestige is maintained by limiting those who have access to the group. An extension of membership might be viewed as a dilution of the prestige of other members and of the whole.

The idea of a prestige economy is to an extent applicable to the heads of institution themselves. It was clear that being from a particular background or having had some key leadership and management experiences would stand an individual in better stead. Heads' level of salary does indicate that there is a high demand for one who is thought capable of generating success. Those who were already heads and were approached to take up a headship role elsewhere realised that they were in a strong position, both before and after appointment.

Personal prestige, within and beyond the institution, was an identifiable factor. The head's ability to act depends on his or her individual prestige within the institution. On the whole, heads tended to feel that they had gained a certain amount of prestige during their academic career, to which was added the prestige that came with the role itself. Heads of post-1992 institutions were most likely to comment on the extent to which they felt that the role gave them particular permissions and tended to encourage deference.

No interviewee professed to doing anything in order to accrue prestige – and this is in keeping with the generally equivocal relationship that most people tend to have with the term. Rather, prestige tended to come incidentally, as a consequence of particular achievements or association with highly regarded institutions. The almost universal belief that prestige within an institution required academic credibility was striking, in an era when one might suppose that the role of head of institution is becoming much more clearly business-focused. Perhaps this is another example of prestige trumping reputation. A small number felt negatively about the idea of prestige, and one felt that being a head of institution actually meant that one had to forego prestige, of the sort that is accrued by a highly successful academic career that leads to what he termed 'permanent fame'.

The institution provides a bounded area, even if the boundaries are in many ways highly permeable. Within it are many forms of capital, social, cultural and symbolic, represented by the many outcomes and outputs of university activity, but also by the many individual and group relationships within and beyond the institution. Prestige is relevant in a number of ways to effective leadership performance, as an aim, a component of the leader's environment and a personal resource. For many, particularly in pre-1992 institutions, the generation of institutional prestige was one of the main aims of institutional leadership, the fruits of which were being of high standing beyond the institution. The achievement of institutional goals frequently meant that one had to deal with systems of prestige, that would motivate individuals and groups to behave in particular ways, or not. These might be the prestige economy within an individual discipline or professional group, or the economy formed by the interaction of disciplines and professions within the institution.

A further way of using the concept is to consider a particular initiative, or feature of the organisational landscape, as a prestige economy. Thus one might evaluate the prestige economy that is generated by the Research Excellence Framework or the QS rankings. Each of them values particular forms of capital and can powerfully influence behaviour. Another approach might be to explore prestige from the perspective of an individual, each of whom will have a different conception of their institution and their place within their working environment more generally. Perhaps one could think of each individual as having a prestige economy, delineated by their own perceptions of what is important in their life world.

In summary, the focal points of a prestige economy might be:

- system, institution, discipline, profession or other organisational unit;
- an aspect of policy and practice, including a specific initiative;
- an individual's life-world.

With such a range of potential uses, the idea of a prestige economy is clearly a highly elastic and versatile term, bringing obvious advantages and disadvantages with it.

It is hard to draw a boundary around prestige, to determine what should be included in an account of it. Firstly, prestige shades into reputation, esteem, status and a number of other terms. A judgement has to be made, making use of the broad distinctions between prestige and reputation that have already been discussed. Secondly, given the ideological baggage that is sometimes associated with the word, and the noted tendency for individuals to deny or not to perceive that they are motivated by prestige, it is highly likely that there will be disagreement in accounts of whether prestige exists or, where it is held to do so, how it operates. A maxim might be that a prestige economy is real if it has real effects, including the fact that some would believe it to exist, and so be more likely to behave in accordance with its supposed values. An important aspect is that these were the perceptions of individuals. To be able to talk more robustly of a prestige economy would require the gathering of others' perceptions, to triangulate.

It was clear that heads of institutions found much to discuss about prestige, whether their institution had it, sought it or did not seek it. They needed to pay attention to their own personal standing in order to be able to work effectively. Heads were highly aware of the many constituencies in their university and the need to act even-handedly across the institution. Beyond, it was increasingly important to help to project the institution. The study appears to indicate that an exploration of the working of prestige can help to illuminate values, attitudes and behaviours in universities.

References

Brewer, D., Gates, S. and Goldman, C. (2002) *In pursuit of prestige: Strategy and competition in US higher education*. London: Transaction Publishers.

Pickles, E. (2012) *Local Enterprise Partnerships (LEPs) and enterprise zones*, https://www.gov.uk/government/policies/supporting-economic-growth-through-local-enterprise-partnerships-and-enterprise-zones/supporting-pages/local-enterprise-partnerships, accessed 1 May 2015.

Chapter 10

Students and prestige

A growing higher education market with a wide range of provision increases the complexity of the processes through which students are matched with institutions and programmes of study. Recent growth in the number and influence of league tables has been accompanied by the development of sources of advice for parents and potential students on how to make choices, including how to interpret tables. The idea that students choose where they will study is central to a neo-liberal view of education as a market with consumers. Underlying this is an assumption that choice-making consists of the careful consideration of data that have been organised to permit comparisons across institutions. However, the nature of that choice needs some investigation, as the central idea of rational benefit maximisation, whilst relevant, is not an adequate explanation of the process. Although there is a significant literature on the social and economic factors that enable or constrain student choice, relatively little research has been undertaken either on the psychology of student choice or on how universities select students. It is a complex field. Firstly, students cannot be assumed to be a homogeneous group. In the UK, the student market is commonly divided into school leavers, local mature students and international students (Veloutsou et al., 2004) and within those groups there may be immense variety in social and educational background and in aspiration. Secondly, there may be many influencing factors in play, as studies of student choice indicate. Maringe (2006) identifies three models, each with its own focus and collectively illustrating the complexity of the issue: a structural model focuses on the socio-economic and other constraints on an individual that influence choice; an economic model assumes that students make calculations based in part on rates of return; and a personality or subjective judgement model emphasises the preconceptions and filtering that an individual applies to information. Probably all of them have some value, and an analysis based on only one may obscure as much as it illuminates. Decision-making is likely to be a much more complex and nuanced process than making a survey of comparative data, since a decision of this kind is as much a social decision as an educational one. One of the tensions in choosing an institution lies between prestige maximisation on the one hand, and the choice of an institution and programme that best meets a student's interests and educational needs on the other. Exploring the way that prestige operates at an individual level may offer insights into how students make some of their choices and indeed to the ways in which they frame their conceptions of educational opportunities.

Institutional differences

Education systems and institutions worldwide vary considerably in their structure and organisation, presenting potential students with a range of institutions that have more or less prestige. Institutions distribute life opportunities when they select students, withholding them from others whom they do not select, and variation in the standing of institutions influences the nature and extent of that opportunity. Whether intentionally or not, systems and institutions tend to distribute opportunities in ways that benefit students from particular backgrounds, for both structural and socio-cultural reasons – the two being closely related. Perhaps the most significant structural aspects in relation to students and prestige are the extent to which systems are vertically stratified and horizontally differentiated. Vertical stratification describes the tendency for some universities to have a higher standing than others, often expressed through division into mission groups. Obvious examples include: the UK, with its Russell Group, other pre-1992 institutions and post-1992 institutions; Australia's Sandstones, Gumtrees, Unitechs and New Universities; and the US Carnegie classification of doctorate-granting universities, master's colleges and universities, baccalaureate colleges, associates colleges, special focus institutions and tribal colleges. Some systems are more stratified than others. For example, the UK and US systems are strongly stratified, and the Dutch, German and Swiss systems, whilst having some institutional distinctiveness, are much less so. A fundamental difference in the latter list of systems, as in a number of other EU countries, is that in most disciplines students achieving required grades have a right to study in an institution of their choosing. As a result student bodies tend to be more homogeneous among institutions than in those countries where universities select their students.

Although the proportion of the population participating in higher education has increased significantly in most countries over the last thirty years, it could be argued that the growth has increased stratification, in that much of the expansion has occurred outside the longer-established research-intensive institutions, increasing the range of institutions and students within higher education (Arum et al., 2007). Therefore, concerns over access have not gone away as systems have expanded and student numbers increased. Rather, they have become ones of differential access. Ambitions to encourage the development of 'world-class' institutions may also increase stratification. Thus the current German government excellence initiative, selecting a small number of universities, including nine 'elite' institutions, to receive additional national funding is designed explicitly to favour a limited number of institutions so that they can compete better internationally. This must inevitably increase institutional diversity across German higher education (Mechan-Schmidt, 2012) and increase the probability of differential access.

Horizontal differentiation reflects the differing focus and emphasis of particular institutions, rather than their status. Thus it is common for national systems to include institutions that are professionally focused. Some are specialist institutions, catering for only one or a few disciplines or professional groups. For a number of socio-cultural and economic reasons, there tends to be a relationship between differentiation and stratification, in that some disciplines and professions are more likely to be represented in the highest status institutions than others. Overall, then, there is variation from one country to another in the range and kinds of institution that are available for students, and the nature and extent of the social and cultural capital that can be gained by attendance at a particular institution.

Elite education

The tendency for elite institutions to exist in higher education systems is unsurprising and almost inevitable. Hirsch offered the insight that as a society becomes wealthier, satisfaction in what is consumed does not lie only in the product or service, but also in the extent to which others in the society consume it. The usefulness of spending on education as a means of job advancement decreases, the more people have that advantage (1976, 3). Thus, elite education is a scarce social good with a differentiating effect, since not everybody can attain a position of advantage at an elite institution. Hirsch differentiated between absolute and relative dimensions of education. Whilst the quality of education can be increased in absolute terms, if quality in one area rises more than in another, then the other becomes relatively disadvantaged. Every gain entails a loss. Elite provision cannot be expanded significantly. As discussed earlier, prestige, unlike reputation, cannot be held by all.

The idea that elite higher education is a scarce positional good has been used to illuminate the causes and effects of competition in higher education worldwide. Marginson (2006) examines both national and global competition and, noting that institutional reputation is a more known factor than is the quality of teaching in an institution, suggests that a student who is offered the choice of a prestigious institution that teaches less well against a less prestigious one that has better teaching, will almost always choose prestige. The student is choosing a positional good. Marginson cites both US and Australian research into students' attitudes in support of the claim. Carefully collated information that is designed to make it easy to make a rational choice is not likely to be influential in such a decision. The student is being entirely rational, but is valuing things other than are captured in institutional evaluation data. The current construction of most international league tables makes this approach more likely. When universities are ranked principally through aspects of research, the student is presented with data that encourage a prestige-driven, positional choice. Thus some parts of an education market function on a prestige basis, in which price may have a signalling effect. Institutions will tend to behave in keeping with the nature of the market. As Marginson points out, an elite institution can afford not to reduce its charges or improve its service. For as long as the institution is prestigious, there will be eager customers. Indeed, as with luxury goods, a high cost generates exclusiveness and desirability.

The increasing prominence of a small number of 'world-class' universities now provides another arena for positional competition, with the additional feature that English is now the dominant language of higher education. This, and the seeking out of positional goods, helps to explain why so much global student movement remains one-way, with major 'exporting' and 'importing' countries. As a contrast, Marginson notes the more equal levels of exchange that occur among European countries on the whole. Elite institutions may also achieve positional advantage through spending on facilities that are not entirely necessary, such as impressive sporting facilities, a practice that has been blamed for the rapidly rising cost of US higher education (Archibald and Feldman, 2011).

Return on investment

One obvious way to frame the student consumer's choice is to consider it to be an investment, in money and in time, on which the student would want to see a return. The cost of higher education, set against the benefits it brings to individuals and to society, is of continuing interest in many countries. It can be a muddled debate, with interventions from those who have a vested interest in proving that higher education is or is not too expensive, and made the more complex because of the immense difficulty of assessing the value of a degree in an individual's life and expressing it in terms of money. A recent Organisation for Economic Co-operation and Development study suggests a strong positive return to both, in twenty-five countries (OECD, 2012). In the UK, a 2013 Department for Business, Innovation and Skills report concluded that the return on a graduate remains substantial – £168k for men and £252k for women – with even larger social benefits to the government, exceeding the cost of providing the education (BIS, 2013).

A smaller number of studies have attempted to estimate differences in return, comparing one part of a higher education sector with another. This is of course highly contentious politically. Elite institutions may be challenged if it can be shown that students attending 'lesser' institutions benefit more from doing so, as measured through the level of salary they later achieve. Such a sensitivity could be seen in the reception given to the Boyer report in the US, which claimed that research-intensive institutions were in some cases short-changing their students by not providing access to senior members of faculty (Boyer, 1998). The results of studies differ widely. In 2003, during the UK debate on the introduction of tuition fees, in which research-intensive institutions argued that they should be allowed to charge higher fees than others, Conlon and Chevalier (2003) asked whether it paid to attend a prestigious university and, noting the dubious practice of grouping really rather disparate universities together into a single type of institution, concluded that the effect was overstated, and made up to 6 per cent difference to a male student's earnings and 2.5 per cent to a woman's. The study accounted for variation in personal characteristics, including ability, subject and family background. The authors explored the possible reasons for the difference, suggesting that it could be attributed to better teaching or to the additional social and cultural capital that a student might gain, which might include both a signal of worth to a potential employer and the availability of an increasingly influential peer network. On the basis that the benefit appeared to be constant over time as those surveyed carried on through their careers, they concluded that the cause was an increase in capital. In another study, Hussain noted the difficulty in defining institutional quality, and the inadequacy of using student academic ability on entry as a proxy, before showing for UK universities a 6 per cent or £35,207 difference in earnings for those from highly ranked institutions. However, compared with the overall estimated benefit of £281,594 the figure was relatively small. This study surveyed only students six years from graduation, and so did not attempt to capture long-term effects (Hussain et al., 2009). A more recent BIS report concluded that once student differences in background had been accounted for, there was no significant variation in return from one mission group to another (BIS, 2013).

In the US, this debate can be seen in an influential RAND report that concluded that students attending an elite private institution received a 'significant economic return' and that this was increasing over time (Brewer et al., 1999, 104). However, a study in the same year using similar data and examining the earnings of students of equivalent abilities who attended more and less prestigious institutions found that there was no difference in the level of earnings. On the other hand, there appeared to be a significant relationship between the cost of tuition and the student's earnings (Dale and Krueger, 1999). A study the following year (National Center for Educational Statistics, 2000) concluded that choice of college made up to a 16 per cent difference in earnings for men and up to 12 per cent for women, but noted that the subject chosen was significant, too. A more recent study by Hoekstra (2009) investigated the effect on earnings of people between the ages of twenty-eight and thirty-three who had attended a flagship state university, concluding that there was a 20 per cent advantage for white men. An interesting feature of the study was that those studied had narrowly either gained or been denied a place, and so were presumably broadly comparable in other ways.

Thus there is no clear answer on the financial benefits of higher education. As costs rise, debate increases, as can be seen in recent public discussion about return on investment and, in the US, in calls for this to be made known at the outset. More recent publication of data showing return on investment broken down by discipline within institutions may help to encourage more nuanced choice (Payscale, 2014), especially as costs continue to rise. A further concern, currently under investigation in the UK, is the feasibility of measuring the added value of a degree, since it can be argued that a university should be recognised for successfully raising the standards of lower-achieving students rather than 'polishing gold'. A recent research report (Gambin et al., 2014) has drawn attention to the assumption in the work of the Department for Business, Innovation and Skills that all of the increase in a graduate's earnings can be attributed to their enhanced productivity, as against their education having provided a signal to an employer that the individual is likely to have some valuable qualities. As discussed later, this reflects a tension between human capital and signalling theories, and in a sense between universities as providers of reputation or prestige.

Students as consumers

The increase in neo-liberal approaches to university organisation, governance and funding in many national systems has been accompanied by a dominant metaphor of the student as consumer. This can be placed within a long tradition of mistrust in those who provide public services and a wish to 'empower' those who use them. An aspect of recent UK government policy has been to transfer the cost of education to the student, with an accompanying rhetoric about student choice (Browne, 2010), whilst maintaining a significant degree of control over the nature of the education that is provided. As signalled earlier, the assumption lying behind the idea of the student as consumer is one of rational action – that if students are presented with accurate data about the educational experiences that are on offer, they will take a rational decision, as consumers in a market might be supposed to do. There are a number of difficulties in achieving this. The 'positional good' aspect of higher education has already been explored. Baldwin and James point out that in higher education one is dealing with 'intangible, non-observable qualities' (2000, 142). Measurement of the outcomes of education is extraordinarily difficult and values-based and requires a long-term perspective. Even if evaluation focuses on the outputs of a university, on what the institution actually provides, the provision of accurate data that can be turned into information requires decisions on what is held to be the most important to measure, moderated of course by what it is actually possible to measure. The quality of teaching is, for a number of reasons, very hard to evaluate. Some of these arguments have already been rehearsed in the discussion on league tables. There is clearly also a tension between the provision of data that are sophisticated enough to be meaningful, and yet straightforward enough to be understandable to the non-specialist reader. For these and other reasons, education is a 'credence good' (Emons, 1997), a term coined to describe services, the quality of which cannot accurately be determined even after they have been received.

At system level, too, there are practical constraints on students making the choices they might like. Despite the rhetoric of student choice, a free market in students would be extremely difficult to manage in a nation state. If it were allowed to operate, it would not really be feasible for less successful institutions to be closed. This perhaps explains why a 'voucher' approach has often been advocated for school admissions as well as universities, but has never been implemented. In any case, government quotas often govern the availability of places in particular disciplines and professions, particularly at an undergraduate level, with the aim of managing national workforce skill requirements (Baldwin and James, 2000).

Notwithstanding the rhetoric, choices are unevenly distributed among the population for many reasons that are both economic and socio-cultural. In addition, variation among students makes it unwise to assume that all study choices are taken on the same basis. It may be that structural, economic and subjective concerns will have different weightings and will play out differently, from one student or group of students to another, and this may help to explain why research on student choice tends to have produced a varied range of outcomes. For example, some parts of the education market may well be more conventional in their sensitivity to price than others. There are a limited number of places available in the 'best' institutions, so usually those universities select, rather than the student. Thus a distinction is sometimes drawn between selecting and recruiting institutions – between those that have many applicants for each available place and those that need more actively to attract students. The relationship between the student and the institution is fundamentally different in these two cases. A selecting institution may make itself more attractive by charging a high price. A recruiting institution may have to be more sensitive, in that students may not be able to afford, or not be prepared to afford, a higher price. The selecting institution is in a prestige economy. The recruiting institution deals in reputation.

Students are now faced with a vast amount of data, including the results of student satisfaction exercises, together with a prospective return on investment. All of it can be interrogated relatively swiftly where it is web-based. A literature review of more than twenty years of US research on the process of choosing a college (Cabrera and Nasa, 2000) took a human capital approach (Becker, 1975) to identify a three-stage process of predisposition, search and choice, starting in the seventh grade and heavily influenced by available data and by parental encouragement and support, as well as a number of other factors such as cost. Many other US studies have investigated college choice and persistence, and the relationship between the two (St John et al., 2000). However, the decision of where to study is even more complex and nuanced. Even where accurate and relevant data can be supplied in a form that is sufficiently nuanced yet digestible, it is not at all clear that students do actually behave as rational actors making logical consumer choices. Students may fall back on an holistic view or impression or overall image of an institution. This may in part be because the evaluative judgement is too complex and tedious to make. This is where an institution's prestige signalling, rather than the solidity of its reputation, may be influential. Brennan's study of Australian students' choices of universities in Victoria found that students had sets of 'consideration' institutions that they would consider attending and 'inept' ones that they certainly would not (2001, 192), adding strength to the suggestion that often an overall view is taken that is not closely linked to factual detail.

Some suggest that students match themselves with an institution as a way of choosing. Choices may be made for cultural reasons, with students desiring to attend institutions to which they feel most closely attuned in terms of social class. Ball et al. (2002) distinguish between choice and decision-making, seeing the latter as a better term including constraints and power. Their study of over 500 students in a range of schools drew from Bourdieu to propose that choice of university is a highly complex and nuanced decision that in some respects has to do with 'taste' and the selection of a matching lifestyle. Whilst a distinction is sometimes drawn between less prestigious institutions being chosen by a student, and more prestigious institutions selecting students, the process is likely to be a mix of the two, in that a student is likely to apply to the 'best' institution that is likely to accept him or her (Brennan, 2001). The process is therefore one of matching rather than straightforward choice, and highly likely to be influenced by students' self-perceptions of personal worth and academic ability. The same study found that high-achieving students' approaches to researching universities were not significantly different from those of the less highly achieving. It has also been argued that student motivation in choice of institution is best understood as containing both rational action and cultural aspects (Croxford and Raffe, 2014; Foskett and Hemsley-Brown, 2001). Ball et al. emphasise that self-exclusion is a feature of many decisions, as students select from those options they find acceptable or that they believe are open to them. Students may feel uncomfortable with the ethnic mix of an institution, or its historic and traditional ambience, for example. The influence of close social connections is strong, with young people informally absorbing attitudes. Knowledge of the implicit differences in status of institutions is unevenly spread. Those from private school backgrounds are better versed in the placings of institutions in a prestige pecking order. They do not even consider attending a new university. It is simply impossible to imagine. All in all, a powerful process of social reproduction is at work, through the selections that individuals make, both what they accept and what they reject. The writers conclude that as opportunities for the most desirable jobs become more competitive, the 'scripts and grammars' about institutions and choices will become 'instilled or supervised with ever greater vigilance' (2002, 69).

A small-scale study of students in a range of UK universities intended to explore the effect of the introduction of £9,000 per year tuition fees, also found that students' choices on the whole were influenced by perceptions of the potential cultural and academic alignment that the student might feel in relation to the university, as well as by institutional data. Students in high-prestige institutions were highly aware of the positional advantage they had gained, and those who were not so fortunate knew that they had to do everything they could to make up for their position of comparative disadvantage. Although ideas of the student as consumer were widely held, there was an equally significant awareness of the need for each individual to be personally responsible for getting the best out of the experiences on offer, a conclusion supported elsewhere, where research has suggested that study habits and ability are the most important determinants of success in higher education (Need and De Jong, 2001).

A study of applications to the eighteen universities in Ontario (Drewes and Michael, 2006) found students preferring universities closer to home, and spending more on teaching, scholarships and services. Female applicants preferred small classes. High research activity levels discouraged applications. The most interesting finding from a prestige perspective is that negative reports of teaching quality as reported in league tables had different student preference effects according to type of institution. The rankings were treated relatively lightly by those applying to comprehensive universities, but taken more seriously by those at principally undergraduate institutions. For older universities, with broad doctoral programmes and medical schools, there was a reverse effect, suggesting that applicants had a greater familiarity with those institutions and thus paid less attention to reports. For less well-known institutions, high scores were much more important.

Universities, in their actions, show an awareness of the importance of overall attractiveness. Wilkins and Huisman note the growth of marketing in universities as a means of attracting staff and students (2014, 2), and the relative lack of research on institutional image in comparison with student identity. They claim that the image of a branch campus may gain from a 'halo' effect from a prestigious parent institution. It may also be that membership of a particular mission group, such as the Group of Eight, Ivy League or Russell Group, may confer heightened prestige on a group of institutions that are projected together as examples of excellence, and taken by employers to be a proxy measure of a 'good' graduate. The attainment of a prestigious image is not easy for institutions wishing to increase their academic status. A study of Israeli higher education showed that institutions conveying an image that was at odds with current reputation would not be taken seriously and could even damage their reputation further (Oplatka, 2002).

Social reproduction

Whilst there has been a major increase in the proportion of young people attending university in all developed and developing nations in the last thirty years, it can be argued that universities tend to reflect and to reproduce the dominant class structure. Thus it remains the case that a little under 50 per cent of Oxford's undergraduate intake is from private schools (University of Oxford, 2014), even though most young people attend state schools in the UK. As noted earlier, it may therefore be that the disadvantage that many young people experienced by not having the opportunity to go to university is now being seen in another form in that some social classes may be most likely to attend particular kinds of institution, a phenomenon that has been called 'effectively maintained inequality' (Lucas, 2001, 1680).

There is evidence of continuity in the nature of student groups attending universities. Croxford and Raffe use the example of the UK to point out that the status of institutions remains stable over time, in what they term an 'iron hierarchy', under which 'Subjects and institutions vary along a single dimension of status, associated with the educational backgrounds, social class, non-local origins and (young) age of many students' (2014, 13). They ground the claim by examining student characteristics, as recorded by the National Universities and Colleges Admissions System (UCAS), rather than institution descriptors, to examine full-time undergraduate cohorts between 1996 and 2010 in the various mission groups: the Russell Group of research-intensive institutions, other pre-1992 institutions and the institutions that achieved university status after 1992. They found no evidence of separate social and academic hierarchies, but instead identified a dimension that consisted of both educational and social background. The social, ethnic and demographic characteristics of the various mission groups have remained very stable throughout that time. There was also little change in the statuses of subject areas over that time. There were only weak associations in relation to ethnicity. The writers conclude that this supports the view that universities have a role of social reproduction.

A recent study of fair access to prestigious UK universities, defined as Russell Group institutions (Bolliver, 2013), noted the difficulty in defining access, and took a conservative path of considering it to refer to the experiences of those who are equally well qualified to apply, rather than taking account of the different life chances and experiences of students from differing backgrounds. The study differentiated between the likelihood that a prospective student would apply, on the one hand, and be accepted, on the other. The writer suggests that increases in university fees may encourage those from lower socio-economic backgrounds to study nearer to home. At the same time, universities are under increasing pressure to demonstrate fair access. Analysis of Universities and Colleges Admissions Service data from 1996 to 2006 appeared to show that access is not fair, but barriers are different from one group to another. Those from lower social class backgrounds are less likely to apply to Russell Group institutions, while those from black, Pakistani and Bangladeshi backgrounds seem to receive different treatment during the admission process. State school applicants appear to receive unfair access both for application and for admission. One possible explanation offered is that non-traditional students may be predicted to achieve lower grades, a problem that would be solved by post-qualification application. Over the period of the study, tuition fees were introduced in the UK, first at £1,000 per year and then £3,000 from 2006. The study found that there is no sign that tuition fees have deterred those from state schools and lower social classes from applying to Russell Group institutions.

Increased fees have stimulated an interest in their effects. A study of almost 2,000 final year further education and sixth form UK students (Callender and Jackson, 2008) confirmed earlier research by finding that student tuition fees, now paid by all students in England, had a more constraining effect on students of lower social status than of those from wealthier backgrounds. They were likely to be influenced by the living costs of an area and the possibilities of gaining term-time employment. Choice of institution was likely to be constrained.

However, choice of subject and of qualification were not constrained. A Scottish study (Forsyth and Furlong, 2000, 2003) of disadvantaged young people also found that they were more likely to take less prestigious courses at lower-status institutions. An important conclusion of the Callender and Jackson study in relation to student motivation is that students on low incomes would be more likely to regard the cost of a degree as a debt, whereas those with higher incomes would tend to see it as an investment. Of course, subsequent increases in tuition fees may have heightened these effects. US studies have also modelled the effects of higher tuition costs, and other factors, on student choices of institution (Cabrera and Nasa, 2000).

Discussion of participation in higher education often makes use of Bourdieu's analysis (1977), in which a family's cultural capital is held to be a highly significant factor in academic success. A study of admissions to Oxford (Zimdars et al., 2009) found that broad cultural knowledge within the dominant culture was related to success in admissions, especially in arts subjects. In practical terms, vagueness in admissions criteria made it harder for those from the lower social classes to gain admission. However, cultural capital did not explain differentials between males and females and the lower level of success of applicants from South-East Asia, which were most strongly present in the sciences. Private schooling was linked negatively to the chance of an offer, a change from previous studies, but consistent with previous findings that students from state schools tend to perform better than those from private schools, given equivalent attainment at the start.

A further study of Oxford admissions (Zimdars, 2010), that included interviews with admissions tutors and observations of meetings, was not able to find evidence of the inequalities in admission that are associated with social class, ethnicity and gender. The writer notes that post-qualification applicants have an advantage, presumably because they carry lower risk. It is suggested that some selection practices may be attempts to reduce the possibility of failure. This might mean homophily – the tendency for tutors to make offers to people they see as being like themselves, and also as being like other students who have previously been admitted and been successful.

The extent to which particular sources of information are used and trusted may differ among students from particular social groups. Claims that students of lower social status tend to use unofficial and informal information, including friends and family (Callender and Jackson, 2008), may offer an example of how some forms of networking can be more powerful than others. Access to others who think as you think and do not have wide knowledge may not be very helpful, and may remove the more prestigious institutions from consideration.

Comment

The growth of a world market in higher education, and its function in the allocation of social advantage, raises a number of difficult questions for governments and for universities. At present, while some countries take measures to make access fairer, however defined, global student flow circumvents such arrangements. Thus, whereas many governments have at times considered the social equity of the allocation of university places nationally, this has been less well considered in relation to full fee-paying international students, whose presence may provide financial security for the host institution. Marginson (2006) asks how equity can be found between national and international students, and what part parental income and status plays in obtaining the educational advantage. The solution to global-level stratification, he suggests, has to be international policy action.

International and national league tables continue to exert a powerful influence on universities' behaviour, and probably on student behaviour too, although this has been less thoroughly researched than one might expect. The idea of the 'world-class university', identified by measures that have little to do with teaching quality, will continue to signal where the most prestigious educational goods are to be found. At a national level it is thus a challenging task for institutions to keep in mind issues of equity and access if this disadvantages the institution in the more prestigious league tables. There are immensely strong pressures to model an institution so that it scores highly in a contest that is not designed with equity and access in mind, but rather the reverse. This feature of higher education is not likely to change in the foreseeable future.

One possible consequence of a highly marketised system that emphasises student choice is a risk-averse culture, in which institutions are reluctant to take a distinctive position but instead describe themselves and act in ways that are indistinguishable from one another. Thus it may seem safer to chase student satisfaction than to take a distinctive position. Baldwin and James note the problem of institutional prestige distorting student choice and offer a response. They argue that universities should not publish bland descriptions of themselves and what they do, but should instead have teaching approaches that are appropriate to the curriculum and should make clear what is actually on offer to students. A fully justified range of options will, they believe, 'disrupt the sterile and destructive status hierarchy which is currently dominant in Australian higher education' (2000, 146). This is a brave proposal. It may be that the sheer number of league tables and other indicators will dilute their effect, and will also provide a range of options for demonstrating excellence from which an institution can select, but some league tables are likely to continue to hold the highest prestige, and to confer it, in a way that will tend to drown more nuanced messages.

A major problem for national league tables is in the difficulty of measuring teaching quality. At present a number of the proxy measures that tend to be used are of dubious value. Referring to the proportion of first-class degrees awarded encourages institutions to award more of them and says little about educational quality, especially since the problem of measuring 'value added' has not been solved. Some other measures reward a particular way of allocating human and other resources that may not necessarily be the most educationally sound way of providing a curriculum. Thus, staff–student ratios are a crude, although often significant, indicator of support for student learning that may come in other perhaps equally effective forms. So, at present students are invited to make choices on the basis of data that are in many ways misleading. It may be that the development of robust indicators of teaching quality will be helpful. Presumably the predominance of research indicators in most league tables reflects the difficulty of obtaining reliable data on teaching rather than any inherent wish of the publishers to favour research. There are obvious advantages in attempting to measure the quality of teaching, in that it then becomes possible objectively to demonstrate excellence in teaching, in the same way that grant income and citations provide a basis for claims of research excellence. Indeed, it could be argued that success in measuring teaching, particularly in a quantitative way, would be a prestige benefit for teaching as an activity in universities where it is often seen as an area of 'soft' knowledge, and therefore intrinsically of lower status, whilst also making it a difficult area for staff to gain recognition. On the other hand there are obvious dangers in the closer measurement of teaching. Unless it is very carefully done, there is a likelihood of performativity which might include the constriction of teaching and assessment approaches to those that are likely to trigger the highest score rather than those that might be more educationally beneficial.

An important aspect of the development of indicators would be a reduction in reliance on student satisfaction data. Whilst there is a strong argument for paying careful attention to student views, there is risk in presenting an idea of higher education as a service to be provided, rather than an activity in which active participation on the part of the learner is required. This is the essential difference between the UK's National Student Survey (NSS) and the US National Survey of Student Engagement (NSSE) (Kuh, 2001), on which the Australasian Survey of Student Engagement used in Australia and New Zealand (AUSSE) (ACER, 2014) is also modelled, and which in turn has influenced the Irish Survey of Student Engagement (ISSE) (HEA, 2013). In passing it is worth noting that surveys of student opinion make the assumption that students will provide their objective view of the quality of their institution. However, it has often been remarked that there is a conflict of interest. A thoughtful student will be aware that a poor rating for teaching will find its way into league tables and will detract from the prestige of the institution and thus, indirectly, will help to devalue the student's degree.

In conclusion, prestige has become an even more powerful and increasingly overt factor in differentiating among institutions. Competition is global and intense, and as the most prestigious institutions seek internationally to attract students who can afford expensive provision, issues of equity of access are not addressed. The ways in which students are actually matched with institutions appears to be considerably at variance with the rational choice model that has spawned so many quality indicators, and their presentation and analysis. This is not to argue against the provision of clear and accurate data about what universities provide, but to note that it does not of itself lead to greater equity. That will be more effectively pursued by focusing on the ways in which students actually do decide that particular institutions are, or are not, for them.

References

ACER (2014) Australasian Survey of Student Engagement (AUSSE), http://www.acer.edu.au/ausse, accessed 24 November 2014.

Archibald, R. and Feldman, D. (2011) *Why does college cost so much?* Oxford: Oxford University Press.

Arum, Y., Gamoran, R. and Shavit, A. (2007) *Stratification in higher education: A comparative study*. Stanford, CA: Stanford University Press.

Baldwin, G. and James, R. (2000) The market in Australian higher education and the concept of student as informed consumer, in *Journal of Higher Education Policy and Management* 22, 2: 139–48, DOI:10.1080/713678146.

Ball, S., Davies, J., David, M. and Reay, D. (2002) 'Classification' and 'judgement': Social class and the 'cognitive structures' of choice of higher education, in *British Journal of Sociology of Education* 23, 1: 51–72.

Becker, G. (1975) *Human capital: A theoretical and empirical analysis, with special reference to education*, 2nd edition. New York: National Bureau of Economic Research.

BIS (2013) The impact of university degrees on the lifecycle of earnings: Some further findings. BIS research paper no. 112, https://www.gov.uk/government/uploads/system/uploads/attachment_data/file/229498/bis-13-899-the-impact-of-university-degrees-on-the-lifecycle-of-earnings-further-analysis.pdf, accessed 30 October 2014.

Bolliver, V. (2013) How fair is access to more prestigious UK universities?, in *British Journal of Sociology* 64, 2: 344–64.

Bourdieu, P. (1977) Cultural reproduction and social reproduction, in J. Karabel and A. Halsey (eds), *Power and ideology in education*. Oxford: Oxford University Press.

Boyer, E. (1998) *Reinventing undergraduate education: A blueprint for America's research universities*. New York: Stony Brook.

Brennan, L.M. (2001) How prospective students choose universities. Unpublished PhD dissertation, https://minerva-access.unimelb.edu.au/bitstream/handle/11343/39537/81402_720.pdf?sequence=1, accessed 13 November 2014.

Brewer, D., Eide, E. and Ehrenberg, R. (1999) Does it pay to attend an elite private college?, in *Journal of Human Resources* XXXIV, 1: 104–23.

Browne, J. (2010) *Securing a sustainable future for higher education: Independent review of higher education funding and student finance*, https://www.gov.uk/government/uploads/system/uploads/attachment_data/file/31999/10-1208-securing-sustainable-higher-education-browne-report.pdf, accessed 20 February 2015.

Cabrera A. and Nasa, S. (2000) Understanding the college-choice process, in *New Directions for Institutional Research* 7: 5–22.

Callender, C. and Jackson, J. (2008) Does the fear of debt constrain choice of university and subject of study?, in *Studies in Higher Education* 33, 4: 405–29.

Conlon, G. and Chevalier, A. (2003) *Does it pay to attend a prestigious university?* Centre for the Economics of Education (CEE) discussion paper P0033.

Croxford, L. and Raffe, D. (2014) The iron law of hierarchy? Institutional differentiation in UK higher education, in *Studies in Higher Education*, DOI: 10.18080/03075079.2014.899342.

Dale, S. and Krueger, A. (1999) *Estimating the payoff to attending a more selective college: An application of selection on observables and unobservables*. NBER working paper 7322. Cambridge, MA: National Bureau of Economic Research.

Drewes, T. and Michael, C. (2006) How do students choose a university? An analysis of applications to universities in Ontario, Canada, in *Research in Higher Education* 47, 7: 781–800.

Emons, W. (1997) Credence goods and fraudulent experts, in *Rand Journal of Economics* 28, 1: 107–19.

Forsyth, A. and Furlong, A. (2000) *Socio-economic disadvantage and access to higher education*. Bristol: Policy/Joseph Rowntree Foundation.

Forsyth, A. and Furlong, A. (2003) Losing out: *Socio-economic disadvantage and experience in further and higher education*. Bristol: Policy/Joseph Rowntree Foundation.

Foskett, N. and Hemsley-Brown, J. (2001) *Choosing futures: Young people's decision-making in education training and career markets*. London: Routledge Falmer.

Gambin, L., Beaven, R., Hogarth, T., May-Gillings, M. and Long, K. (2014) *Methodological issues in estimating the value added of further education, higher education and skills: A review of relevant literature*. BIS research paper 166. London: Department for Business, Innovation and Skills, https://www.gov.uk/government/uploads/system/uploads/attachment_data/file/305635/bis-14-668-methodological-issues-in-estimating-the-value-added-provided-by-higher-education-further-education-and-skills-intervention.pdf, accessed 24 March 2015.

HEA (2013) *Launch of new national student survey*, http://www.hea.ie/en/news/launch-new-national-student-survey, accessed 24 November 2014.

Hirsch, F. (1976) *Social limits to growth*. Cambridge, MA: Harvard University Press.

Hoekstra, M. (2009) The effect of attending the flagship state university on earnings: A discontinuity-based approach, in *Review of Economics and Statistics* 91: 717–24.

Hussain, I., McNally, S. and Telhaj, S. (2009) *University quality and graduate wages in the UK*. IZA discussion paper 4043, http://ftp.iza.org/dp4043.pdf, accessed 2 November 2014.

Kuh, G. (2001) Assessing what really matters to student learning inside the National Survey of Student Engagement, in *Change: The Magazine of Higher Learning* 33, 3: 10–17.

Lucas, S. (2001) Effectively maintained inequality: Education transitions, track mobility, and social background effects, in *American Journal of Sociology* 106, 6: 1642–90.

Marginson, S. (2006) Dynamics of national and global competition in higher education, in *Higher Education* 52: 1–39, DOI 10.1007/s10734-004-7649.

Maringe, F. (2006) University and course choice, in *International Journal of Educational Management* 20, 6: 466–79.

Mechan-Schmidt, F. (2012) Excellence – but those missing out don't see it that way, in *Times Higher Education*, 1 March, http://www.timeshighereducation.co.uk/419204.article, accessed 24 March 2015.

National Center for Education Statistics (2000) *College quality and the earnings of recent college graduates*. Washington, DC: NCES.

Need, A. and De Jong, U. (2001) Do local study environments matter? A multilevel analysis of the educational careers of first-year university students, in *Higher Education in Europe* XXVI, 2: 264–78.

OECD (2012) *Education Indicators in Focus* – 2012/06 (June), http://www.oecd.org/edu/skills-beyond-school/Education%20Indicators%20in%20Focus%206%20June%202012.pdf, accessed 30 October 2014.

Oplatka, I. (2002) Implicit contradictions in public messages of low-stratified HE institutions: The case of Israeli teacher training colleges, in *International Journal of Educational Management* 16, 5: 248–56.

Payscale (2014) *College salary report*, http://www.payscale.com/college-salary-report, accessed 30 October 2015.

St John, E., Paulsen, M. and Starkey, J. (2000) The nexus between college choice and persistence, in *Research in Higher Education* 37, 2: 175–220.

University of Oxford (2014) *Undergraduate admissions statistics*, http://www.ox.ac.uk/about/facts-and-figures/admissions-statistics/undergraduate-admissions-statistics, accessed 24 March 2015.

Veloutsou C., Lewis, J. and Paton, R. (2004) University selection: Information requirements and importance, in *International Journal of Educational Management* 18, 3: 160–71.

Wilkins, S. and Huisman, J. (2014) Factors affecting university image formation among prospective higher education students: The case of international branch campuses, in *Studies in Higher Education*, DOI: 10.1080/03075079.2014.881347.

Zimdars, A. (2010) Fairness and undergraduate admission: A qualitative exploration of admissions choices at the University of Oxford, in *Oxford Review of Education* 36, 3: 307–23.

Zimdars, A., Sullivan, A. and Heath, A. (2009) Elite higher education admissions in the arts and sciences: Is cultural capital the key?, in *Sociology* 43, 4: 648–66.

Chapter 11

Prestige in academic life
Excellence and exclusion

Introduction

Prestige plays a major part in universities worldwide. It is a scarce and often intangible quality that, unlike reputation, cannot be possessed by all. It takes time to gain and, generally, to lose. It exists within groups that have a shared sense of what is prestigious. That sense may even be what defines and limits the group, which is highly likely to have defined what it holds to be prestigious. Prestige-related perceptions often frame decisions about higher education. When the universities that produce the most Nobel prize winners are routinely cited as being the 'best' institutions, as if everything that they do is thus validated, then prestige has shaped perceptions. When national funding is strongly directed to basic research rather than to applied research and development, prestige is in play. When institutions use teaching income to support research and when faculty believe that their promotion prospects are dependent principally on their research performance, prestige is shaping values and priorities. In these cases, and elsewhere, prestige trumps reputation.

Prestige is deeply rooted in all forms of social organisation and is a centrally important aspect of both individual and group psychology. It cannot be wished away. Neither should it be, necessarily, because excellence generates prestige. However, prestige can lead to inequity and exclusion, through deliberate action or circumstance. So, although a list can be made of the less than helpful effects of prestige in academic life, this commentary does not take a dystopian view of the future for universities. Neither does it speak against difference. Universities have many and varied roles and a range of types of institution is needed to undertake them all. Instead, the working of prestige needs to be recognised, understood and dealt with in ways that help universities to be more efficient and effective, celebrating excellence and minimising exclusion. The study of prestige can be an increasingly valuable way of understanding and gaining the potential to modify attitudes, values and behaviours in a complex world.

Policy and practice issues

Arguments for paying attention to prestige may be made on the basis that parity of esteem, equity and inclusion are desirable features of higher education, but also for entirely pragmatic reasons. In many areas of academic life practice is less efficient and effective than it might be, and often does not contribute to the wellbeing of academic communities or of those they serve. Many policy intentions are thwarted and a great deal of funding is wasted because prestige concerns prevent or limit desired change. Examples can be found across the range of academic activity – teaching, research, leadership and service. Most of the issues have been known about and discussed for many years. Some are matters of national policy and can be influenced strongly by that means, particularly through funding. Others are deeply culturally held and may best be tackled at the level of the institution, department or discipline. Preceding chapters have explored some of the main areas in which prestige is at work and have identified some of the associated tensions. Some of the most important of these, discussed earlier in the book, are summarised below.

At national level:

- The cost of higher education tends to outpace the rate of inflation, partly for prestige reasons, a tendency that increases as systems become more differentiated and competitive.
- There is an overemphasis on data systems that are intended to make the choosing of institutions easier for students, when much student-matching with institution does not make use of rational choice decision-making. The issue, is in part, one of how students decide on the kind of institution in which they feel at home.
- Basic research continues to be favoured over applied research, with insufficient attention paid to the ways in which the former can lead to the latter.
- Whilst the notion of the world-class university producing growth in the knowledge economy is attractive to policymakers, this vision does not extend much beyond the role of the 'top' institutions. The economic and social contribution that other higher and further education institutions can make is comparatively neglected.
- The world-class university concept and its associated league tables discourage and disadvantage universities with other more local missions.
- Governments that are striving to produce the conditions in which wealth can be created look to universities to support the knowledge economy. However, triple helix collaboration, the bringing together of government, industry and universities, often does not happen effectively, especially in the UK because of the ways in which enterprise is supported at a local level, where universities often do not have a substantive role.
- Universities do not collaborate as often or as effectively as they might with one another, particularly when there are perceived to be differing levels of

prestige. Collaboration is as likely to be based on the prospect of sharing or gaining prestige as it is on choosing an appropriate partner for what they might bring to a collaborative endeavour.

At institutional level:

- Research continues to be favoured over teaching, even in many institutions that gain most of their income from teaching. Academic conceptions of being professional continue to be centred largely on research excellence and the levels of training for teaching in universities and of qualifications in teaching remain low.
- Leadership and management have low status in many parts of the academy, limiting the supply of able members of the academy into senior positions and encouraging a division between university leadership and the academy.
- Emphasis on and reward and recognition for single-discipline research means that interdisciplinary working does not happen as extensively as is warranted. Similar cultural and motivational barriers inhibit interprofessional work.
- Overseas student recruitment does not take note of access and equity issues. In the UK there is an attempt to ensure fair access for home students but not overseas students. In some cases universities are rebalancing intakes towards overseas students, thus increasing overall inequity in their student body.
- Efforts to broaden curricula to incorporate skills-based, interdisciplinary and vocationally connected elements are inhibited by prioritisation of the requirements of single-discipline study.
- Traditional views of academic role are not keeping pace with the large number of blended roles, or reflecting or encouraging careers that include work both within and beyond the academy.
- Academic and administrative parts of institutions do not always hold each other in mutual esteem.

How the prestige problem is growing

The growth of mass education, the forces of globalisation and the working of the knowledge economy make prestige an ever more important aspect of higher education as competition among graduates, institutions and nation states intensifies. Most of the above problems are increasing in scale and the need to tackle them is becoming more urgent. Almost worldwide, the demand for higher education appears at present to be insatiable. In all developed countries and most developing ones, ever larger numbers are attending higher education institutions. Paradoxically, an age of opportunity for many is also one of increasing elitism. As national systems grow, the disparity between those who have the opportunity of a university education as against those who do not is now accompanied by another concern, about differential access to particular kinds of higher education experience. Higher education inevitably distributes economic and social opportunity, in systems that provide either equity in the quality of provision or an acceptance of diversity. Worldwide there are two broad models – the egalitarian and the elite. They are illustrated by the continental European tradition of entry to all those who are qualified, as against a more sharply differentiated US-style system, the latter now much more the norm in the wider world. This leads to a central question of whether a society wants higher education to distribute broadly equivalent opportunity or offer differentiation and, if the latter, who should have access to what kinds of provision.

It may appear parochial to attribute such a decision to a national level when the economic forces that are increasingly shaping universities operate well beyond the borders of the nation state and when student flow and research-funding are increasingly international. There are certainly some policy questions that can no longer be entirely settled at a national level for these reasons. However, a nation state will still have a concern for its overall prosperity, for the value for money of whatever public investment it makes and, perhaps, for the ways in which social and economic opportunity are distributed among its population. Inescapably, therefore, it is necessary to have a view nationally on the kind or kinds of university that are encouraged or required to exist and the ways in which public, and perhaps private, money is spent within those institutions.

As the amount and cost of the higher education provided increases, the trend towards a relative increase in private provision is likely to continue. This in itself has a prestige dimension, varying with national context, to do with the openness of a higher education system to new entrants, particularly private ones. The UK retains a mainly public university system and its most prestigious higher education institutions are public ones. Most private provision growth in the UK, and in some other national systems, has been in vocational and professional fields such as law and business studies. Conditions may be changing but a more traditional instinct that private provision is by its nature less prestigious remains, in much the same way as did resistance to the reality of massification in the 1990s (Scott, 1995). In mainland Europe, an unwillingness both within and beyond universities to see private sector growth accompanies a strong tradition of public funding of higher education. The US system has always been largely private and many of its most prestigious institutions are private ones. There is no perceived conflict in the US between prestige and the private status of a university, although it is necessary to differentiate between 'for profit' and 'not-for-profit' institutions. Many other countries that are encouraging major growth have chosen either a mixed or a largely private system, and there appears to be far less of a prestige issue than in Western Europe between the two forms of provision.

Even where there is a strong public tradition, the distinction between public and private is rapidly being eroded. Although UK universities remain public institutions, the introduction and growth of student fees and reduction in capital funding allocations to universities means that they are encouraged to act increasingly like private institutions. The granting of degree-awarding powers to private institutions in the UK and government policy intending that quality assurance arrangements should not disadvantage private provision are clear signs of a determination to encourage private providers to enter the market. Governments elsewhere that have encouraged mainly private sector university growth have nevertheless to intervene on quality, to maintain national reputation, to ensure that whatever public funding is invested is used appropriately, to ensure minimum standards are maintained and to encourage comparability and portability of awards and qualifications. This convergence suggests that any prestige advantages enjoyed by either public or private provision because of their governance will lessen over time.

Although the playing field may be becoming more level, some long-established institutions have a head start in prestige. New private providers may find it challenging to attain a prestigious position quickly, and will have to attempt to do so on the basis of indicators such as high levels of graduate employment in high-prestige professions, given that some traditional markers of prestige such as institutional longevity and illustrious alumni are not yet available to them. Where higher education growth in a system is substantial and from a small base, or where prestigious education was always previously bought abroad, there is likely to be less residual historically based prestige impeding the growth in the status of new provision. However, for most new entrants prestige may not be available and the best that can be hoped for is reputation. The standing of new entrants may be retarded when private for-profit providers are seen to be of poor quality, receiving large amounts of public money and using too little of it for educating students, as some US experience has shown (Harkin, 2010) and as has been seen in recent UK government concerns over the quality of alternative providers (BIS, 2015). Where funding of public institutions is inadequate to sustain them so that the experience they provide is obviously worse than that offered by newer entrants to the market, there is likely to be a change in relative status over time, although this may be cushioned by the residual social and cultural capital possessed by more established institutions.

The way in which research funding is distributed is an important factor influencing the location of academic prestige. Current policies are helping to produce a strongly two-tier system in public universities in the UK. Arguments for the concentration of research funding to achieve excellence and thus global status have led to a highly selective research evaluation method with most research funding now allocated to a small number of institutions. A clearer line can thus be seen to be emerging between prestige- and reputation-orientated universities, broadly meaning research- and teaching-led institutions. Despite the developing trend to treat private, including private for-profit institutions, on comparable terms with state-funded institutions, at present government research funding is available only to public institutions. This is likely to have two effects. Firstly, if private higher education providers do not engage in research, as happens in some cases in the US but not in the UK, they are unlikely to be as attractive as employers to research-active staff. Secondly, growth in the private sector will produce a much more challenging and competitive reputation-orientated climate for teaching-led institutions, especially in more high-volume and profitable subjects, whilst the most prestigious research-intensive institutions have a more sheltered experience (King, 2009).

The increasing cost of higher education has become a concern for governments and individuals, with prestige playing a major part. The experience of the US in recent years suggests that the cost of higher education tends to rise more steeply in a differentiated system, a feature of health systems, too. Thus an increase in private provision does not necessarily lead to cheaper higher education. Nevertheless, the world trend is towards more differentiated systems, but with the cost borne increasingly by the student or their family, rather than by the state. Cost still weighs heavily even on those governments that have taken this path, because of the need to make loans to students. So, unless government is willing to step away from the funding of higher education altogether, leaving it entirely to the market to decide how much a higher education should cost and to the user to fund it, there is a problem of either controlling the number and cost of students who are supported or allowing institutions some flexibility in recruitment and fee levels, and seeing the cost of higher education rise. Prestige is inflationary in its effect, increasing the cost problem for government and for students. For a limited number of institutions there is keen competition for student places, and thus little need to contain fees or pay close attention to costs. It is in the interest of such institutions to acquire prestige items that sustain this level of demand. This may include investment of teaching income in research activity that paradoxically produces no teaching benefit but increases the prestige of the institution and its attractiveness to students. Further, a degree from a prestigious institution can be a form of 'costly signalling', so the more it costs the more it is valued, producing a further upward pressure on cost. Prestige is therefore expensive, for governments and for students.

Current concerns over cost, particularly when students are very directly and obviously paying for their education, inevitably leads to an interest in whether a university education adds value. Difficulties in containing the cost of higher education are increased because it is almost impossible to measure added value, particularly in a comparative way, making higher education even more susceptible to prestige-related inflation. If it were possible to do this, governments would know what they were paying for, universities would experience pressure to improve what they offer and students could make more informed choices, as consumers in a transparent and well-informed market. This rationale underlies the growth in widely available comparative data about institutions and their achievements. At present most attempts at comparison rely on proxy measures, such as the extent to which a higher education increases individual income or the percentages of those who achieve graduate-level jobs within a particular timescale. However, these indicators contain a signalling element, as they may be influenced by employer perceptions of the quality and standing of a graduate's former institution, and so are not measures of value that has been added through the university's teaching. Perhaps it may become possible to devise some defensible way of measuring the added value of a programme or course, although there are formidable problems in doing so, especially across a range of disciplines. The obvious alternative to testing knowledge and skills within a disciplinary or professional context is to attempt to measure improvement in such universal desirables as critical thinking or problem-solving. However, even if the problem of achieving independence from socio-cultural aspects could be solved, it is extremely debatable whether these would have predictive relevance for future performance in particular contexts. Further, if these were built into quality indicators, the dangers of performativity are obvious, with a risk that curriculum provision would be skewed towards student achievement in such tests at the expense of other purposes. So, whilst measuring added value may seem a desirable path from a free market economist's standpoint (Duncan, 2015), it does not seem either feasible or desirable. Thus education remains in part a credence good, the value of which cannot be ascertained even after the event, and very much open to the working of prestige.

Even if a value-added measure can be found, prestigious institutions can largely side-step the value-for-money debate. A prestigious university degree may be little more than an expensive sifting process, a form of costly signalling, that marks out people who are of a particular sort rather than indicating what they have learnt at a university. Thus, attempts to measure value for money may do a great deal of damage, whilst prestige-driven student decisions continue to be made that are unaffected by such judgements, for even if added value could be specified, its effect on many individual choices of institution or programme would probably be limited as it would not drive out the prestige that is associated with costly signalling. Indeed, it could be argued that an individual's propensity to be influenced by the results of such value-added tests would be a marker of whether they were moved by reputational or prestige concerns. So whilst it seems likely that a choice between two broadly similar sources of provision might be influenced by a value-added measure, especially among those whose room to choose is limited financially or for other reasons, price would probably remain a strong signal of prestige for some parts of the higher education market, meaning that some would continue to seek the advantage that comes with a prestigious education, irrespective of what a value-added figure might say. This is in keeping with what we know about how students appear to make institutional choices and is a common consumer behaviour – we are able to measure the relative performances of cars but that does not remove the wish of some buyers to own one that is inefficient in fuel consumption but that has a prestige benefit. One might expect value-added measures to affect institutions to varying extents, too. Reputation-seeking institutions would be most influenced. There would be some effect even on the most prestigious institutions. For example, the Boyer report in the US (Boyer Commission, 1998) forced a response from the research-intensive institutions that were criticised. However, the prestige value of a degree from an elite institution would act as an insulator against such criticism.

The drive to create and sustain 'world-class' universities increases the tension between excellence and equity. Driven partly by national and institutional hubris, it is a distorting influence that may result in skewed spending at national level to ensure success in a highly public international contest. The desire for world-class universities is also in part fuelled by a belief that universities can make a major contribution to the knowledge economy of a nation state through the supply of useful research and skilled graduates. Governments seek an answer to the problem of economic growth, and universities offer a plausible one. To enable this, some universities need to be large and wealthy, in order to afford expensive research programmes and to attract the highest-quality staff to work in them. At the same time it is in the interests of those institutions that can mount a serious claim to be contributing to such growth to argue that they can, and to organise themselves for the purpose. It is an appealing prestige-infused arrangement for both government and those universities involved. However, it can be argued that concentrating investment in a small number of high-prestige institutions is not the most effective way of producing economic growth through a system of higher education and research. It could equally be claimed that an advanced economy requires that all of its citizens be as highly skilled as possible, both those who are entering the labour market and those who are already in it. The thrill of achieving success in world league tables may be accompanied by relative neglect of the far less prestigious but economically vital contributions to be made by the rest of the higher education sector and by further education, funding for much of which is far less fashionable and far more constrained (Wolf, 2015). This is not to argue against the support of high-prestige institutions, but to point out that a drive for prestige makes it hard to achieve a balanced approach that is influenced by an objective assessment of economic and social benefit.

The increased pressure for research excellence, a principal means of demonstrating world-class status, has consequences that are not always helpful at an institutional level. It usually suggests that researchers should be freed of other distractions, an approach likely to be supported strongly by many faculty, especially where it is clear that research rather than teaching will be rewarded. Thus research tends to become separated from teaching, so that increasingly it is undertaken by different people, with differing terms of employment and expectations. The primacy of research also encourages a move away from large undergraduate populations, or at least a decision not to expand, in order to avoid the distracting effect of large-scale teaching. Prestige is based on scarcity, providing a further incentive for the most prestigious institutions not to extend their provision. If they do, there is a risk of a diminution of prestige. Therefore, keeping undergraduate numbers low also ensures scarcity and increases the prestige value of such a degree. A recent trend in UK research-intensive institutions to recruit more undergraduates may perhaps decline when concerns about dilution of prestige start to outweigh the advantages of additional income. League tables that reward selectivity provide a further incentive for institutions to encourage a large number of applications but to admit relatively few. Thus a number of factors contribute to the emergence or confirmation of a relatively small number of elite, research-focused institutions, increasingly differentiated from a much larger number of more teaching-focused institutions.

Access to higher education is not a new problem. Excellent higher education has always been in short supply and many governments have been concerned to equalise access. However, it is becoming much more acute and difficult to manage as higher education worldwide becomes more international and more differentiated. Internationally focused universities tend, unsurprisingly, to recruit overseas students extensively, often encouraged by being able to charge higher fees than for home students. As the proportion of international students in a national system rises, national-level attempts at managing equity among the home student intake are circumvented, so that an elite higher education becomes something that is purchased by the wealthy. Without a very major effort to ensure that opportunity is available to those who are not as advantaged, these aspects of globalisation will further drive exclusion and opportunity will increasingly be distributed on the basis of ability to pay.

The status of teaching is an important prestige issue in both teaching-led and research-intensive universities. Institutions of all kinds have been relatively slow to introduce teaching-led promotion routes and indeed have often used teaching-only contracts as a place to put those who are not believed to be sufficiently active in research. A prestige nettle to be grasped is that of whether all members of faculty should have the opportunity to undertake research. This sense of the tripartite role, of which research is a part, has remained strong in the academy as faculty numbers have grown significantly, with massification. However, there is no reason to suppose that the amount of research that is needed in a nation state grows in direct proportion to its student population and the number of those who are employed to teach them. Yet it is an article of faith in higher education that its teaching is distinctive because it is research-informed, and there is of course a strong argument that staff who are up to date in their field and its research are likely to teach better. However, dealing with this requires a finer-grained view of research, and a full acceptance of the value of scholarship that is linked with teaching. When staff are graded very publicly against criteria that value only internationally significant research, scholarship lacks prestige, and the status of teaching is a casualty.

It might be supposed that the growth of communications technology and its application in education would make a significant difference to patterns of higher education worldwide. In many ways it has done so, but prestige and related aspects limit the extent of change. It is now possible for any institution to project its teaching worldwide, by making lectures and other stimulus material available through Massive Open Online Courses (MOOCs) and supporting communication through virtual learning environments and other widely available media for individual and group interaction. It is entirely possible to develop a strong reputation for the provision of distance learning, as the UK's Open University has demonstrated over many years. Some parts of the higher education market are particularly responsive. For example, continuing professional development provision finds a market among those for whom attendance at a campus is not feasible, owing to geography and to other commitments. In countries where a major expansion of higher education is required at the lowest possible cost, it may well be that the use of communications technology can help greatly in providing mass higher education, although it is far easier and cheaper to 'deliver' teaching material than it is to provide discussion, tutorial support and assessment. However, this does not intersect with the prestigious parts of higher education. Physical attendance at an institution remains a highly popular option, as is demonstrated by continuing high levels of application for prestigious institutions and the major and continuing growth of the international student market worldwide. Higher education provides benefits beyond access to knowledge – the social cachet and the close connections that are gained through physical attendance are not easy to reproduce. Once again there may be a more strongly emerging difference between prestige-maximising and reputation-maximising institutions. Mass education through communication technologies may increasingly be advocated for others by those who choose to send their own children to more traditionally delivered and prestigious provision. This is a separate issue from the 'blended' use of technologies that are used to enrich more traditional provision. MOOCs also provide an invaluable tool for the projection of prestige, when prestigious institutions make lectures and other teaching material freely available online in a display of costly signalling.

What might be done

The power of prestige can be seen in some of the policy intentions that have not succeeded, even where a strong case could be made for them. The continuation of large lectures as the main method of teaching in much of higher education suggests that student-centred approaches have made surprisingly little headway. The proportion of state-school students remains stubbornly low at the most prestigious institutions (Zimdars, 2010). The professionalisation of higher education teaching has more than a twenty-year history in the UK and yet progress is very patchy. Governments have encouraged universities to launch two-year degrees, to little effect. Universities are urged to consider mergers, in order to achieve economies of scale, but rarely do. In 2000 the UK government invested significantly in an e-university that closed in 2004, having recruited only a thousand students (Garrett, 2004). Credit accumulation and transfer, a highly rational way in which students can gather credit from a number of institutions, has never become established (Bekhradnia, 2004) after many years of effort, its main uses confined largely to low-status courses (Field, 2004). Clearly there are other factors in play in each of these cases, but prestige plays a significant part.

Universities are being expected to deliver more than ever before, yet achieving change in higher education can seem infuriatingly difficult, as the list above suggests. A straightforward response to a need to achieve productivity is simply to increase directive pressure. The size of national higher education systems, the resources they require and the outcomes that are looked for produce an understandable tendency for governments to measure and control, so that management becomes managerialism. Institutions acquire strengthened structures and more explicit roles and responsibilities, emphasising the necessity for all parts of the organisation to be contributing to the institutional mission. In effect this means the adoption of a machine metaphor of organisation. An overarching statement of mission heads a range of interrelated strategic documents detailing policy and strategy in all key areas. They reach out to the furthest parts of the organisation, through systems of performance management and appraisal, where individual targets are set that contribute to the work of the team, the department, the school, the whole institution. Usually, formal approaches to internal communication are strengthened, with the aim of ensuring that all members of the organisation are clear about its mission and its priorities, and are regularly seeing feedback about the quality of teaching and the level of research income. For ease of management and transparent accountability at institutional level, it is likely that all parts will be treated as if they were the same. This is an entirely understandable reaction, given the demanding environment for universities.

However, patterns of motivation are a forgotten aspect of a drive for greater efficiency and effectiveness. No matter what the strength of the structures, targets and messages, prestige does not go away. It is hard-wired into each individual and is an enduring feature of organisational life. Prestige concerns influence the career pathways that individuals choose to take, making some avenues much more attractive than others. Prestige factors influence who works with whom, what gets the most attention and what discretionary time is spent on. As a positive force, the drive to seek and maintain prestige is a strong motivator for individuals and groups to achieve the best of which they are capable. The excellence of an institution absolutely requires this effort at all levels. The negative aspects are many. Prestige can maintain unhelpful hierarchies and traditions that stifle change and growth. Prestige may encourage tribalism and parochialism, meaning that those who might usefully work together to be more than the sum of their parts do not feel inclined to do so. Most importantly, it frustrates initiatives like those listed earlier and is at the root of the policy problems listed at the start of the chapter. The ubiquity of prestige in life may suggest that it is simply part of the human condition and may as well be accepted, rather like the weather. However, although prestige-related behaviours, beliefs and attitudes will always exist, they are open to influence, in part through thoughtful management action. Taking more account of prestige, naming it and working with it, may perhaps reduce some of the unhelpful tensions in organisational life, through a better understanding of individual and group motivation.

Government policy affects patterns of prestige whether it intends to or not. So in reviewing the nature of prestige in a field, one might ask what a system or an institution is already, perhaps unwittingly, doing to influence prestige patterns. A number of areas have been outlined in previous chapters and listed at the start of this conclusion. Changing prestige patterns is not straightforward, because it is complex and involves human relationships. John Field has noted that social capital is 'particularly slippery as a focus for policy' (Field, 2008, 142). Where government seeks to influence social capital, it should do so through the support of existing networks rather than attempting to build new ones where there are none already. Field suggests: 'it is prudent for governments to ensure that it seeks to do as little harm as possible to people's stocks of social capital' and to avoid making connections that produce consequences that are more negative than positive (2008, 155). These words of caution may well be transferable to working with prestige, where attempts to influence what is valued may mean replacing one kind of performativity, or conformity to the method of measuring, by another.

If a great deal of what is felt to be prestigious has its meaning at local levels, it becomes ever more important to be able to communicate effectively at those levels. This does not mean an ever larger institutional megaphone, the augmentation of standard broadcast methods of getting an institutional message out across the university, because messages tend to be evaluated according to their source. It requires attention to spanning organisational boundaries, where they have to exist, and making use of and valuing staff who have that boundary-spanning ability. There are major opportunities for the strategic management of staff motivations if those motivations are understood, noting that prestige-desiring and prestige-seeking behaviours may differ even within the same department. Thus many actions can be taken at an institutional level, but some have to be negotiated quite locally. Performance-related pay may be an ineffective instrument in achieving change. It has long been recognised that money is a hygiene factor, but does not of itself provide enduring satisfaction. To append financial incentives to activities that do not confer prestige of any kind on the individual who is being performance-managed is likely to be a less than fruitful exercise.

One way of encouraging desired values and activities may be to develop alternative patterns of prestige. If an institution consistently, publicly and in practice values particular things, then there is a possibility that values can be shifted provided any countervailing forces are less strong. These might include the effects of government policy and also the influence of other loyalties within and beyond the organisation. The positional advantages accrued by individuals and groups in a prestige-generating institution may be in tension with ideas of inclusiveness. One way of shaping prestige is to ensure that prestige that can be shared and that has wide benefits is viewed and commended more positively. This might, for example, be put into effect in performance review schemes that are at present always set at an individual level, thus validating individual rather than collective endeavour. However, some features of prestige economies are quite enduring and may not be amenable to change or be extremely resistant to it, so that one has to consider whether an attempt at change would be worthwhile.

Co-operation can be a major casualty of prestige. Strong identification with belief systems is often accompanied by stereotyping and othering, as groups and individuals bolster their own sense of identity and worth at the expense of others. Co-operation is most likely to happen where negative stereotyping and othering are at their minimum. This does not mean the elimination of differences across the various occupational groups in a university. Difference will remain, for all the sociological, psychological and practical reasons advanced here. Co-operation does, however, require mutual respect across groupings: within the academic body, which tends to mean in inter- and multi-disciplinary and interprofessional co-operation; within the administration, across its varying functions; and, very importantly, between the academy and the administration. Many prestige systems are involved and attention has to be paid to them if openness is to be achieved, rather than closure and the missing of opportunity.

Attention is also required to the importance of the academic case. Many plans and targets tend to be justified on the grounds of government policy, financial need or perceived stakeholder benefits. However, the motivation to teach and research well may be felt, by those who do this work, to be an end in itself, to be judged on its own terms by those who are expert in that activity. Thus, if it is not clear that a particular change will result in better teaching, as it is understood by those who are doing the teaching, or better research, as those researchers conceptualise research, then it is not likely to attract support. The brute reason of external pressure for change may fail to engage groups that are strongly socialised around other values. It can be argued that some necessary changes are too radical or difficult to achieve agreement upon in advance. It may be necessary to force through a change, so that afterwards the advantages in practice are the best advertisement for the change. However, it may well be worthwhile at least to attempt to make the academic case, and to explore what a change may mean to the main interest groups involved.

A future

If a concern for prestige is an enduring feature of individual motivations and social relationships, it may be that thinking about prestige may help to indicate some aspects of likely futures for universities. Prestige may both drive and inhibit change. Some of the former have been touched upon – increasing global competition among nation states and among students, competing for limited amounts of prestige. Prediction seems increasingly difficult for not only is the pace of change quickening in most national systems, some of the fundamentals of organised life are changing utterly. Certainly developments in communication technologies, both in increased capability and decreased cost, offer astonishing possibilities for communication and for learning that could only have been dreamed of even twenty years ago. Vast amounts of educational materials are now available at no cost to the user. The world's libraries can be explored from a home computer, removing one of the major advantages for so long enjoyed by universities as sources of knowledge. Rifkin's claim (2014) that a capitalist model is increasingly hard to sustain is apparently being borne out in many areas of culture and communication that have radically changed in recent years. The printing industry offers an excellent example in which a combination of new technologies and changing working practices has produced a completely different model of production. The market for recorded music has also changed immensely, to the extent that most music is almost free at the point of use, and can easily be copied at no cost, driving producers to gain income by other related means. The speed and extent of such changes makes them seem revolutionary rather than evolutionary. Have we reached a decisive tipping point where we can expect radical change in universities worldwide, so that higher education will look totally different in a few years' time? Are we about to experience an avalanche in which universities are transformed by globalisation and technology, as Barber et al. have predicted (2013)? Are our currently prestigious institutions about to be swept away?

Complex changes are happening quickly, as the preceding discussion has suggested. However, there are conservative influences, many of which have to do with prestige. Older ideas of the university may be in ruins (Readings, 1997) as globalisation challenges the importance of nation states, but there remains a need to denote excellence in research and teaching, both to identify what has the greatest value and to provide a benefit for those associated with it. Prestige is slowly gained and usually slowly lost, and longevity is itself often a component of prestige. Excellence comes in preferred forms, especially when prestige is being sought and accorded. A skeuomorph is an architectural term that refers to the mimicry of one object or way of manufacture in the making of another. For example, plant pots may continue to be made circular even when they are moulded rather than turned. We also use mimicry to signal quality. Thus laminate flooring may be made to resemble wood by the inclusion of a photograph of wood grain. So durability and cheapness are combined with the appeal of tradition. Prestige may well increase the use of deliberate skeuomorphism in universities. That is to say, technological change may make many things possible, but the ways in which students and others experience a university may still need to feel relatively traditional. We already have this, of course, in that most of the more prestigious institutions have iconic old buildings that were originally constructed for very different conditions of learning. The public lecture, which has for so long been critiqued as an ineffective form of teaching and learning (Bligh, 2000), continues to thrive, supplemented but not replaced by video capture. The graduation ceremony, attended by faculty resplendent in gowns and caps that have been rented for the day, remains an important event in a student's journey and in the experience that the university offers both to students and their families.

Prestige is here to stay, with good and bad consequences, and it cannot be driven out. It is too much a fundamental part of the psychology of being human. This book has not attempted to prescribe what should be done, although in places a preferred ethical position has been taken on some matters. Instead, it has described some prestige practices and explored their consequences. The effects of prestige can be managed, and a starting point is to name it, working to gain its benefits and minimise its harmful consequences.

References

Barber, M., Donnelly, K. and Rizvi, S. (2013) *An avalanche is coming*. London: Institute for Public Policy Research, http://www.ippr.org/images/media/files/publication/2013/04/avalanche-is-coming_Mar2013_10432.pdf, accessed 5 May 2015.

Bekhradnia, B. (2004) *Credit accumulation and transfer, and the Bologna Process: An overview*. London: Higher Education Policy Institute.

BIS (2015) *Alternative providers of higher education: Improving quality and value for money*. Sheffield: Department of Business Innovation and Skills, https://www.gov.uk/government/uploads/system/uploads/attachment_data/file/407730/bis-15-97-alternative-providers-of-higher-education-improving-quality-and-value-for-money-consultation.pdf, accessed 7 April 2015.

Bligh, D. (2000) *What's the use of lectures?* San Francisco: Jossey Bass.

Boyer Commission (1998) *Reinventing undergraduate education: A blueprint for America's research universities*. Stony Brook, NY: State University of New York at Stony Brook for the Carnegie Foundation for the Advancement of Teaching.

Duncan, E. (2015) Excellence v equity: Special report universities, in *Economist*, 28 March–3 April.

Field, J. (2004) Articulation and credit transfer in Scotland: Taking the academic high road or a sideways step in a ghetto, in *Journal of Access Policy and Practice* 1, 2: 85–99.

Field, J. (2008) *Social capital*. Abingdon: Routledge.

Garrett, R. (2004) The real story behind the failure of the UK e-University, in *Educause Quarterly* 4: 4–6.

Harkin, T. (2010) Emerging risk: An overview of growth, spending, student debt and unanswered questions in for-profit higher education. Washington, DC: United States Senate, http://www.help.senate.gov/imo/media/doc/HELP%20Emerging%20Risk%20Report%20with%20exec.%20summary.pdf, accessed 7 April 2015.

King, R. (2009) *Presentation to the all-parliamentary group: Private higher education: Private gain or public interest?*, https://www.open.ac.uk/cheri/documents/roger-king-presentation.pdf, accessed 7 April 2015.

Readings, B. (1997) *The university in ruins*. Cambridge, MA: Harvard University Press.

Rifkin, J. (2014) *The zero marginal cost society*. New York: Palgrave MacMillan.

Scott, P. (1995) *The meanings of mass higher education*. Buckingham: Society for Research into Higher Education/Open University Press.

Wolf, A. (2015) *Fixing a broken training system: The case for an apprenticeship levy*. London: Social Market Foundation, http://www.smf.co.uk/wp-content/uploads/2015/07/Social-Market-Foundation-Publication-Alison-Wolf-Fixing-A-Broken-Training-System-The-Case-For-An-Apprenticeship-Levy.pdf, accessed 14 August 2015.

Zimdars, A. (2010) Fairness and undergraduate admission: A qualitative exploration of admissions choices at the University of Oxford, in *Oxford Review of Education* 36, 3: 307–23.

Index

Abu Dhabi 76, 80
academic capitalism 8, 23
'academic oligarchy' 58
academics 22–3, 66; barriers to interdisciplinarity 107–9; division between academy and administration 145; as facilitators 129, 131; motivation 41, 183; personal prestige 67; prestige brokering 33; research stars 146–7, 151; research-teaching nexus 132; role of 2; *see also* faculty
access 164, 166, 173, 179
accountability 89, 181
accreditation 70
added value 89, 99, 159, 166, 176–7
administration 145
admissions criteria 165
Adonis report 121
agency 22, 69
Aghion, P. 60
Alderfer, C. 41
alliances 62–3, 150
Altbach, P. 60
altruism 27, 46–7, 52
applied research 39, 102, 120, 125, 134, 135, 172
apprenticeships 121
arenas 32–3
Argyris, C. 42
arts 107, 112–14
Asch, S. 45

Asia 85
assessment 112, 113, 128
Australia 2, 55; Australasian Survey of Student Engagement 167; funding 58; Learning and Teaching Fellowships 33; overseas students 56; rankings 87; Sandstones 59, 156; status hierarchy 166; student attitudes 157; student choice 161; Universitas 21 network 90; Worldwide Universities Network 91
Australian National University 91
Austria 97
autonomy 22, 50, 110; curtailing of 135; institutional 58, 64; openness 68; professional knowledge 111

Bahrain 81
Bailey, F. 26, 32, 33, 104–5
Baldwin, G. 160, 166
Ball, S. 162
Barber, M. 184
Barnett, Ron 6, 132
basic research 9, 39, 51, 70, 114, 133–4, 172; claims about 118; economic impact 120; funding 171; LERU 90–1; purpose of research 125–7; *see also* research
beliefs 50, 52, 62, 102–3, 112, 123
Bernstein, B. 35
Bess, J.L. 41

bias 48–50
Biglan, A. 106
BIS *see* Department for Business, Innovation and Skills
Blackmore, P. 21
bonding capital 28
Botswana 81
Boud, D. 132
boundaries 21–2, 30, 31–2
bounded rationality 43
Bourdieu, Pierre 11, 15, 20, 25–8, 35, 46, 103–4, 113, 162, 165
Boyer Commission 131, 158, 177
brain processes 46
Brandes, D. 128
Brazil 81, 85
Brennan, L.M. 161
Brew, A. 132
Brewer, D. 4–5, 13, 140
bridging capital 28
brokering 33
Browne Review (2010) 120–1
Bruner, J. 20
Burnard, P. 114
business 106, 107, 111; *see also* employers; enterprise

Callender, C. 164–5
Cambridge University 91, 104, 142
Canada 90, 163
Capalleras, J. 41
capital 5, 21, 24–9, 103, 150–1, 153; *see also* cultural capital; social capital; symbolic capital
capitalism 8, 23, 65, 68, 70, 183–4
Carnegie Foundation 98, 156
CBI *see* Confederation of British Industry
chemistry 106
Chevalier, A. 158–9
China 56, 64, 72, 74, 78–9, 81, 85, 87
citations 89
Clark, Burton 58, 104

classification 98
closure 29, 66, 68, 69
cognitive efficiency 43–5
Cohen, M. 102, 125
Coleman, J.S. 27, 28
collaboration 46–7, 68, 110, 122–3, 134, 152, 172–3
collectivist ethos 51
collegiality 6–7, 19, 27, 60–1, 70
commensuration 93
committees 32–3
commodification 130–1
communication technologies 1, 7, 23, 65, 67, 179–80, 183
competence movement 111–12
competition 12, 150, 173; elite education 157; global 64, 67, 81, 85, 167, 183; international 54, 56–7; league tables 86, 88, 95; positional 158
competitions 9, 33
competitive altruism 47
competitiveness 1, 4, 61, 134; capital 26–7; economic 133, 135; league tables 85; overseas campuses 75–6, 77; research 62
complex model of motivation 40
Comroe, J. 126
Confederation of British Industry (CBI) 120
conference keynotes 32
conflict 45–6
Conlon, G. 158–9
conservatism 63, 113, 148
'conspicuous production' 47
consumer pressure 121
consumers, students as 61, 160–3
co-operation 47–8, 182–3
cosmopolitan prestige 23
'costly signalling' 47, 52, 70, 176, 177, 180
costs 51–2, 158, 172, 176; *see also* fees
Cottrell, S. 25

creative commons 65–6, 70
creativity 63, 68–9, 112, 113, 114
'credence goods' 62, 160, 177
credibility 141, 143, 153
Croxford, L. 163–4
cultural approval 25
cultural borrowing 64
cultural capital 21, 26, 153, 157, 159, 165, 175
culture 18, 19, 75
curiosity-driven research 42, 43, 109, 118, 119, 125, 127, 130; *see also* basic research
curriculum 8, 55, 63, 129; collaboration with business 123; constructive alignment 129–30; Hong Kong 78; performativity 177; single-discipline study 173
Czech Republic 97

data 9, 151–2; 'big data' 67, 68; league tables 86–7, 88, 90, 92, 95, 151; measurement issues 176–7; return on investment 159; student choice 160, 161, 166–7, 172; student satisfaction 167; U-Multirank 96–7
Deci, E. 41
decision-making 43–5, 48–50, 155–6, 162, 172
Department for Business, Innovation and Skills (BIS) 158, 159–60
departments 30, 32, 51
developing countries 8, 119, 173
Dewey, John 128
discipline, Foucauldian concept of 93
disciplines 2, 20, 27, 39, 106–7, 114; boundaries 31; language 35; loyalty to disciplinary community 55; myths 105; prestige brokering 33; prestige economies 30, 151–2; single-discipline study 173; tribalism 144–5; *see also* interdisciplinarity

display 47, 61, 62
distance education 179–80
dramaturgy 34
Dubai 76, 80–1

earnings 158–60
economic capital 26
economic growth 8, 60, 80, 85, 118–38, 172, 178; basic research 125–7; higher education response 122–4; Hong Kong 79; reports 119–22, 133; Singapore 74
economic view of prestige 58
education 106, 107
egalitarianism 174
Egypt 72
Eisner, E. 112
elite education 157–8
elitism 6, 13, 28, 173, 174
Elliott, J. 111–12
employability 19, 120, 122, 123, 134
employers 94–5, 123, 152
engineering 106, 109, 111, 144
English, James 3, 33
English literature 106, 107
enterprise 6–7, 123, 131, 134
entrepreneurialism 64
epistemic relations 35
equity 166, 172, 173, 174, 178, 179
equivocality 4, 25
Espeland, W.N. 92–3
ETH Zurich 91
ethnicity 164, 165
Etzkowitz, H. 110
Europe: egalitarianism 174; geography 107; League of European Research Universities 90–1, 97, 149, 152; league tables 87, 89
European Union (EU): league tables 85, 95; public and private provision 58; students' right to study 156; U-Multirank 86, 96–8

European University Association 84, 86–7
excellence 1, 135, 171, 173, 178, 181, 184
exclusion 171, 179
expertise 25–6, 43–4, 49, 70, 105, 129

faculty 10, 11, 20–1, 30, 61; barriers to interdisciplinarity 8–9, 107–9; disciplinary teaching 134; league tables 92, 95; mastery of knowledge 129; mobility of 55, 56; openness 68; promotion prospects 171; research excellence 135; research-teaching nexus 132, 179; *see also* academics; staff
fair access 164, 166, 173, 179
fees 61, 92, 158–9, 162, 164–5, 174, 176, 179
Feldman, K. 41
Field, John 27–8, 29, 182
financial incentives 51, 182
Foucault, Michel 92–3
framing 44–5
France 56, 59, 60, 90, 97
Fullan, M. 25
funding 1, 8, 58–61, 66, 70, 175–6; awarding of research grants 13–14; basic research 125, 171; concentration of 60, 132; economic outcomes 120; German 'elite' institutions 156; HEFCE 124; Hong Kong 79; Mode 2 knowledge 110; science research 84; for teaching 19; U-Multirank 97; wasted 172

Garfield, E. 126
Gates, S. 13
geography 107
Germany 55, 60, 72, 156; modes of knowledge 110; overseas students 56; sciences 106; students' right to study 61; U-Multirank 97
Giddens, Anthony 20
Ginnis, P. 128
Glazer, N. 111
'global hubs' 7, 16, 19, 56, 80, 81; Hong Kong 77–9; Malaysia 77; Singapore 73–6; United Arab Emirates 76
globalisation 1, 8, 54, 62–6, 72, 173, 184; increased exclusion 179; openness 67, 68, 69; opportunities from 22, 23; rankings 84
Goffman, Erving 33–4
Goldman, C. 13
gossip 48
governance 5, 59–60, 74, 85
government influences 8, 24, 58, 60, 62, 69–70, 74
grants 13–14, 32, 89, 126–7; *see also* funding
Greene, J. 50
group approbation 41, 48
Group of Eight 163
Guest, D. 42
Gulf states 58

habitus 20
halo effect 49, 89, 163
Hargreaves, A. 25
Hargreaves, D. 45
Harvard University 87
Hattie, J. 132
Hayes, J. 45
Hazelkorn, E. 84–5, 92, 94, 95
heads of institutions 139–54
HEFCE *see* Higher Education Funding Council for England
Henkel, Mary 20
Hertzberg, F. 41
Heseltine report (2012) 121–2
hierarchy of needs 40, 46
Higher Education Funding Council for England (HEFCE) 121, 124

Hirsch, F. 157
historical perspective 1–3
Hoekstra, M. 159
Hong Kong 33, 55, 58, 77–9, 80
honorary degrees 32, 33
horizontal differentiation 157
Huisman, J. 163
humanities 20, 35–6, 89, 106, 144, 152
Humboldt, W. 131
Humboldtian model 55, 59
Hussain, I. 159
hybrid organisations 110

IARU *see* International Alliance of Research Universities
identity 19, 20–2, 135
'illusio' 104
India 56, 81, 85
individual agency 22, 69
inequalities 29, 171
In Pursuit of Prestige (Brewer et al.) 4–5
innovation 121, 124
INSEAD 74
intellectual capital 25, 26
interdisciplinarity 8–9, 30, 107–9, 145, 173; climate for 114; co-operation 183; curriculum 63; U-Multirank 97; valid knowledge 36
International Alliance of Research Universities (IARU) 91
International Ranking Expert Group (IREG) 90
internationalisation 7–8, 55–7, 72, 98, 148; *see also* globalisation; overseas students
internet 67–8, 70
interprofessionalism 109
IREG *see* International Ranking Expert Group
Ireland 97, 167
Israel 163

Ivy League 17, 59, 163

Jackson, J. 164–5
James, R. 160, 166
Japan 55, 80, 89, 97
job satisfaction 41, 106
John Hopkins University 55
journals 24, 36, 108

Kahneman, D. 44, 45
Kandiko, C.B. 21
Klein, J.T. 108
Knight, J. 72, 73, 81
knowledge 6, 35–6, 84, 105–14; arts 112–14; economic expectations 118; globalisation impact on 65; 'hard' and 'soft' 106; identity and 21; interdisciplinarity 107–9; mastery 129; Mode 2 knowledge 107, 109–10, 129; MOOCs 70; myths 105; professional 107, 110–12, 127–8; Sainsbury report 119; U-Multirank 96, 97
knowledge economy 57, 73, 102, 113, 114, 125, 172, 173, 178
Knowles, Malcolm 128
Korea 56, 72, 81

Lambert review (2003) 133
Lane, J. 76
language 35–6
law 111
leadership 14, 104–5, 173; heads of institutions 139–54
Leadership Foundation for Higher Education 139
League of European Research Universities (LERU) 90–1, 97, 149, 152
league tables 1, 5, 33, 39, 84–101; employer behaviours 94–5; heads of institutions 149–50; internal effects of ranking 92–3; international 7–8, 12, 19, 55,

56–7, 66–7, 79, 84, 87–8, 151; national dimension 88–90; objectivity 19; perverse effects of 86; prestige clubs 90–1; prestige economies 151; rational choice approach 43; student choice 9, 94, 155, 157, 163, 166; U-Multirank 96–8; weaknesses of 86–7, 98, 166–7
learning: commodification of 130–1; constructivist theories of 129–30; learning objectives 129; research-teaching nexus 132; specificity of learning outcome 134–5; student-centred 128–9
legitimation code theory 35
Leitch review (2006) 119
LEPs *see* local enterprise partnerships
LERU *see* League of European Research Universities
Leydesdorff, L. 110
Lieberman, M. 46, 48
local enterprise partnerships (LEPs) 121, 122, 123, 124, 133, 150, 152
local government 122, 133, 150, 152
local prestige 23

major professions 111
Malaysia 58–9, 72, 75, 77, 80
managerialism 6, 22, 181
Marginson, S. 55–6, 62–4, 68–70, 80–1, 157–8, 166
Maringe, F. 155
marketing 9, 10, 92, 130–1, 163
marketisation 66, 70, 79, 89, 166
markets 10–11, 17, 155
Marsh, H. 132
Maslow, A. 40, 46
Massachusetts Institute of Technology (MIT) 74
massification 6, 179
massive open online courses (MOOCs) 68, 70, 179, 180
mathematics 106, 109

Mathew effect 49
Mauritius 81
McInnis, C. 40
McNay, I. 58
mechanistic view of organisations 18–19
medicine 106, 109, 111, 125–7, 144
memoranda of understanding 63
mergers 147
Merton, R. 49
Michigan State University 80–1
minor professions 111
mission statements 6
MIT *see* Massachusetts Institute of Technology
Mode 2 knowledge 107, 109–10, 129
Monash University 62
MOOCs *see* massive open online courses
moral capital 104
'moral tribes' 103
motivation 11, 12, 14, 40–3, 50–1, 52, 181, 182
multiranking 86, 96–8
music 45, 106, 113–14, 184
myths 103–5, 118, 124, 127, 131–2

Naidoo, R. 131
nation states, role of 63–4, 72
national prestige 72–83
National Student Survey 92, 94, 140, 146, 167
national systems 19, 54, 56, 85–6, 173, 180–1
National Universities and Colleges Admissions System (UCAS) 164
neo-liberalism 65–6, 67, 69, 155, 160
Netherlands 59, 61, 90, 97, 156
networks 7, 18, 19, 32, 90; collaboration 68; globalisation 69; social capital 27–8, 81; structural holes 28; trilateral 110
new public management 66
New Zealand 72, 167

Nissani, M. 107
normalisation 93
norms 35
nursing 106, 109

occupational prestige 57–8
Odena, O. 113
OECD *see* Organisation for Economic Co-operation and Development
Open University 179
openness 66–9, 70
Organisation for Economic Co-operation and Development (OECD) 158
organisational culture 39
'organisational sagas' 104
organisations 18–19
Orr, S. 113
outreach 12–13, 98
overseas campuses 58–9, 64, 73; competitiveness 75–6, 77; Malaysia 77; Singapore 74, 75; United Arab Emirates 76, 80–1
overseas students 56, 66, 72–3, 94, 166, 173, 179
Oxford University 91, 142, 163, 165

patents 66
Paulsen, M. 41
pedagogy 128–31
peer learning 129
peer review 27, 33
performance management 51, 61, 181, 182
performativity 9, 167, 177, 182
performing arts 107, 112–14
permeability 31, 32
personal prestige 5, 67, 141–4, 152
philanthropy 52, 68
physics 106, 107
policy 1, 55–6, 60, 69–70, 80, 91, 133, 172–3, 180–3
political context 79, 80
political systems 18, 19

polytechnics 2, 59; *see also* post-1992 universities
positional goods 157, 158, 160
positivism 112
post-1992 universities 141, 142–3, 148, 152, 164
postgraduate provision 66, 73
power 19, 31, 32, 58, 107
pre-1992 universities 141, 142–3, 144, 146, 148, 153, 164
prestige 1, 12–16, 17–18, 70, 171; alternative patterns of 182; arenas 32–3; arts 113; attitudes to 140–1; barriers to interdisciplinarity 108–9, 114; basic research 133–4; brokering 33; capital 24–9; communicating 9–10; current concerns 7–9; defining 3–5; economic perspective 133, 134; future of 183–5; globalisation 54, 62–6; growing problem of 173–80; heads of institutions 139–54; historical perspective 1–3; Hong Kong 79; international comparisons 57–62; language 35–6; league tables 86, 87, 89–90, 93, 95, 99; local and cosmopolitan 23; Malaysia 77; motivation 181; national 56, 72–83; openness and closure 66–7, 69; organisations 18–19; pedagogic practices 128, 129; personal 5, 67, 141–4, 152; policy and practice issues 172–3; professions 112; psychology of 39–53; roles 23–4; scarcity 104, 178; self-presentation 33–4; social permissions 102; student choice 157–8, 161, 162–3, 166, 167; symbolic capital 103; trust 105; two paradigms 5–7; United Arab Emirates 76
prestige clubs 90–1
prestige economies 10–11, 15, 17, 29–30, 150–4, 182; boundaries

31–2; identity development in 21; league tables 86, 95; national systems 19; roles 23–4; selectivity 161
priming 45
private institutions 5, 51, 174–6; Hong Kong 78; Malaysia 77; United Arab Emirates 76; United States 56, 58
private schools 162, 163, 165
prizes 1, 10, 33
productivity 88, 121, 180
professional knowledge 107, 110–12, 127–8
professionalism 34
professions 2
promotions 11, 30, 32, 51, 108, 171
propositional knowledge 111, 112
psychological contract 42, 50
psychology 15–16, 18, 39–53; bias 48–50; cognitive efficiency 43–5; conflict 45–6; co-operation 47–8; motivation 40–3
publications 24, 32, 55
Putnam, R.D. 27, 28

Qatar 81
QS 87, 153
quality assurance 36, 60, 175; Hong Kong 79; league tables 89, 92; Malaysia 77

Raffe, D. 163–4
RAND report 159
rankings *see* league tables
rational choice approach 43, 121, 155, 157, 160, 172
rational economic model of motivation 40
reactivity 93
reciprocity 29, 47–8
recognition 51, 52, 173
REF *see* Research Excellence Framework

regulation 58
reputation 3–5, 13, 48, 51, 150, 154; academics 23; competitive altruism 47; decision-making 43; government influences 8; heads of institutions 140, 141, 147, 151, 153; league tables 88, 93, 94–5; national 175; recruitment of students 161; 'reputational reservoir' 104; student choice 94, 157; tensions 42, 43; trumped by prestige 153, 171; value-added measures 177
research 20, 62, 173, 178–9; applied 39, 102, 120, 125, 134, 135, 172; awarding of grants 13–14; concentration of resources 90; economic focus 120, 178; funding 1, 60, 61, 84, 175–6; globalisation impact on 65; government influences 24; heads of institutions 141, 145–7; Hong Kong 78; 'impact' 12, 19; institutional goals 66; international importance 22; league tables 87, 88, 167; Mathew effect 49; motivation 183; promotions 30; purpose of 125–7; research-teaching nexus 131–2; Sainsbury report 119; student choice 157; U-Map 98; U-Multirank 96, 97; what counts as 19; white paper 121; *see also* basic research
Research Excellence Framework (REF) 33, 108, 120, 135, 140, 146, 153
return on investment 158–60
reward systems 51, 52, 182
Richards, R. 77
Rifkin, Jeremy 65–6, 67–8, 69, 70, 183
risk, avoidance of 130–1, 166
Rogers, Carl 128
Rottingen, J.-A. 127

Rousseau, Jean-Jacques 128
Rowley, J. 41
Russell Group 17, 59, 90, 123–4, 140, 148–9, 152, 156, 163, 164
Ryan, R. 41

Sainsbury report (2007) 119
salaries 60
Salmi, J. 60
Sandstones 17, 59, 156
satisficing 43
Sauder, M. 92–3
Saudi Arabia 56, 72
Schein, E. 40, 42, 111
Schneider, J. 44, 49
Schon, Donald 110–11, 112
sciences 35–6, 106; academic careers 20; basic science 111; Hong Kong 78; league tables 89; modes of knowledge 109–10; research funding 84
Scotland 2, 165
Scott, Peter 6
selectivity 61, 89, 156, 161, 165, 178
self-actualisation 40, 41
self-determination theory 41
self-fulfilling prophecy 93
self-interest 27, 47, 48, 52, 103, 135
self-presentation 33–4
Shanghai Jiao Tung index 17, 87, 95
Shay, S. 113
Sidhu, R. 74
Simon, H. 43, 45
Singapore 55, 58–9, 72, 73–6, 80
skeuomorphism 184
Slovic, P. 45
Snow, C.P. 106
social capital 26, 27–9, 68, 81, 153, 157, 159, 175, 182
social class 161–2, 163–5
social connection 46
social establishment 34
social inclusion 86, 89, 99
social model of motivation 40

social relations 35
social reproduction 162, 163–5
social sciences 35–6, 75, 89
social standing 11, 46
social status 34, 35, 48
social work 106
sociology 15, 18, 106
'soft power' 55, 72, 74, 79
solidarity 27, 48
South Africa 55
South America 58
specialisation 59, 62
spill-over effects 49
sporting facilities 92, 158
Sri Lanka 81
stability 2–3
staff 2, 104; administrative 145; league tables 92; relationships with heads of institutions 144; turnover 51; unconscious beliefs and values 52; see also academics; faculty
stakeholders 85, 95, 96, 114, 120
Stenhouse, L. 112
stereotyping 49, 52, 182–3
stratification 58, 59, 87, 156–7, 166
strong ties 28–9
structuration 22
student-centred teaching 128–9, 130, 180
students 1, 9, 120, 155–70, 172; as consumers 61, 160–3; elite education 157–8; institutional differences 156–7; league tables 94; mobility of 56; National Student Survey 92, 94, 140, 146, 167; return on investment 158–60; role of 2; selection of 61, 89, 156, 161, 165, 178; social reproduction 162, 163–5; value-added measures 177; see also overseas students
'Students at the heart of the system' (white paper, 2011) 120–1
Sunday Times Good University tables 88

surveillance 93
Sweden 97
Switzerland 156
symbolic capital 103, 153
System 1/System 2 processing 44

taste 11, 26, 46, 113, 162
teacher-centred teaching 128, 129, 130
teaching 39, 102, 134, 171, 173; claims about 119; competitions 33; funding 19, 61, 175–6; globalisation impact on 65; heads of institutions 145–6; institutional goals 66; interdisciplinary tensions 109; league tables 87, 88, 166; measurement of 166–7; motivation 183; pedagogy 128–31; quality assurance 36; research-teaching nexus 131–2; role of the nation state 63; Sainsbury report 119; status of 179; student choice 94, 120, 157, 160, 163, 166–7; U-Multirank 96; value added 176–7; white paper 121
Technical University of Munich 74
technology 1, 7, 23, 65, 67, 69, 179–80, 183
Teichler, U. 86, 87, 98
Times Higher Education rankings 78, 81, 85, 95, 97, 121
Toutkoushain, R. 84
transparency 9, 85, 90, 96–7
Treiman, D. 57–8
tribalism 144–5, 181
'triple helix' 102, 110, 152, 172
Trowler, P. 107
trust 105, 131
tuition fees 61, 92, 158–9, 162, 164–5, 174, 176, 179
turnover 51
two-system view of intuition and reasoning 44
two-tier system 119–20, 175

Tyler, R. 129

UCAS *see* National Universities and Colleges Admissions System
U-Map 98
U-Multirank 86, 96–8, 99
United Arab Emirates 72, 76, 80–1
United Kingdom 2, 55, 180; basic research 127; economic perspective 119–24, 133; external monitoring of quality 27; funding 58, 59, 61, 175; heads of institutions 139–54; IARU 91; league tables 87, 88, 89, 96, 97–8; LERU 90; massification 6; National Student Survey 92, 94, 140, 146, 167; overseas students 56, 173; private provision 174–5; recruitment of students 178; Research Excellence Framework 33, 108, 120, 135, 140, 146, 153; research impact 19; return on investment 158–9; Russell Group 59, 90; salaries 60; social reproduction 163–4; stratification 156; student choice 155, 160, 162; tuition fees 158–9, 164–5; Universitas 21 network 90; Worldwide Universities Network 91
United States 2, 4–5, 55–6; Boyer Commission 131, 158, 177; elitism 174; IARU 91; institutional autonomy 64; Ivy League 59; league tables 84, 85, 87, 89, 96, 97–8; learning objectives 129; National Survey of Student Engagement 167; private provision 56, 58, 174, 175; research spending 126; return on investment 159; rising costs 92, 165, 176; salaries 60; sciences 106; sporting facilities 158; stratification 156; student attitudes 157; student choice 161; Times Higher

Education rankings 81; Universitas 21 network 90; Worldwide Universities Network 91
Universitas 21 network 90, 95, 149, 152
Universities UK 122
University College London 62
University of California Berkeley 91
University of Chicago 74
University of Copenhagen 91
University of Hertfordshire 124
University of Liverpool 75
University of London 142, 147
University of Melbourne 64
University of New South Wales 74, 75
University of Nottingham 64, 75
University of Peking 91
University of Singapore 91
University of Tokyo 91
University of Warwick 75, 133
University of Waterloo 80

value added 89, 99, 159, 166, 176–7
values 15, 50, 62, 102–3; alternative patterns of prestige 182; arts 112; economic aspirations 123; internal 5; leadership 105; liberal 12–13; prestige economies 29–30; shared 51; societal 46, 106; unconscious 52

Veblen, T. 26
vertical stratification 156
vice-chancellors 142–3, 148
visual and performing arts 107, 112–14

Watson, D. 104
weak ties 28–9
Webber, K. 84
websites 61
Whitfield, J. 47, 48, 50
Wilde, Oscar 51
Wilkins, S. 163
Wilson report (2012) 122–3, 133, 134
women leaders 143
Woolcock, M. 28
World University Rankings 95
'world-class' universities 54, 62, 133, 146, 178; economic growth 172; European Union 97; international league tables 7, 19, 57, 86, 87, 88; positional competition 158; public funding 59, 79; stratification 156; student choice 166
Worldwide Universities Network (WUN) 91

Yale University 91